HERO
IN
DISGRACE

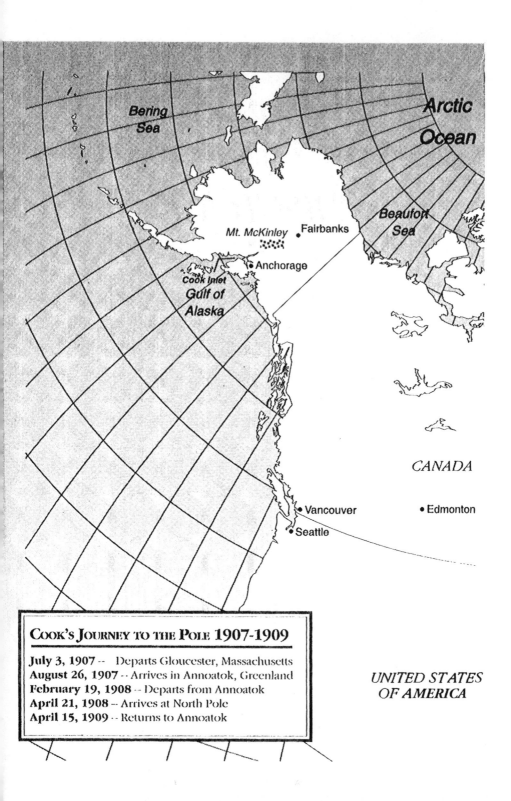

Bering Sea

Arctic Ocean

Beaufort Sea

Mt. McKinley • Fairbanks

• Anchorage

Cook Inlet

Gulf of Alaska

CANADA

• Vancouver • Edmonton

• Seattle

COOK'S JOURNEY TO THE POLE 1907-1909

July 3, 1907 -- Departs Gloucester, Massachusetts
August 26, 1907 -- Arrives in Annoatok, Greenland
February 19, 1908 -- Departs from Annoatok
April 21, 1908 -- Arrives at North Pole
April 15, 1909 -- Returns to Annoatok

UNITED STATES
OF AMERICA

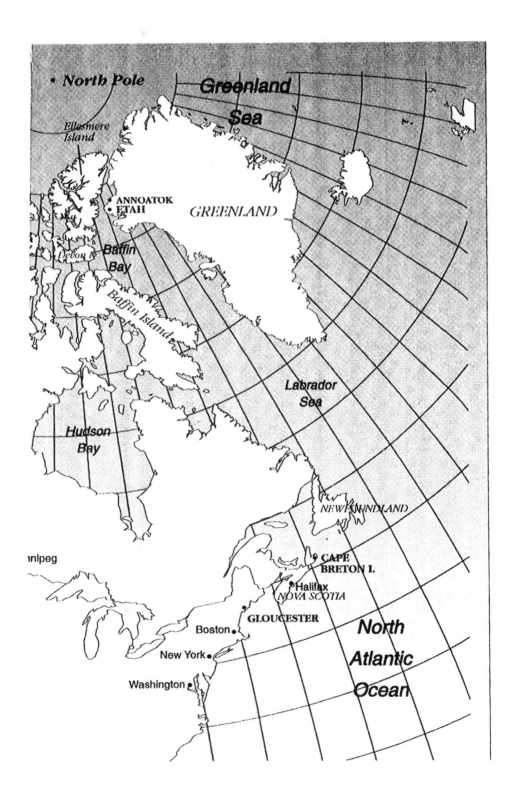

HERO IN DISGRACE

The True Discoverer of the North Pole

FREDERICK A. COOK

Howard S. Abramson

Foreword by Warren Cook Sr., president of the
Frederick A. Cook Society

toExcel

San Jose New York Lincoln Shanghai

Hero in Disgrace
The True Discoverer of the North Pole, Frederick A. Cook

Published by toExcel Press,
an imprint of iUniverse.com, Inc.

For information address:
iUniverse.com, Inc.
620 North 48th Street
Suite 201
Lincoln, NE 68504-3467
www.iuniverse.com

ISBN: 0-595-00092-4

This book is dedicated to my parents,
who taught me to pursue the truth.

Contents

Acknowledgments

It is impossible to cite all the people who helped me complete this project in ways large and small over the four years I was actively involved with it. But at least a few of them must be singled out, and the rest—from the United States to Denmark to some unlikely spots in Greenland—noted in a sweeping and heartfelt thank you.

I must specifically thank Sheldon Cook-Dorough, the historian of the Frederick A. Cook Society, and his many compatriots at the society for their help. Janet Vetter, Cook's granddaughter, was extremely helpful to me, and I am sorry that she did not live to see this book in print.

The staff of Greenlandair and Scandinavian Air Service were incredibly kind and helpful; there is no way I would have made it to Annoatok without the cheerful help of the staff of Greenlandair and some wonderful people in Greenland, including Philip Lauritzen.

Carl Kramer, a photography pro of the first order at the *Washington Post,* gave me some important help, as did people at Fuji Film USA.

And, once again, I must especially thank my wife, Martha, for her selfless assistance and support, and my three children—Nelson, Daniel, and Allegra—for their forbearance in letting their daddy play hookey long enough to fix this chapter in history.

Howard S. Abramson
North Potomac, Maryland

Foreword

The passage of over eighty years has not dispelled the controversy nor quelled the search for the truth as to who was the first to discover the North Pole. In an era when planes can land upon and submarines pass underneath the polar cap, one might ask if the issue remains a relevant one. The answer is a resounding yes. The heroic deeds of those early century adventurers exploring unknown terrains under the most difficult and life-threatening circumstances warrant our attention not only because of the great courage displayed in and of themselves, but also because the truth in history must be served.

Hero in Disgrace, Howard Abramson's well-researched examination of the Frederick A. Cook and Robert E. Peary controversy, sheds new light on the claims of these two explorers to the title of first to reach the pole. In a distinctively articulate and adventuresome style of writing, Howard Abramson gives us a chronicle covering the wide scope of events in Dr. Cook's life ranging from the achievements of his four expeditions to the Arctic to his courageous leadership on a journey to the Antarctic Region with Roald Amundsen. We are also treated to Cook's Mt. McKinley climb, his successful expedition to the North Pole in 1908, and a banquet testimonial dinner given by his peers when pardoned from Leavenworth Prison in 1930.

As one of Dr. Cook's few living relatives (he was my paternal Grandfather's brother), as a ten-year-old I recall his warmth, kindness, deep sense of integrity, and unselfish concern for others. His live and let live approach to life is perhaps best summed up by a letter he sent to a writer interested in the Cook/Peary controversy. Despite the venomous character assassination waged against Dr. Cook by the Peary forces, he wrote:

> I note you are to reopen what you call the Cook-Peary controversy. Now, I have no controversy on hand. It is all on the other side and I would like you to treat the matter in that spirit. My case will eventually rest on its own merits without reference to rival interests. As to Mr. Peary, my feeling for him is that of pity rather than revenge. He is nearing 60, has lost his toes in the service. He has striven against awful odds and finally according to Hensen, Peary's disability was such that he was carried to the Pole and back on a fur cushioned sled. The man who can succeed under such a handicap deserves all the glory that comes his way.

Hero in Disgrace represents the culmination of research earlier presented in the works of Edwin Swift Balch, Thomas F. Hall, J. Gordon Hayes, Andrew Freeman, Hugh Eames, Theon Wright, and of the ongoing efforts of the Frederick A. Cook Society. The facts are here and the reader will be able to form his or her judgment. As Dr. Cook said, "The facts are written. They are the truth. You be the judge." My suspicion is, that when the verdict comes in, this hero will be extricated from his grave of disgrace.

Warren B. Cook, Sr.
President,
The Frederick A. Cook Society

Introduction

Little has changed in northern Greenland since the days when Frederick A. Cook and Robert E. Peary walked the frozen surface of the Arctic as they challenged the odds, and each other, in the race to be the first man to stand at the North Pole.

Walking in their footsteps today at the end of the Earth only heightens the irony that the controversy their long-ago race ignited has now outlived them by almost a century. That the controversy is surely not settled was clearly evident by the furor that erupted recently on the front pages of America's newspapers, when the first great cracks appeared in what has been one of modern history's greatest pair of lies: that Peary discovered the North Pole and that Cook's prior claim to have done so was spurious, unworthy even of serious consideration.

The controversy continues to fascinate us, even though at first glance more than eighty years later, it would seem not really to matter who got to the North Pole first. But it obviously does matter to many of us, and for an array of reasons. Any doubt about the nation's, and the world's, continuing interest in the issue was dispelled in late 1988 and throughout 1989, when the primary remaining spear carrier of the Peary myth—the National Geographic Society—temporarily altered its long-standing, die-hard support for Peary's claim, admitting, finally, that Peary never got nearer than thirty to sixty miles of the North Pole.

Close examination of the historical record shows the ludicrousness of Peary's original claim and makes a mockery of the National Geographic Society's continuation of its fabrication of history. But just how widely accepted the Peary myth is was obvious when even the society's relatively minor adjustment of its Peary tale in 1988 immediately made headlines on the front pages of newspapers in all regions of the United States and in many publications around the world.

Some months later, in late 1989, the National Geographic Society recanted its earlier admission, basing its new change of heart on dubious data produced—at the society's expense and direction—by an unknown organization of so-called experts that the society said "proved" that Peary had, indeed, made it to the North Pole.

Scrutiny of the National Geographic Society's latest claim to having staked the Pole in Peary's name quickly tarnished as convincingly as history has undone the society's awarding of that same prize to the same pretender in the past. Outside experts strongly criticized the mountain of assumptions that the apologists for Peary used to "prove" the claim and dismissed the results as worthless.

The current Gilbert Grosvenor who runs the society today used some of the same words that his father and his grandfather had used to support Peary. During a press conference he termed the work of the society's handpicked and paid group "unimpeachable" and added, "I consider this the end of a historic controversy and the confirmation of due justice to a great explorer."

It was with just such language that the society and its agents presented Congress with Peary's claim to the North Pole in 1911, when it sought to have his award officially recognized by the nation. A key member of Congress, Ernest W. Roberts of Massachusetts, waived aside the efforts of both the man and the group after hearing all the evidence. In his minority committee report, he wrote that Peary's testimony was "delightfully vague and uncertain . . . [and provided] very conclusive evidence that the examination of his records [by the National Geographic Society, which had unilaterally taken on the role of arbiter] was anything but minute, careful and rigorous."

When presented with another opportunity in 1988 to undo this historic wrong, the society, instead of honestly seeking to resolve the long-contentious issue, again chose to take the expedient way out, still apparently afraid to admit that Peary—one of its patron saints—was a cheater and a liar.

This recent episode underscores why history must be corrected. For even while many of the last diehards of the Peary conspiracy are finally admitting that their man never really made it to the North Pole, Cook's claim is still dismissed by many writers with a quick wave of the hand. This continued slight so many years later proves just how effective the campaign of lies by Peary's apologists was and why it is worth the effort to overcome historical inertia to force the rewriting of this chapter of our world's past.

When one encounters the enormous physical difficulties involved in traveling around Greenland today and experiences the isolation of a nation without a single intercity road or a mile of railroad track, one is all the more amazed at the courage of the men who braved the harsh realities before and after the Cook-Peary fiasco. It is all the more astonishing that nearly all the explorers who braved the elements did so simply because they wanted to make the claim of being number one at something: touching the completely imaginary North Pole, the very top of the world.

And it goes on today, as modern adventurers strive to be the first to ski to the Pole or the first to "prove" they made a successful land journey to the North Pole, thanks to satellite tracking, or the first to travel by submarine and touch the Pole from below.

In my journey to Greenland in 1987, I discovered that it is more difficult to get to Etah—the key "town" on the northwestern coast of Greenland where both Cook and Peary landed to begin the last and most important phases of their northward treks—today than it was one hundred years ago. While one could catch a ride there on a whaling ship in the nineteenth or early twentieth century or come over from Europe on a blubber ship making a scheduled run, Etah is now abandoned, the casualty of a Danish policy of forcing the Inuit to settle in larger towns to make delivery of social services by the government more efficient.

Not that Etah was ever a thriving metropolis. At the turn of the century, the whole town consisted of three or four stone huts and several tents. In modern times, the town had grown to around a dozen wooden houses and a trading post before it was shut down as a permanent settlement. These days, only an occasional hunter disturbs the tranquility of the strikingly beautiful and protected bay that spreads out from Etah, which made it such an attractive haven for explorers.

Today, traveling anywhere in Greenland is difficult. Were it not for Greenland's trusty airline, Greenlandair, and the company's charter helicopters, as well as the services of the U.S. Air Force, it would be almost impossible to travel north of the U.S. Air Force base at Thule in summer, except aboard one of the small boats used by the Inuit to hunt in years when the summer season is warm enough to break up the pack ice.

Thus, having seen and traveled in some of their footsteps, one's inclination is to say nothing disparaging of either Cook or Peary, for their sacrifices were many and their achievements historic. Were all the world's histories to record some form of ironic tie in the contest to be the first to reach what the Inuit call the "Big Nail," it would seem only fitting to let the moving hand's words remain unchallenged, no matter what new evidence is brought to light or what reconsideration of old evidence is made.

But, alas, that is not the way history was recorded. And that is the primary reason why it must be corrected.

While it is the fashion in some countries to say simply that both Cook and Peary claimed to have reached the North Pole around the same time, most histories—and all those published up to now in the United States, the home of both contestants—proclaim flatly that Peary discovered the Pole. When Cook is mentioned, it is usually only to point out that he made a false claim around the time of Peary's great accomplishment.

Even that might be acceptable to students of the quest were it not that Peary's claim to the North Pole was accepted only after his supporters had methodically and underhandedly destroyed Cook's reputation and stolen from him his well-deserved spot in history through a grand conspiracy.

As a result of the campaign by Peary's financial and social backers, Cook lost credit in most people's eyes not only for any rights to the North Pole, but for the rights to several other unrelated accomplishments. He was one of the few explorers to make historic contributions at both the North and South Poles and was the first human to spend the long winter's night at both ends of the world. He rediscovered the cure for scurvy and single-handedly saved the 1898 Belgian Antarctic Expedition. He also made noteworthy expeditions around Alaska's Mount McKinley, the highest peak in North America, and claimed to be the first man in history to climb to its top. Furthermore, he did the first ethnographic studies of the Eskimos of northern Greenland and wrote several exciting books about his ventures, which still pulse with the first-person verve of the brave, wide-eyed explorer.

The only thing Cook did to bring disrepute upon himself was to claim that he discovered the North Pole. And he refused for the rest of his life to recant, no matter what the reward offered for doing so or the price exacted for continuing the claim, and there were many of both.

Crawling through the passageway and sitting down in what remains of the hut in northern Greenland from which Cook launched the overland portion of his journey to the North Pole, one can feel the echoes of history and can almost hear the reverberations of Cook's calls for justice. Until the day he died, Frederick A. Cook not only maintained that he had told the truth about his trek to the North Pole, but he also believed that history would eventually be corrected and all his claims restored.

This is his true story, the portrait of Frederick A. Cook, Hero in Disgrace.

PART ONE

CHAPTER 1

"I Am Beginning Again"

Leavenworth Federal Penitentiary had never seen anything quite like it. Staff members and prisoners alike had contributed money and time to make the hastily arranged farewell party something special, to let the guest of honor know that all his good works had been appreciated. More than a few rules were bent that Saturday night in March 1930 to provide as close to a feast as was possible within the bleak prison's walls.

After the unaccustomed gaiety of the banquet, the large hall was hushed as federal prisoner 23118—among the oldest of the four thousand inmates—rose to speak. There was an unmistakable twinkle in the prisoner's eyes and a fire in his voice that night, as the man, who was clearly not a neophyte at addressing large crowds, implored his colleagues to obey the prison's rules and support its staff. His five years in prison had not been lost ones, he told his comrades, because he had learned much from them. He urged the men to spend their remaining days behind bars preparing themselves to reenter society and not to waste precious time bemoaning their fates. And when he finished his short, contemporaneous speech, the prisoner and guest of honor—known to the world outside those prison walls as Frederick Albert Cook—was mobbed by well-wishers.

It had been a long road for Cook, from years of desolate isolation

3

to the fishbowl life of prison; from celebrated feats at the Arctic and Antarctic and atop Mount McKinley to aiding the many drug addicts among the prison population; and from acclaim as the first man in history to claim explorations's greatest remaining prize, the North Pole, to infamy as a supposed plunderer of widows and orphans and a convicted felon.

When the tall prison gate swung open soon after noon on Sunday, March 10, 1930, what the waiting newspaper reporters saw in the Kansas sunlight was a spry man, looking surprisingly fit for a sixty-five-year-old professional who had just spent five years in a federal prison. Although his borrowed suit was faded and did not fit perfectly, the reporters unanimously agreed that he looked well, with ruddy cheeks and a discernible bounce in his step.

Cook was caught in a whirlwind of activity from the moment on Saturday, March 9, that Warden Thomas B. White had officially received word from Washington that Cook, who was sent to prison for allegedly using the U.S. mails to defraud oil company investors, would soon be released on parole. The decision to free Cook had been announced in Washington on Friday by the attorney general of the United States.

Cook's fellow prisoners and the staff members of the prison hospital had insisted on holding the banquet to honor him after they learned of his imminent release. And reporters had been constantly calling the prison staff, clamoring for an opportunity to talk with Cook, a man who had been on the front pages of newspapers around the globe since the end of the nineteenth century, for his explorations and for the mail-fraud case.

Warden White told the ten reporters who were at the prison that March morning awaiting Cook's release that he would drive Cook from Leavenworth to a hotel in the center of the like-named Kansas town for a press conference. Cook's release papers from Washington reached Leavenworth at 10 A.M., but his fellow prisoners refused to let him go without last embraces and proper farewells. Finally, just after noon, Cook slipped out of the prison alone and took a cab to the National Hotel, and the waiting press corps.

To no one's surprise, the first question the reporters asked Cook was whether—after five years in prison and some twenty years of disgrace—he still claimed to be the first man to have reached the top of the world, the North Pole. From the minute Cook had made his claim to the Pole in 1909, his own world had been turned upside down.

Cook spent one full hour answering that first question, as he forcefully restated, for what must have been the millionth time, that he had, indeed, reached the North Pole, or a place quite close to it, no matter what lies were spread by the cabal supporting the other claimant, Robert E. Peary.

"I am broke, gentleman," he told the reporters, "I am beginning again. . . . I have written of my life and my discoveries, not in a controversial vein. Time will bear out claims I have made for myself; time, and a final examination of the records."

He said recent trips to the North Pole by airplane—conducted by the Americans Richard E. Byrd and Floyd Bennett (a claim that is disputed by many historians today)—and by airship—conducted by the Norwegian Roald Amundsen—had served to confirm his original observations during his 1908–09 trek and rekindled his desire to prove that he had reached the North Pole first. "I still feel an impulse to explore, but at 65, one must abandon such things." And then he again challenged the nay-sayers to call his bluff.

"I only wish to send those who doubt me back to the records I left and Peary left" [in their writings after returning to civilization in 1909, he told the reporters.] "Mine were printed before Peary's; I had no opportunity to see his first. And our reports tally."

With that, Cook departed by car for Chicago, after posing for photographs in front of the hotel at the request of the seven news photographers who had come to witness his release. And with his reemergence, the flames of controversy over the discovery of the North Pole instantly reignited from the embers that have refused to die, to this day.

CHAPTER 2

Skill, Patience, and Coolness

The destinies of Frederick A. Cook and Robert E. Peary began what would prove to be a lifelong entanglement on June 6, 1891. Cook was among Peary's crew of five unpaid volunteers who, along with nine scientists—who were paying for their rides—were aboard the steam-powered barkentine *Kite* as it sailed out of Brooklyn's harbor. Cook, an inexperienced physician and novice explorer, was hardly a noteworthy member of Peary's complement of voyagers, however.

The star of the show was indisputably Josephine Diebitsch Peary, Peary's handsome wife, whom he had decided to take along on his first full-scale expedition to the Arctic. Peary had caused quite a stir in Victorian America when he announced he would take Josephine along on the journey, which would make her the first white woman known to have visited the Arctic.

The Pearys were married soon after the budding explorer had returned from his first unsuccessful foray into northern Greenland in 1886. After he announced he would take Josephine, Peary was loudly praised in some quarters for encouraging the tradition of the pioneer women, those hardy, brave females who had been instrumental in settling the American West. To others, however, he seemed a grandstanding fool, who was needlessly exposing his wife to peril for the sake of publicity for his own exploits. Whatever the case, Josephine's inclusion certainly garnered the budding explorer a great deal of news coverage, something Peary strived for, both for the glory and to help him raise money.

In a nation thirsting for homegrown accomplishments to help justify its expanding world role, controversy was the next best thing to achievement, and Peary quickly became an American star. Also, the nation was looking for a way to erase the memory of the tragedy of the first official American attempt to map a route to the North Pole, which had been conducted under the direction of Adolphus W. Greely. After Greely and his men established what was to be a permanent station at Fort Conger on the east coast of Ellesmere Island far north, the mission ended in disaster and cannibalism, with nineteen of the twenty-six members dying by 1884 of starvation and disease during the two years it took to effect a rescue.

Peary's chief goal, in what became known as his First North Greenland Expedition, was to take some of the sting out of an earlier bitter personal disappointment by crossing Greenland on a course farther north than that blazed by Norwegian explorer Fridtjof Nansen. Nansen, who would become a major figure in Arctic exploration, earned Peary's unbridled wrath as a result of his own successes over territory on which Peary had failed.

Peary's first attempted crossing of Greenland in 1886, which was financed with money provided by his mother, had failed miserably. Peary made his attempt with Christian Maigaard, a young Danish government official who was based in Greenland and who decided to join Peary after he helped Peary obtain the necessary official permission to undertake the expedition. Attempting to cross from west to east, Peary and Maigaard managed to get less than a hundred miles before they abandoned their efforts. Storms had delayed them, and Peary had seriously underestimated the physical strains of crossing the ice cap. When they turned back, far short of their goal, they had only about six days' worth of supplies left.

Two years later, Nansen made his own attempt to cross the island. He ignored conventional wisdom and made his attempt from east to west, and succeeded.

After Nansen's successful march, Peary made the first of what would become a lifelong series of unsubstantiated attacks on his fellow explorers. This time, he accused Nansen of having appropriated his, Peary's, plan. Wrote Peary in 1898: "Nansen effected the crossing of southern Greenland, starting on the shortest of my indicated routes. . . . This forestalling of my work was a serious blow to me."

Peary charged that Nansen had usurped him, even though Nansen had published his intention to attempt the crossing several years before Peary revealed his plans. But now, to keep the others away, Peary was determined to claim priority in the Arctic from Nansen through his next expedition and to establish his quest for the North Pole as the exclusive franchise.

Several years later, explorer Roald Amundsen, who was unquestionably the first man to reach the South Pole, wrote, "Peary has got it into his head that he is entitled to a monopoly of everything up there in the North." Cambridge Professor J. Gordon Hayes, in one of his books about Peary, said, "No consideration for the rights of other explorers caused Peary any concern."

Peary also wanted to determine how close to the North Pole Greenland's land mass extended, so he could prepare himself for his eventual assault on the Pole. He intended to create maps of the area in preparation for his later journeys, which he expected would start over the same territory. And at this point, Peary was convinced that if he searched northern Greenland hard enough, he would find an "imperial highway" of smooth ice that would allow him to speed to his goal.

After stopping at several Eskimo and Danish settlements in southern Greenland on the journey from Brooklyn, the *Kite* made it into Melville Bay near Cape York on July 1, 1891. The ship struggled through large fields of ice floes in the bay and was then frozen in for several days. Soon after the ship broke free of the jam, a large chunk of floating ice slammed against the ship's rudder, tearing the heavy iron tiller from the helmsman's grasp and crushing Peary's ankle against the deckhouse.

Cook discovered that Peary had suffered a double fracture of his leg, just above the ankle. He set it and did his best, along with

Josephine Peary, to make the patient as comfortable as possible. Each time the ship collided with the ever-present ice floes as it inched its way northward for the next three weeks, however, Peary suffered from stabs of pain caused by the jarring of the ship. But he was a solid, powerful-seeming man, who endured pain well. He appeared taller than his six feet, and the most notable feature of his appearance was, no doubt, his walrus mustache, which looked like the one worn by German Kaiser Wilhelm.

Finally, the *Kite* neared Peary's chosen destination, a tiny Eskimo settlement on Whale Sound, from which he planned to launch his overland expedition in the spring. However, as Peary quickly learned, even in summer, weather conditions in Greenland are unreliable and unpredictable. That year, because of heavy ice in Whale Sound, it was impossible for the *Kite* to enter, and Peary had to alter his plans; he ordered the ship to travel farther north, where it finally put in at McCormick Bay.

Cook's next important duty, after fixing Peary's broken leg, was to act as ambassador for the expedition. The crew's first attempt to enlist help from the local Eskimos—without which the expedition was doomed to failure—was unsuccessful. This inability to make friends had contributed to Peary's decision to abandon Whale Sound as a harbor and to journey northward instead. Peary ordered Cook to make contact with any Eskimos he could find in McCormick Bay and to convince at least one family to move their home near the large house Peary's crew had constructed.

The Americans had named their abode Red Cliff House, in recognition of the strange color of the snow there, which was caused by millions of mites that were imbedded in the frozen earth. The house had private quarters for the Pearys and a large bunk room for the rest of the travelers. Much of the structure had been prefabricated aboard the *Kite* while the crew waited for a change in ice conditions that would allow them to come ashore and unload the ship.

Within hours of leaving the *Kite,* Cook, as leader of the small expedition, was engaged in crude but effective conversation with several members of a small nearby village he had come across. He quickly convinced one couple, whose names were Mane and Ikwah, to accompany the crew. Cook and Mane patiently spoke back and forth in their native tongues until each had a rudimentary vocabulary of the other's words, which allowed Cook to make himself understood. His new companions took Cook to their village, where he slowly explained to the Eskimos that if they agreed to help the Americans, the crew would pay them for their furs and their labor with tools and other manufactured goods.

The Pearys invited the young Eskimo couple to dinner on their first night at Red Cliff House after the Eskimos had pitched a tent nearby and settled in. During the dinner, Ikwah was attracted to Mrs. Peary and, clearly expecting his host to follow the universal Eskimo tradition of sharing wives, tried to put his arms around Josephine. The Pearys attempted tactfully to explain their own customs to the clearly disappointed Ikwah and were apparently successful, since the couple remained near Red Cliff House, despite the rebuff. Two weeks later, when the bay was completely frozen over as winter approached and overland travel became easier, others from the Eskimo village joined the crew of the *Kite.*

These Eskimos labored long and hard to supply the visitors with suitable clothing for the approaching winter and for the planned expedition in the spring. They were already used to the sudden appearance of boatloads of peculiar white men from distant shores and had even coined a name for them: *Oopernadlett,* or "men who come in the spring."

During this first visit to the Arctic, Cook developed an immediate and deep interest in, and fondness for, the Eskimos of Greenland and their way of life. First, he concentrated on mastering their language. Cook marveled at all the accommodations they had made to the harsh environment. And because of his interest and friendliness and his willingness to learn without judging them or attempting to change them, he was accepted by the Eskimos as hardly any other white man had been. He was even allowed to enter what the Eskimos called their birth igloos, which until then had been forbidden territory to anyone but expectant mothers. Cook later wrote that when labor began, a pregnant woman would enter a newly built birth igloo alone; if all went well, the mother and child would eventually emerge; if not, the igloo would simply be sealed up, without any other person ever venturing inside.

And, with few moral judgments thrown in, Cook wrote of the Eskimos' practice of temporary marriages and of their generally communal society, which placed little emphasis on individual ownership and much emphasis on the survival of the group. At a time when Western man was still suffering the restrictions of the Victorian age, the Eskimos had few social restraints against sexual intercourse. Indeed, the crew of the *Kite*—and of nearly all the other expeditions of that age—could attest to this aspect of Eskimo life. Even the straight-laced Peary and his servant and chief aide, Matthew Henson, would indulge themselves in this unrestricted sexual climate and sire children during expeditions.

Cook was able to accept that rather than being a sign of some inherent degeneracy—as others had claimed—the Eskimos' sexual practices were understandable in a place where life expectancy was short and perils were plentiful. These liberal liaisons, coupled with the flexible marriages that were encouraged especially between members of different villages, also helped to minimize the genetic problems of inbreeding. Cook saw that the Eskimos' sexual interests were aroused most when the spring dawn began to erase the four months of winter darkness, just as the sexual interests of the Arctic's animals were being reawakened. As a result of this cycle, nearly all the Eskimo babies were born in deep winter, when the villagers were spending much of their time indoors, away from the howling storms.

Cook also studied why these Eskimos seemed not to be affected by the explorers' scourge: scurvy. There were no fresh vegetables to be found, and about the only greens he ever saw his Eskimo companions eat were partially digested grasses that they removed from the stomachs of slain game. In what would turn out to be an important discovery that would save many of his colleagues' lives during his career, Cook surmised that the large amounts of raw or barely cooked fish and meat the Eskimos ate must provide some benefit in preventing scurvy. He had unknowingly uncovered one benefit of vitamin C, which had itself not yet been discovered.

Cook learned of the Eskimos' many superstitions and of their large store of folklore, which would serve him well later. He discovered that shadows were special to these people because they believed that shadows housed an individual's spirit, what the white man referred to as the soul. This belief also made his Eskimo companions more fearful of the dark months of winter, when their shadows would not accompany them on hunts. He learned that the Eskimos rarely traveled upon the ice cap that made up the vast interior of Greenland because they knew there was little to eat there and there were no landmarks they could use as reference points. The Eskimos would not travel far out on the sea ice, either, unless they could see land, by which they could determine their position.

Peary made full use of Cook's strong ties with the Eskimos, although he seemed to look upon them as more akin to the pack animals that explorers in balmier climates utilized than as the exotic torchbearers of civilization in the frozen wasteland, as Cook viewed them. According to one writer who interviewed Cook about this expedition fifty years ago,

> Peary called them "my Eskimos" and referred to himself as their benefactor. Although the simple articles he brought to them [steel needles, wood and metal scraps, steel knives and, eventually, guns] may have made their lives easier, he was no philanthropist. They called him "nali" (rich man) and found that he drove a stiff bargain. For a seal or blue fox skin he paid one steel [sewing] needle. He bought a day's work or a week's work with an empty tin or a piece of board from a packing case. To him the Eskimo was a means to an end which he described this way: "I have often been asked: 'Of what use are Eskimos to the world?' They are too far removed to be of any value for commercial enterprise, and furthermore they lack ambition. . . . But let us not forget that these people . . . will yet prove their value to mankind. With their help the world shall discover the Pole."

These basic differences in principle were to persist throughout Cook's and Peary's respective careers. In many ways, they help to define these two explorers.

In addition to learning how the Eskimos talked and lived, Cook used this trip to learn how to stay alive in the harsh environment of the Arctic. He learned to guide a team of dogs pulling a sledge;

he studied the designs and constructions of Eskimo sledges and later made important improvements on his own; and he discovered how to make snow houses, which served him well at both Poles and in Alaska. He was taught how to hunt the game and birds that inhabited the Arctic during the daylight of summer, both to provide fur and feathers for the special garments required to survive in the Arctic and to fill his stomach and those of his dogs, and he learned from his companions how to keep warm and dry and what clothes to wear in what conditions and how to care for them.

But most important, Cook began to read the environment, to sense where the game was, to know when danger lurked near and unseen. In other words, he began to think like an Eskimo and began to be at ease on the ice. He combined this native knowledge with the best that Western man had devised for use in cold environments, and he learned how to ski and to use snowshoes and a sextant. In short, he turned himself into a first-class explorer during this maiden voyage to the Arctic.

Finally, in early May, the overland journey of Peary's First North Greenland Expedition began. Peary was accompanied by Cook; Matthew Henson, Peary's black servant, whom he met when he visited a Washington, D.C., men's clothing store, where Henson was working as a clerk; Eivind Astrup, a young Norwegian skiing champion; Langdon Gibson, brother of the illustrator Charles Dana Gibson, who created the famous Gibson Girl; and several Eskimos. After the group reached a cache of supplies on the inland ice above McCormick Bay, the Eskimos refused to go any farther, saying that evil spirits occupied the interior of the Greenland ice cap. Peary sent them back to Red Cliff House, along with Henson, who had suffered a frozen heel.

The four remaining members of the party then set out to trek across Greenland. After they had traveled about 130 miles from McCormick Bay, Peary announced that he would continue the quest with only one companion. This practice, too, would become a Peary hallmark. He had originally planned to take the loyal Henson along with him, as he did in future expeditions. But with

Henson not available, Peary chose Astrup, although all three of his companions had immediately volunteered to accompany him when he revealed his plan. Cook and Gibson returned to their base, while Peary and Astrup continued onward with some 1,200 pounds of supplies on two sledges pulled by thirteen dogs.

On July 4, 1892, after sixty-five days, Peary and Astrup made it across the northwestern corner of Greenland to a point where a wide channel slides into Greenland from the Greenland Sea. Peary named the area Independence Bay, in honor of the United States's celebration of the anniversary of its Declaration of Independence from Britain. To honor himself, he named both an island and the body of water that separated it from the Greenland mainland. Peary said the channel was surely the northern boundary of Greenland that he had been seeking. After surveying his domain, including Peary Channel and Peary Land, the explorer later wrote, "I could understand the feelings of Balboa as he climbed the last jealous summit which hid from his eager eyes the blue waves of the mighty Pacific."

However, subsequent explorations let some of the air out of Peary's balloon: "Peary Channel" was found, years later, to be a solid, waterless land area, and "Peary Land" thus became a small tip of Greenland. Some doubts have been raised about whether Peary and Astrup actually made it all the way to Independence Bay, although there is no doubt that the journey was a noteworthy effort, by far the longest trek across the giant island that had been completed up to that time. By it, Peary proved himself to be a leading overland explorer.

As Peary and Astrup neared McCormick Bay on their return to Red Cliff House, they spotted a search party that had been sent from the *Kite,* which had just returned from its winter stay in Newfoundland. There was a joyful reunion as Peary and Astrup detailed their claimed successes. In all, the expedition had covered some 1,100 miles from Red Cliff House to Independence Bay and back, over eighty-five days of marching. Thus, Peary and Astrup had averaged more than fourteen miles a day, a breakneck speed by Arctic standards. Their rate was more than twice Nansen's, but the Norwegian had not used dogs to pull his sleds.

Peary returned home triumphant, virtually assured that his future efforts would attract more sponsors—and attention from the press. He was in such a good temper that he even managed, uncharacteristically, to spread a little praise on at least one of his companions, Cook. The dour Peary, never known to lavish compliments on underlings, wrote some nice things about his surgeon and ethnologist, but, as was usually the case, his praise was not presented in a positive, endearing way.

In his book about this expedition, Peary wrote, "To Dr. Cook may be attributed the almost complete exemption of the party from even the mildest indispositions, and personally I owe much to his professional skill, and unruffled patience and coolness in an emergency. In addition to his work in his special ethnological field, in which he has obtained a large mass of the most valuable material concerning a practically unstudied tribe, he was always helpful and an indefatigable worker."

CHAPTER 3

The Split

The *Kite* returned to the United States in late September 1892, and Peary immediately began making preparations for a return journey to the Arctic. He obtained a new leave of absence from the U.S. Navy, but only after his growing stable of influential men helped him convince the military brass that the pursuit of his dream of reaching the North Pole was worthy of their assistance. Free of navy duties, Peary began the first step necessary for the launching of what would become known as Peary's Second North Greenland Expedition: He started looking for money.

Cook, meanwhile, returned to his fledgling medical practice in Brooklyn and discovered that his newfound fame had also attracted a following of new patients who wanted to be treated by the celebrity doctor and Arctic explorer. Cook also found himself in modest demand as a speaker throughout the area, although, true to his word to Peary, he lectured only on the medical and social aspects of Eskimo life, not on the group's explorations. To maintain his monopoly on such material, Peary required all his companions to sign an agreement that prevented them from publishing any accounts of their journeys with him.

For Cook, these busy days were a far cry from his pretrip experiences of an empty waiting room and more than enough spare time to read about the Arctic exploits of others.

Peary undertook a rigorous fund-raising schedule, which included his parading through the streets of American cities in full Arctic paraphernalia, and in a dog-driven sledge when he could, on his way to lectures for which he charged admission. While Cook spoke to audiences about his experiences in the Arctic without charge, Peary was earning large fees. Peary's agent reported that the explorer was not satisfied unless he earned at least two thousand dollars a day from his own lectures, a tidy sum in the 1890s. Between stops on the endless campaign for money, Peary pressured Cook to join him on his new expedition.

Cook told a biographer, many years after the events, that he had not been excited about the prospect of returning to Greenland, but agreed only after Peary visited him several times and offered him the post of second in command of the expedition. Perhaps as part of his campaign to enlist Cook, Peary, in a report to the Philadelphia Academy of Natural Sciences, once again praised Cook's work in Greenland, calling him a "patient and skillful surgeon, indefatigable worker, earnest student of the peculiar people among whom we lived; he has obtained, I believe, a record of the tribe unapproachable in ethnological archives."

But a short time later, when Cook sought Peary's permission to publish that very same ethnological record, after being urged to do so by other physicians who heard him speak, Peary refused to give it. Peary said that if he approved Cook's breaking of the terms of the contract that prevented his companions from publishing accounts of their journeys with him, he would be besieged by such requests from the other members of the expedition. Cook argued that his report had little commercial value and would not lessen the worth of Peary's own reports, but to no avail. In response to Peary's refusal, Cook resigned from the upcoming return voyage.

Cook then tried to settle down to his growing medical practice, to make some money and to get on with his life. But the magical draw of the Arctic, which had lured so many men to challenge it, had claimed another victim. In a 1910 interview, Cook explained this siren call. Rather than the "call of the wild" that some had speculated drew men north, he said, "It is more the voice of the Arctic, the thirst for that great icy expanse, the Polar Sea. It is an acquired taste. If I was born with it, it was so latent that I never perceived it. . . . But it came to me in my first Arctic trip, and it has never left me."

After his abrupt split with Peary, Cook considered trying to mount his own campaign to the Arctic but, apparently in an effort to avoid a direct competition with Peary, he turned his attention to the other end of the world, the South Pole. Antarctica had been subject to much less exploration than had the Arctic, and Cook saw an opportunity to make his mark without getting into competition with Peary. He formulated a plan to export the ways of the Greenland Eskimos, which he had learned so well, to the South Pole: to bring Eskimo clothing and dogs and sledges to the Antarctic. To accomplish this goal, he knew, he would first have to travel to the Arctic to buy dogs to pull the sledges and furs with which to make the clothes for the expedition.

Then, in what must have seemed a magical stroke of good fortune to him, James H. Hoppin, a professor at Yale University, visited Cook at his medical offices in early 1893 and asked him to lead an expedition to Greenland in the summer for his son, Benjamin, a student who had become interested in exploring the Arctic. Cook was only too happy to comply and promptly chartered the *Zeta*, a seventy-eight-foot Nova Scotia schooner, for the voyage.

Just before joining the ship, Cook visited Peary's new ship, the *Falcon*, on which Peary planned to conduct his second expedition. The *Falcon* was then docked in Brooklyn harbor, where visitors were being charged twenty-five cents each to tour it, part of Peary's seemingly never-ending commercialism. Peary had been reduced to charging admission to his ship by anxious creditors, while he searched for enough money to conduct the new expedition. On board, Cook paid his respects to Eivind Astrup, who was again accompanying Peary, and to the Pearys. During his visit, Peary told a reporter that he was sorry Cook was not coming with him to Greenland. Among other reasons, Peary no doubt would have liked to have Cook along in case something went awry with his latest publicity gimmick, which again involved his wife: Josephine was coming along on the expedition, only this time she was pregnant. It was the Pearys' plan that Josephine would give birth in

Greenland to the first white child known to have been born above the Arctic Circle.

Cook joined the *Zeta* in Halifax, Nova Scotia, and on July 10, 1893, embarked on what was scheduled to be a three-month sail. They cruised north along the coasts of Newfoundland and Labrador before crossing Davis Strait to Greenland. On August 16, the *Zeta* anchored at Upernavik, well north of the Arctic Circle and at that time the most northerly Danish trading station on the giant island. There, the captain refused to sail farther north, claiming that to do so would endanger the ship by exposing it to treacherous ice conditions. Despite the urgings of his paying guests, led by Cook, who said there was no worrisome ice in the waters around Upernavik at the time, the captain refused to alter his decision, and two days later the *Zeta* headed southward.

The *Zeta* stopped next at a small village, and Cook bought six dogs to start his sledge team and many bear, seal, and caribou hides and bird skins from the Eskimos. Cook then had the ship sail to Uummannaq, where he and young Hoppin explored a large fjord in a long canoe that was rowed by Eskimo women and steered by tribal elders.

Then the *Zeta* recrossed Davis Strait to Canada, and at a small trading post operated by the Hudson Bay Company, Cook made arrangements with an Eskimo family to take two of their children to New York. In return for having them accompany him on the lecture tour he was already planning to help finance his expedition to the South Pole, Cook told the family he would care for the two children and return them the next summer. Then the *Zeta* set sail for Brooklyn, with Cook satisfied that he had made notable progress toward his own expedition, and his paying guests pleased with their unique summer's adventures.

Upon his return, Cook began his fund-raising efforts in earnest. He estimated that he would need twenty-five thousand dollars to launch the Antarctic expedition, and he attracted the immediate support of several newspapers. One of Cook's strongest boosters was a man who would play a pivotal role on Peary's side in later events, Herbert L. Bridgman, who ran and was part owner of the newspaper, the *Brooklyn Standard Union*.

Bridgman wrote an appeal to New York's wealthy businessmen, which he published in his newspaper: "The work of unlocking the great mystery of the South, the final problem of the surface and structure of the globe, could be entrusted to no more competent hands than Dr. Cook's. Those who know him know that he combines the patience, judgment, and zeal of the explorer with thorough medical and scientific knowledge, added to a practical experience of priceless value with the Peary expedition."

But even that appeal was not enough to loosen a sufficient number of purse strings. Cook later reported that billionaire Andrew Carnegie, during a meeting at the Union League Club in New York City, declined to assist him, saying he could not see any possible benefits to humanity from expeditions to either Pole that were worthy of his money.

So, Cook turned his inventive mind to other possible avenues of funds. He came up with the idea of conducting the world's first strictly pleasure cruise to the Arctic, chartered a steamship named the *Miranda*, and set the fare for this exotic voyage at five hundred dollars per passenger. In quick order Cook had fifty-five paying passengers—mostly students from rich families and faculty members from leading eastern universities—and enough money for his Antarctic voyage; all he had to do now was deliver the planned tourist journey to the north.

But the voyage of the ill-fated *Miranda* became a nightmare, worthy of a *Perils of Pauline* movie. As soon as the lines were cast off in New York harbor on July 7, 1894, and the *Miranda*'s engines were started, the ship struck the dock. There was no apparent damage, however, so the ship resumed its journey. But a few days later, the ship's compass stopped working, so the *Miranda* put into St. John's, Newfoundland, for repairs. There, Cook hired an ice pilot, Michael Dunphy, to steer the vessel safely through the dangers the *Miranda* was sure to encounter in the waters around Greenland. Dunphy had been second mate on the *Kite*, when that ship carried Peary and his entourage, including Cook, to Greenland in 1891.

But the *Miranda*'s passengers had not even lost sight of New-foundland when it struck an iceberg in the strait between New-foundland and Labrador, off Bell Isle. Several of the *Miranda*'s protective hull plates were damaged, and it was hauled back to St. John's for repairs once again. One week later, the *Miranda* was under way again and managed to cross Davis Strait safely and anchor at Maniitsoq, Greenland, a small town south of the Arctic Circle, which was then known by its Danish name, Sukkertoppen.

After several days ashore exploring the area, the *Miranda*'s passengers reboarded the ship, which resumed the voyage northward on August 9. However, when the ship was barely out of port, the *Miranda* struck a submerged rock and suffered serious damage to the hull at her waterline. The ship limped back to Maniitsoq, so the passengers could scramble ashore if the *Miranda* started to sink. Cook's passengers quickly became alarmed about their prospects for a safe and speedy return, and rightly so. At this time there was but one hotel in all Greenland, and it was far from Maniitsoq. Obtaining another vessel from the United States or Canada could take many weeks, and there was not much time before ice would begin to clog the passageway between North America and Green-land, making travel difficult, if not impossible.

Cook and the *Miranda*'s crew agreed that it would be best if another ship shadowed the injured ship on her return voyage after makeshift repairs were made, in case the *Miranda* began to sink in the icy and always dangerous waters. Cook was told that there was a large fishing boat in port at Sisimiut, a larger village some one hundred miles to the north. So, in a canoe paddled by Eskimos, Cook braved the frigid waters and piloted the boat to the town the Danes called Holsteinsborg, which is still a major settlement on Greenland's west coast. There, with the help of local officials of the Danish government, Cook obtained assistance from the captain of the *Rigel,* a Gloucester fishing schooner.

Cook's efforts so inspired the gratitude of his passengers, that one of them, G. Frederick Wright, a professor at Oberlin College, later wrote a letter on Cook's behalf to a committee of the U.S. House of Representatives. In a letter to Representative William J. Fields of Kentucky, Wright said that following the *Miranda*'s collision, "the courage and skill which he showed in venturing 100 miles northward along the rugged coast of Greenland in a small boat to get relief prepared me for believing that he could accomplish any daring enterprise that was within the reach of human effort."

The *Rigel* reached the *Miranda* on August 20, eleven days after it had hit the rock. After deliberations between the two crews, it was decided that the *Miranda*'s passengers should be transferred to the *Rigel* and that the fishing vessel would accompany the *Miranda* as she made for Sydney, Nova Scotia. Since the *Rigel* had no engine, it was decided that the *Miranda* would pull the schooner, and on August 28, the two entwined ships left Greenland.

On the second night out, the *Miranda* was taking on water, and her captain decided that she could go no farther, that she was sinking. The crew was taken aboard the *Rigel,* and the *Miranda,* still afloat, was cut loose. Now, more than one hundred passengers and crewmen were wedged into the *Rigel*'s accommodations for twenty. Finally, after seventeen stormy days under sail, the *Rigel* reached Sydney.

But the fates were still not through with the *Miranda*'s voyagers. Many of the veterans of the world's first "pleasure cruise" to Greenland sailed on the steamship *Portia* for New York. The *Portia* rammed and sank another vessel during the trip, and four crewmen were killed. On September 11, the *Portia* finally reached New York. To mark their harrowing voyage and to keep in touch with each other, the veterans of the *Miranda* cruise founded the Arctic Club of America, with a Yale University professor, William A. Brewer, as its first president.

Cook was now wiser about the perils of the Arctic and thankful that all his passengers had returned safely, but he was again without enough money to conduct his expedition to the South Pole, since he returned much of the money he had collected to the passengers.

Peary, meanwhile, was having serious troubles of his own on his second foray. He had reached Bowdoin Bay, twenty-five miles north of Red Cliff, where his first expedition had been based, on August 3, 1893. That was the very time Cook was leading his charges aboard the *Zeta* on his first return to Greenland, the year before the expedition on the *Miranda*. The members of the Second Peary North Greenland Expedition first built their home, which they named Anniversary Lodge, and the *Falcon* departed for home in late August. The first mark the group made on history was the birth of the Peary's child, a girl they named Marie Ahnighto, and who was promptly nicknamed the "Snow Baby" by the press. So, Anniversary Lodge was home to the three Pearys, a nurse, and eleven men—eight members of the expedition and three paying guests.

Peary's goal for this expedition was the same as his goal two years earlier: The group was to make for Independence Bay, where it would split into three groups; Peary would lead the primary team as far north as they were able to go, and to the North Pole if possible.

In spring 1894, the Greenland phase of the expedition began, but it was a disaster from the start. The expedition's ranks were quickly decimated, when Astrup and three other members took sick or suffered frostbite and returned to Anniversary Lodge with the expedition's surgeon. As the survivors trudged on, Mother Nature threw them some Arctic curves. Storms swirled around Peary and his crew, and temperatures reached sixty degrees below zero. Soon they were all suffering from frostbite; many of their dogs became sick or died. By early April, after having traveled only 128 miles from Anniversary Lodge, Peary gave up and turned his bowed party homeward.

While the rest of the expedition members had been away, Astrup, after recovering from a stomach ailment, conducted a topographical survey of the surrounding Melville Bay that, much to Peary's chagrin, was seen by many as the top achievement of the expedition. The only other noteworthy occurrence was that Peary located three meteorites near Cape York—the source of metal for tools used by all the region's tribes—by bribing an Eskimo to show him where they were with the greatest prize Peary had, a rifle.

A dejected Peary decided to remain another year in Greenland so he could try to accomplish at least some of his goals and asked for volunteers to stay with him. A clear indication of how poor the morale was among the group and of Peary's failure to evoke strong loyalty from his underlings was that only Henson agreed to stay with him. Later, one other expedition member was convinced to stay. When the *Falcon* returned to the United States with all but Peary and his two volunteers, one member told a reporter that Peary and his wife were imperious and ate all their meals alone during the stay in Greenland, without ever inviting one of their companions to join them. And there was a shortage of food, at least for the crew, which reduced the menu for the expedition members to unappetizing and bare minimums. Rumors that Peary and his family were eating high off the hog, while the men were barely getting by on boring, stale food, fed their disenchantment with their leader.

William Libbey, Jr., the secretary of the American Geographical Society who was aboard the *Falcon* when it went to retrieve the expedition members, was presumably voicing Peary's feelings—he was clearly voicing Peary's excuses—when he wrote, "At the last a conspiracy was formed with the intention of abandoning Lieutenant Peary, and this would have succeeded if he had not persuaded one of the malcontents to remain with him and his colored man." Peary himself later questioned the loyalty of the men who refused to remain with him, writing that the deserters "had discovered that Arctic work was not entirely the picnic they had imagined."

Throughout Peary's career, failures on his expeditions were always caused by the mistakes of others—at least in Peary's eyes—while all the credit for the successes was his alone. By now, Peary's internal demon was with him all the time, driving him on and warping his perceptions.

Soon after he returned to New York, Astrup published his survey of Melville Bay under his own name, which further incensed Peary when he learned of it. Peary republished the survey—since it was one of the few noteworthy accomplishments of the expedition's members—as part of his own book about the journey and refused to see Astrup again.

Young Astrup, who had clearly idolized Peary, was despondent for some time over this breach with the explorer. Cook wrote later that Astrup, who was then age twenty-four, brooded over Peary's insults for some time, which led to his killing himself: "For days and weeks, Astrup talked of nothing but the infamy of Peary's attack on himself [for publishing his survey] and the contemptible charge of desertion which Peary made against Astrup's companions. Then he suddenly left my home, returned to Norway, and we next heard of his suicide." Cook clearly blamed Peary for Astrup's death, for having taken advantage of Astrup's youth and sensitivity. Another famous Norwegian explorer, Roald Amundsen, also later wrote that he believed Peary was at least partly responsible for Astrup's death.

When Peary sent the *Falcon* home in August 1894, he told Josephine that he and his two remaining companions would try to reach Independence Bay again in the spring. If she was unable to raise enough money to send a relief ship for him the next year, he told her, the trio would sledge to southern Greenland and take a passing ship to Denmark.

But Mrs. Peary would prove even more adept at raising funds than would her husband. At the same time that Cook was pounding on every door he could think of for backing for his dream of an expedition to the South Pole, Mrs. Peary was managing to raise the money she needed to rescue her husband from his uncertain fate. And in the course of raising the ten thousand dollars needed to charter the relief ship, Mrs. Peary forged an alliance with Gardiner Greene Hubbard, a wealthy lawyer who helped his son-in-law, Alexander Graham Bell, establish the Bell Telephone Company. Hubbard was also the primary force behind the fledgling, but growing, National Geographic Society. Hubbard and Morris K. Jesup, the president of the American Museum of Natural History who had already helped Peary, made sure that Mrs. Peary raised enough money to retrieve her husband.

Meanwhile, Peary suffered through another disastrous journey as he again tried to reach Independence Bay. He barely managed to get himself and his companions back to Anniversary Lodge. Sufficient groundwork for the trek had not been done, and Peary and his two fellow travelers suffered the consequences. Peary seemed to believe that determination and stubbornness alone would somehow get him through to the North Pole. The expedition's supplies were inadequate for this journey, and these three brave but foolish men barely escaped with their lives. Of their forty-two dogs, only one survived; the others died of exposure, were fed to the other dogs, or, finally, were eaten by the three adventurers.

One unadoring Peary biographer later wrote of this effort: "There have been many journeys in which men suffered more, but few when such risks were taken. It was one of the worst, not only because of its period and hardship, but because it accomplished nothing. . . . Peary's short cut to fame, up to this time, had not proved a success."

When the ship Mrs. Peary had chartered, the same *Kite* that had carried Peary on his First North Greenland Expedition, arrived in August 1895, the crew found a dispirited, unhealthy-looking Peary, who dreaded the prospects of returning home and once again admitting his failure. To bring back some tangible sign of success, Peary proposed taking the three meteorites he had located the previous year back to the United States, even though they were the Eskimos' only source of iron for their hunting weapons and implements. The two smaller meteorites were placed aboard the *Kite,* but the third proved too large to move without special equipment.

To keep the focus off the failures when he returned, Peary became obsessed with getting the third meteorite to the United States. After Jesup pulled as many strings as he could to force the navy to let Peary have still more time off, Peary returned in August 1896, to retrieve it, but even that effort failed. And when Peary returned to New York, he was met with even worse news: After drifting in the ice for two years aboard the *Fram,* which he was using to check the currents around the North Pole, Peary's nemesis, Norwegian explorer Fridtjof Nansen, and a companion had made a dash over the ice and gotten within 225 miles of the North Pole, the closest anyone had ever gotten to this holy grail.

Peary was crushed. His efforts had been floundering for several years, and now he was again bested, and by Nansen. But Peary had a new plan, which he unveiled in early 1897 in New York. Too much time and effort were spent on every expedition just getting men and supplies in place in the Arctic, he declared. If he could raise $150,000, he would establish a permanent base in northern Greenland from which to launch his assault on the North Pole. If need be, he reckoned, the expedition could remain in the Arctic for five years, so he could make several attempts, if necessary.

To accomplish his dream, however, he needed a five-year leave from the navy, in addition to a lot of money. But the military leadership had long ago lost its patience with the errant Peary, and no amount of string-pulling or arm-twisting by his wealthy backers was working this time. Fortune smiled upon him again, however, when Peary was introduced to a wealthy manufacturer from New York who was both a prominent Republican and a friend of President William McKinley. The man convinced the president of the necessity of freeing Peary from his military obligations—for the sake of national honor—and the explorer was immediately placed on leave to continue his quest. In fact, Peary was to spend precious few days on active duty, even though he always claimed a lifelong connection to the U.S. Navy.

The first thing Peary did with his newfound freedom was to sail back to Cape York and load on his ship the large meteorite that had frustrated him in the past. He gave all three meteorites to Mrs. Peary, and the story they told was that she had lent them to the American Museum of Natural History, which was still being run by Jesup. It was later learned that Mrs. Peary had actually sold the meteorites for fifty thousand dollars to Jesup, who then donated them to the museum. The meteorites are still on display at the museum's Hayden Planetarium in New York City.

CHAPTER 4

A Long Antarctic Night

By the time Peary was making his grandiose plans to establish a permanent base in Greenland, Cook's fund-raising efforts for his South Pole expedition had ended in failure. Cook was disappointed, and he channeled his energies into more mundane pursuits, primarily building his medical practice. Cook had bought a house in Brooklyn and was now treating a number of celebrities, but his wanderlust was far from sated.

Picking up the *New York Sun* on an August morning in 1897, Cook read a dispatch from Belgium about a delay in the departure of the Belgian Antarctic Expedition, caused by the last-minute resignation of the group's doctor. He wasted no time trying to fill the vacancy.

Cook, now thirty-two years old, sent a telegram to the expedition's commander, Adrien de Gerlache, a leading oceanographer of his day and a naval officer, who had conceived the expedition. Cook offered to serve without pay and to join up with the expedition's vessel at his own expense. He said he would bring along his Arctic gear and his dogs, if possible. This latest Scandinavian expedition was designed to make the first detailed studies of the oceans as far south as possible in the Antarctic, to search for any land masses, and to try to locate the South Magnetic Pole. Whether de Gerlache had a more adventurous agenda is still a matter of minor historical dispute.

Two days later Cook received de Gerlache's reply—in French, which was unintelligible to him—asking Cook to meet the ship, the *Belgica,* at Montevideo, Uruguay. Although it had now dawned on Cook that there could well be a major language barrier aboard the ship, and despite his not knowing a single member of the crew, Cook replied with one word: yes. A few days later, de Gerlache changed the rendezvous point to Rio de Janeiro, Brazil, and Cook began to make his preparations.

"To consent by cable to cast my lot in a battle against the supposed unsurmountable icy barriers of the south, with total strangers, men from another continent, speaking a language strange to me, does indeed seem rash," he wrote after the expedition returned. "But I never had cause to regret it. The Antarctic has always been the dream of my life, and to be on the way to it was then my ideal of happiness."

Cook actually became the third physician to sign up for the *Belgica* expedition: The first had been rejected, after his initial acceptance, for mysterious "personal reasons"; the replacement had backed out at the last minute for "family reasons." So Cook, with his Arctic credentials in hand, must have seemed heaven-sent to de Gerlache; the expedition certainly seemed that to Cook.

Three weeks later, taking all the furs he had gathered in Greenland during his trip on the *Zeta* several years earlier, hickory cut from trees in his home Sullivan County with which he intended to build sledges from his own design, material for making snowshoes and tents, and the rest of the gear he had painstakingly gathered in the Arctic, Cook departed for Rio. In his diary, which was published later as the official account of the expedition, the first entry Cook made was this: "At last I am on the way to the land which has been the dream of my life—'the mysterious Antarctic.' I have talked of this journey of exploration so long, have wished for it so persistently, that now, when my one foremost ambition seems on the verge of a realization, I can hardly assure myself that I am not on the road to another of many disappointments."

Cook arrived in Brazil three weeks later, seasick and much the worse for wear from, first, the Atlantic's choppy waters, and then, the tropical heat. In Rio, he waited another two weeks, until October 22, 1897, for the *Belgica* and the start of what all involved expected would be a history-making journey.

The *Belgica* was a ten-year-old, 110-foot long, former Norwegian sealing vessel, originally called the *Patria*. De Gerlache had managed to raise about sixty thousand dollars for the expedition in government and private funds. This amount was barely enough money for the journey, and nowhere near enough to allow the *Belgica* to be outfitted with extra protection against the ice she would face in the Antarctic waters or to buy enough supplies to provide for unforeseen emergencies, such as cold-weather gear for all the crewman. But many of these problems would not be apparent for several months.

After the *Belgica* docked in Rio, Cook came aboard and met the international crew with which he was to brave the uncharted southern fringes of the Earth. In all, the crew consisted of nine Belgians, six Norwegians, two Poles, a Romanian, and Cook—the sole American. That day Cook also set his eyes for the first time on a man who would be a lifelong friend and colleague, Roald Amundsen, the young Norwegian chief officer of the expedition.

Up to this time, the South Pole had generated relatively little interest from explorers or adventurers because of its distance from the naval and economic powers of the age and because there was no commercial incentive of the magnitude of a search for a shorter route to the Orient that would urge adventurers on. But this lack of exploration did nothing to suppress the heartiest imaginings of what would be found at the South Pole. Myths sprang up and grew of an immense Eldorado, a land of milk and honey hidden behind the protecting icebergs and the fog that seemed to shroud all else in the Antarctic. "This land was supposed to be inhabited by a curious race of people who possessed a superabundance of gold, precious stones and other material wealth," wrote Cook. But while similar fantasies drew scores of men to the Arctic to search for treasure, the Antarctic remained mostly unexplored.

In 1739, a French expedition that had been sent south to annex the "South Land" made the first recorded sighting of what the territory was actually like. The crew spied a tiny spit of land that was actually part of a small island far outside the Antarctic Circle; the land was eventually named Bouvet Island, in honor of the commander of the expedition, Captain Jean-Francois-Charles Bouvet de Lozier. But instead of gold and jewels, de Lozier reported icebergs "two or three hundred feet high . . . up to 10 miles long [with] all sorts of shapes. . . . [And] penguins, amphibious animals like huge ducks."

Next, the British, who had taken the lead in Arctic exploration, also cast colonial eyes southward. Under cover of searching for a good spot for scientists to observe an upcoming rare astronomical event—the transit of Venus across the sun, which would provide a spectacular backdrop for studying the planet—the English sent James Cook southward in command of an expedition. Captain Cook had been given secret instructions when he departed in 1768 to beat the French in laying claim to the continent that was believed to cover the bottom of the world.

When he returned to England three years later, Captain Cook forestalled a rivalry with the French: There was no land of milk and honey worthy of serious rivalry, he reported. If a continent even existed, it must be below the fortieth parallel and as frozen as the terrain of northern Greenland, he said. The British admiralty, at Captain Cook's suggestion, agreed to send him south again to settle the question of whether land covered the South Pole region. This, of course, was the same question scientists had about the North Pole. In early 1773, Captain Cook commanded the first ship known to have crossed the Antarctic Circle; the next day he was stopped by a frozen sea. One year later, he traveled almost three hundred miles farther south before he was again stopped by ice.

It was not until January 1820 that man actually set foot on Antarctica, and it was the result of an accident. A British merchant ship, the *Williams,* had been blown off course while rounding Cape Horn and had discovered the South Shetland Islands. A nearby British naval commander decided that the reported discovery was worthy of further investigation, so he privately chartered the *Williams* and put it under the command of his own ship's navigator, Edward Bransfield. It was Bransfield who, on January 30, 1820, set foot on Graham Land. In another one of history's ironic coincidences, a Russian naval officer, Captain Thaddeus Bellingshausen, had apparently also cited the continent of Antarctica three days earlier, but did not identify it as land and did not try to set foot on it.

Except for waves of American sealers and a few forays that got closer to the actual land mass of the Antarctic, that was the extent of exploration efforts in this area before the *Belgica*'s mission.

The first obstacle for Cook to overcome aboard the *Belgica* was the language barrier. This problem was quickly resolved, however, when he learned that all the scientific staff of the expedition spoke German, which he also spoke, thanks to his immigrant parents. He also found that de Gerlache could speak a little English, as a result of a summer he spent on a sealer that operated along the coast of Greenland.

As the ship sailed slowly southward, the members of the Belgian Antarctic Expedition were feted by the Belgian communities of Rio de Janerio and Montevideo and by the Brazilian and Uruguayan governments. When Cook took stock of the ship's equipment, he was impressed by the array of modern machines, which would allow the crew to capture fish and other marine life at various ocean depths, chart submarine currents and temperatures, and study the composition of the water around the ship, as well as by the latest sounding equipment, which would permit the crew to create accurate depth charts.

There was also a well-stocked laboratory for the study of animal and plant life the crew encountered and for meteorological and oceanographic experiments. "When one first steps into the laboratory," he wrote, "there creeps over one a fear to move; for everything seems a frail meshwork of glass; straight and spiral tubes, glass cylinders, thermometers, barometers, test tubes, bottles, and glass articles—too numerous to mention—are attached to all the available surface on the walls, the shelves and even the ceiling." There was also a photography lab, and Cook was tapped as official photographer, in addition to his duties as surgeon; he also found himself once again serving as an expedition's ethnologist.

The *Belgica* stopped at Punta Arenas, the southernmost town on the South American continent, and the crew spent a month exploring the Tierra del Fuego. Cook was once again fascinated by the local Indian tribes, this time the Onas, the Alaculoofs, and the Yahgans. Time had left these Indians pretty much alone, in part because of their reputation among the other residents of the region as unreliable and often unfriendly and, some said, man-eating.

Cook was quite taken with the tribesmen he met, and in his brief stay immersed himself in the local culture, just as he had among the Eskimos of northern Greenland. In the course of his visit, he met Thomas Bridges, a former British missionary, and Bridges's son, Lucas. After twenty-five years of living and working among the tribes, the elder Bridges was awarded a 50,000-acre land grant by the Argentine government in 1886. Bridges had resigned from the clergy and had built his holdings into a 137,000-acre cattle and sheep ranch. He explained to Cook that all three tribes were dwindling in size and that his grand hope was to publish a 32,000-word dictionary of their language so philologists from around the world could study it. Unfortunately, Bridges had not used a standard phonetic system in his work, which would make it unlikely that he would find a publisher. However, Cook told Bridges that he believed the phonetic problem could be resolved and offered to find a publisher for the dictionary when he returned to the United States.

In a book he wrote many years later, Lucas Bridges said that Cook had told his father "there was a society in the United States which made a speciality of American aboriginal languages. . . . He offered to take charge of the dictionary there and then, but father . . . promised to hand it over to Dr. Cook on the return voyage of the Belgica." None of the participants could have guessed that this dictionary would be involved in mystery and intrigue, would become part of the Great North Pole Controversy, and wind up being purloined by the Nazis before finally finding a home in the British Museum.

Eventually, the *Belgica* departed Tierra del Fuego and by the end of January 1898 was in the uncharted waters of the Antarctic. This was relatively late in the season to begin such a journey—since winter descends there as summer approaches in the United States—

but de Gerlache was not about to wait an entire year to begin his primary business. As the ship slowly made its way southward, the crew was immediately reminded of the dangers that lurked in the cold waters that surrounded them. While Cook and First Officer Amundsen were on the bridge of the heaving ship during a storm, they heard a piercing scream and discovered that Carl Wiencke, one of the youngest crew members, had been washed overboard while he was cleaning spilled coal out of the scuppers along the *Belgica*'s deck. Although Wiencke managed to grab hold of a line and despite the heroic efforts of Georges Lecointe, the ship's executive officer, Wiencke was lost.

The *Belgica* continued southward past Bransfield Strait, named after the first man to set foot on Graham Land, and entered a previously undiscovered passage to the Pacific, which they named Belgica Strait. In that strait, the crewmen named various islands and geographic features; one was named for Wiencke, another for the dead Astrup, who had accompanied Peary on two expeditions to the Arctic.

The *Belgica* entered the Pacific on February 17, and despite warnings from Amundsen that the lateness of the season would make navigation treacherous, de Gerlache pressed on, intent upon setting a new farthest-south mark before having to return to friendlier waters. After several close calls with giant icebergs, and despite being nearly blocked by a wall of icebergs one night, de Gerlache took them farther south.

But a big storm on March 1 drove the ship into the main body of the polar ice, and after four days of fruitless maneuvering, they had to accept their fate: "On the fourth of March," Cook wrote in his log, "we were forced to admit our inability to extricate ourselves. Our position . . . [is] about 300 miles across the polar circle and about 1,100 miles from the geographical pole. . . . We are now again firmly stationed in a moving sea of ice, with no land and nothing stable on the horizon to warn us of our movements. . . . We pass no fixed point, and can see no pieces of ice stir; everything is quiet. The entire horizon drifts with us. We are part of an endless frozen sea."

After a few more feeble attempts to free the ship from the firm grasp of the pack ice, the crew settled down to preparing themselves and the ship as best as they could for the long, dark winter ahead. First, the *Belgica* had to be made ready; without the ship, there was no hope of surviving the winter or of sailing home in the spring, for there were no natives to turn to for help. And the chances of the ship's survival seemed remote to Cook, as he and the crew watched the shattering and grinding of giant icebergs against each other in the distance or listened to the booming explosions of their collisions as the many ice chunks ploddingly merged into one enormous, and seemingly endless, island of white. Cook called the *Belgica* "the football of an unpromising fate . . . kicked, pushed, squeezed and ushered helplessly at the mercy of the pack."

Some suspicion has been raised that de Gerlache intended to get the *Belgica* trapped in the ice pack so he and his crew would be the first men in history to spend the winter in Antarctica. But de Gerlache always denied that he had any such hidden agenda.

For now, the crew members spent time getting acquainted with their new home: They hunted, made scientific observations, and marveled at the natural phenomena. And they began to accept that they would be the first humans ever to attempt to live in the Antarctic through the long winter's night.

Cook, meanwhile, was not about to waste this opportunity, and by the middle of March he was testing his polar equipment. To get a better view of the aurora australis that was beginning now that the sun was starting to set for its long sleep and to test his new sleeping bag, Cook left the ship late one night and went to spend the night on the ice. He fell asleep to the eerie quiet that had settled over them in just two weeks as the ice pack hardened. "There was not a breath of air stirring the glassy atmosphere, and not a sound from the noise of the ship, the silence and the solitude were curiously oppressive," Cook wrote. When the wind shifted in the middle of the night and Cook tried to turn himself so he could move his breathing hole away from the breeze, he found that the hood of the sleeping bag was as hard as iron and that his hair, face, and the clothing around his neck were frozen to it.

As he pondered his next move, Cook found himself entranced with the display in the sky: "The aurora, as the blue twilight announced the dawn, had settled into an arc of steady brilliancy which hung low on the southern sky, while directly under the zenith there quivered a few streamers; overhead was the Southern Cross, and all around the blue dome there were sparkling spots which stood out like huge gems. Along the horizon . . . there was the glow of the sun, probably reflected from the unknown southern lands. This was a band of ochre tapering to gold and ending in orange red." By 5 A.M., two hours into this display, he wrote: "The highest icebergs began to glitter as if tipped with gold, and then the hummocks brightened. Finally, as the sun rose from her snowy bed, the whole frigid sea was colored as if flooded with liquid gold."

Cook, still solidly frozen into his sleeping bag, was shaken from his reverie by loud chattering; a group of penguins had come to visit their companion, not realizing that the bundle of skins was actually Cook's sleeping bag. Cook "hastened to respond to the call" of his visitors, he wrote, and freed himself from the bag by pounding his head against the ice and yanking his head back, leaving several tufts of hair behind. He jumped into his fur clothing, "bid the surprised penguins good morning, and went aboard. Here I learned that Lecointe, not knowing of my presence on the ice, had taken me for a seal, and was only waiting for better light to try his luck with the rifle."

The crew remained in high spirits as the hours of daylight decreased steadily every day. By the end of April, when lamps were necessary for reading by 3 P.M., the crew agreed that it was time to get ready for winter. The ship was rearranged, and sleeping quarters were built in places that could be heated efficiently by the ship's stove; little huts were constructed on the ice to shield the crew from the wind and make it possible to make observations during the winter; the ship was weatherproofed as best as it could be; and the crew hunted as many seals and penguins as possible and stored the meat and hides. Snow was banked around the ship before the sun set for good that year on May 15.

The disappearance of the sun sent morale into a tailspin. The initial excitement of discovering what was around them had worn off. The men soon became lethargic and melancholy. They had no appetites and no desire to socialize with each other. Several began to lose interest in their scientific studies. At this point, Cook began the first detailed study of the effects of prolonged darkness on a group of men.

Cook's book about the expedition, *Through the First Antarctic Night,* presents a matter-of-fact recitation of the details of the Belgian Antarctic Expedition and paints a vivid, and apparently accurate, picture of the struggle waged by the crew of the *Belgica.* But one must read the accounts of others, especially *My Life as an Explorer,* by Amundsen, to get a true picture of Cook's crucial and heroic role in the entire crew's survival.

Cook wrote that the two main enemies of mankind in the Antarctic, at least at the beginning of the crew's entrapment in the ice, were isolation and humidity—not, as one might expect, the cold. The dampness when the temperature hovered around the freezing point made life almost unbearable, he wrote, ringing water out of all their clothes and making life inside the *Belgica* most unpleasant. On "balmy" days, when the thermometer hovered near the freezing point, the men prayed for the return of the minus-twenty-degree or minus-thirty-degree days.

Cook noted that when the sun disappeared, the crew members began to suffer from erratic heart rhythms; one day a crewman's heart would be slow and erratic, the next day fast and strong. The men's faces puffed and were oily, their ankles and eyes swelled, and their hair grew rapidly. And he noted a swift loss of conditioning. The crew was actually suffering from the early stages of what we know as scurvy, which is caused by an acute shortage of vitamin C. But there was no understanding of vitamins at that time; in fact, the British had accidentally stumbled upon a cure for scurvy in fresh limes, which are high in vitamin C. To ease the problem of storing large quantities of limes on long voyages, the British had the bright idea of squeezing the limes and putting the juice in tins. The result was that scurvy again became a major killer among seamen because, as we know today, the vitamin C was lost in the tinning process.

As fitness and morale deteriorated, the crew suffered another harsh blow, the death of Emile Danco, who served as the expedition's magnetician. Cook reported that Danco had a chronic heart ailment, which made him less able to withstand the peculiar effects of sunlessness. There are indications, however, that Danco actually died of scurvy. The crew broke a hole in the ice and slipped Danco's sailcloth-wrapped and weighted body through it into the sea. The eerie burial "brought over us a spell of despondency which we seem unable to conquer. . . . We are constantly picturing to ourselves the form of our late companion floating about in a standing position, with the weights to his feet, under the frozen surface and perhaps under the *Belgica*," Cook wrote.

The next depressing event was the death of the ship's cat, Nansen. After months of playfulness and affectionate companionship, Nansen had become irritable and hid in the bowels of the ship for days at a time. The crew was now fully in the grips of despair, and even the hardy Lecointe was sure he was dying; he had already written his will.

Cook, realizing that some action had to be taken quickly if they were to survive, theorized that the heat and light of an open fire might take the place of sunlight and begin to fight the disease he had identified as a form of anemia peculiar to polar regions. After his first experiments proved successful, Cook began to "prescribe" what he called the "baking treatment" for the crew; in less than an hour, he reported, men whose heartbeats were barely perceptible when the process began would return to nearly normal. The heat and light of the fire seemed to have a powerful restorative effect on the men's spirits and energy levels as well.

But the physical effects of scurvy remained; indeed, untreated scurvy is always fatal. Cook, relying upon his experiences in the Arctic and from having observed that the Eskimos of Greenland were unaffected by the disease, had inspired the men to lay in a large stock of seal and penguin meat, although he had been generally unsuccessful in getting the men to eat it. Some of the problem can well be imagined from the description of penguin meat that Cook provided: "The penguin, as an animal, seems to be made up of an equal proportion of mammal, fish and fowl. If it is possible to imagine a piece of beef, an odoriferous codfish and a canvasback duck roasted in a pot, with blood and cod-liver oil for sauce, the illustration will be complete."

Because the crewmen clearly understood they were dying, when

Cook prescribed undercooked penguin and seal steaks as medicine, they willingly consumed them in great quantities. The vitamin C in the unprocessed and undercooked meat immediately worked wonders and restored the crew's fitness.

Amundsen later wrote of Cook during the *Belgica* expedition: "He of all the ship's company was the one man of unfaltering courage, unfailing hope, endless cheerfulness and unwearied kindness. When anyone was sick, he was at his bedside to comfort him; when anyone was disheartened, he was there to encourage and inspire. And not only was his faith undaunted, but his ingenuity and enterprise were boundless."

Thus, by the time the long-awaited sun peeked over the horizon on July 22 for a few minutes, the crew was again healthy and active and prepared to sail home. The plan was to wait until the sun's heat broke open the pack ice and freed the ship. In the meantime, Cook and Amundsen spent much time together perfecting their techniques on the ice and testing Cook's designs for polar equipment.

While Cook's narrative is matter-of-fact and in this case imparts none of the drama of the situation or the importance of his actions, others who were involved and those who have studied the expedition have heaped much praise upon Cook. "It was Cook who now saved the expedition," said one writer who studied the race to discover the South Pole. And Cook's action forged part of a lifelong bond with Amundsen, who often told others that Cook had saved the lives of all the *Belgica*'s crew.

Amundsen wrote in his diary:

It is a pleasure to make excursions with the company that I had. Lecointe; small, cheerful, witty; never losing hope. Cook . . . calm and imperturbable, never losing his temper; and in addition, there are the many small things one can learn in the society of such a thoroughly practical Polar explorer like Cook. In his contact with the North Greenland Eskimos, and in his profound study of everything concerning Polar life, he has, without a doubt, greater insight in these matters than most men in the field. . . . He has advice on everything. He gives it in a likeable and tactful manner; not with fuss and noise. . . .

Together, Cook and Amundsen tried out Cook's new sledge design and built several models with the hickory wood the doctor had brought; together they built a silk tent that Cook had designed that, in an emergency—such as a fast-breaking Arctic storm—could be set up in five minutes by one man; they raced each other to test the value of snowshoes against the progress a traveler could make on skis; and they perfected their techniques as well as their equipment. And Cook constructed sun goggles that were based on an Eskimo design he had seen in Greenland and improved upon by using photographic filters instead of narrow slits. Amundsen was to use Cook's design when he launched his expedition to the South Pole, which prevented his men from suffering the snowblindness that haunted his rival, Robert F. Scott, and Scott's expedition.

Summer came, yet the *Belgica* was still firmly frozen in the ice. The crew began to worry that a second winter in the Antarctic loomed. This was too much for some of the crew; three men were by now insane from the physical hardships and the isolation, and Cook was worried about the condition of several others, including de Gerlache.

In early January 1899, when things looked most hopeless, one of the crewmen spotted a large basin of open water about one thousand yards from the *Belgica*. "The rest of us thought nothing of it," Amundsen wrote, "as naturally water would form here and there. Somehow, though, to Dr. Cook's restless mind this basin seemed an omen of hope. He declared his firm conviction that the ice would break and that, when the opening came, it would lead to this basin. Therefore he proposed what sounded at first like a mad enterprise."

What Cook proposed was that narrow trenches be cut through the thick ice from the bow and stern of the *Belgica* toward the open pool. His reasoning was that the heat from the sun would cause the ice to fracture along the trench line. This escape plan broke the crew's overwhelming lethargy, which had increased when they thought they were trapped indefinitely. For three days, the men worked ceaselessly making the trench. But the sun's heat was not strong enough to accomplish their goal. Then Cook proposed an even more energetic solution: to cut a channel all the way to the basin. The ice was an average of about five feet thick, and since some of the ice in the direct path between the ship and the basin was twenty-five-feet thick, they had to cut a circuitous path about a mile and a half long.

After discovering that the explosive they had taken along with them, tonite, was virtually useless under these conditions, the *Belgica*'s crew began an extraordinary task: actually cutting a channel by hand that was wide enough to sail their ship through. For more than a month they struggled night and day, since the midnight sun burned constantly. Finally, on February 14, the wind shifted the ice pack and provided the last link to the basin; off they went. "We lost no time in steaming out," wrote Cook. "No body of men were ever happier than the officers and crew of the *Belgica* as the good old ship thumped the edge of the ice which had held her a prisoner for nearly a year."

But two days and twenty miles later, they were again caught in the ice. In their new location, wrote Amundsen, "All day and all night we were subjected to a terrific grinding pressure, and the noise of ice cakes battering against our sides . . . was at times so loud as to make conversation trying. Here again, Dr. Cook's ingenuity saved the day. He had carefully preserved the skins of the penguins we had killed, and we now made them into mats and lowered them over the sides of the vessel, where they took up and largely mitigated the impact of the ice."

Finally, after a month, the wind blew the ship free, and the *Belgica,* long given up for lost, sailed into Punta Arenas on March 28, 1899, fifteen months after departing civilization's shores. In their absence, the crew quickly learned, Guglielmo Marconi had invented the wireless and the Spanish-American and Boer Wars had broken out.

Cook left the ship and returned to New York in June. For his many brave deeds, he was later awarded the Order of Leopold by King Leopold of Belgium, the only non-Belgian crew member so honored.

Upon his return from the Belgian Antarctic Expedition, Cook again invested his energies in rebuilding his only source of income: his medical practice. While he received some public acclaim upon his return, it was hardly worthy of the major role he had played in that historic expedition. But much of this lack of fanfare was his own doing, since it was not until years later—when others told their tales—that Cook's heroism became widely known.

Cook traveled to Brussels in February 1900, for a meeting of the commission that King Leopold had created to coordinate the publication of the expedition's many findings. In addition to agreeing to write the first account of the journey, and the only one ever published in English, Cook pledged to write a medical report on the effects of the dark winter on the crew and a paper on the Indians of Tierra del Fuego and to get Bridges's extensive dictionary ready for publication. Bridges died while the *Belgica* was in the Antarctic, but his son gave Cook the manuscript. The commission balked at publishing the dictionary on the grounds that it was not really a product of the expedition. But, Cook reported, "in a friendly spirit toward the late Mr. Bridges and his Indians, I persuaded the Belgians, at great expense, to publish the work." He spent a year working on the dictionary, but by the time of the Great North Pole Controversy, it had not been printed, although, he said, parts of it were at the printer's.

Another interesting part of Cook's story of the expedition, which was published in 1900, was an appendix he wrote on "The Possibilities of Antarctic Exploration." Cook saw great economic potential in the region from its minerals and animal and fish life. And, he said, the Antarctic offered the world's scientists an excellent laboratory in which to study weather and the evolution of life.

Cook's desire to become the first man in history to reach the South Pole had been whetted by his adventures with Amundsen and the rest of the *Belgica*'s crew, and he again tried to find financial backers for his own full-scale assault on Antarctica. Part of his plan involved an invention he was working on: a car modified to travel over the ice. But, once again, he was unable to raise the money required for such an adventure, so he returned his attention to medicine and continued to dream.

CHAPTER 5

Peary's Failed Expeditions

Peary, after obtaining the third meteorite that he and Josephine then sold to Jesup for the American Museum of Natural History in New York, concentrated on raising more money, trying feverishly to enlist a group of wealthy men as long-term sponsors for his plan to establish a permanent base in north Greenland. He proposed that twenty-five backers pledge to give him one thousand dollars a year for the four years that remained of his leave from the navy. But he had signed up only eight benefactors by May 1898, a time when unbeknownst to the world, Cook and the crew of the *Belgica* were awaiting the start of the long winter night in the Antarctic.

Peary was in despair by the time his new ship—the *Windward,* which had been used to rescue explorers Fridtjof Nansen and Hjalmer Johansen three years earlier from their unsuccessful run at the North Pole, during which they had set the farthest north record—had reached the United States, a gift to him from England's Lord Northcliffe. The outbreak of the Spanish-American War was a serious setback to his fund-raising prospects, and it tweaked his conscience as a military officer. However, true to form, Peary looked upon events mainly in light of how they affected him and his plans. In a letter to his wife, he wrote, "Well, Jo, last time [in 1893] they staged a silver panic to keep me from going [by cutting into his fund-raising plans]. Now they're going to have a war!'' As for the struggle between his duty to the navy and his plans to reach the North Pole, Peary found the choice easy to make: onward to the Arctic.

As Peary continued to struggle to find backing for his mission, he learned that Norwegian explorer Otto Sverdrup, who had been with Nansen on the first crossing of northern Greenland, was taking Nansen's old ship, the *Fram,* on what Sverdrup said would be a four-year mission designed primarily to explore and survey the cluster of islands west of Greenland. Peary, believing that Sverdrup was actually secretly pursuing the North Pole, accused Sverdrup of usurping his plan of attack, even though Sverdrup had made his general strategy known several months before Peary unveiled his five-year plan in September 1896. Peary also questioned the propriety of Sverdrup even venturing into "his" northern Greenland, again showing that Peary had come to believe he had an exclusive franchise on the Arctic.

Panic-stricken, Peary had the *Windward* loaded in 1898, and he set sail as fast as he could so he could beat Sverdrup to Greenland. Deciding that the *Windward* could not beat the *Fram,* since Sverdrup had left Norway a few weeks before the *Windward* was ready, Peary chartered a smaller and faster ship, the *Hope.* He arrived in Etah—a tiny coastal village that was the Greenland base for explorers for many years and was at the time the northernmost permanent settlement in the world—just ahead of the *Fram* and the *Windward.*

He bribed a group of Eskimos to accompany him north, where he planned to establish his base. But the *Windward*—to which Peary had transferred—was quickly frozen in by the ice in Smith Sound, the narrow channel between Etah and Ellesmere Island, when they were barely seventy miles north of the settlement. The *Fram* was also frozen in, about fifteen miles south of Peary's ship. Peary then decided to make an all-out run, on foot, for Fort Conger, two hundred miles to the north. He apparently believed that Sverdrup had a similar plan, and he was obsessed with the necessity of beating Sverdrup to it and taking possession of the shelter.

Fort Conger was the base built some twenty years earlier by then-Lieutenant Adolphus W. Greely, who had led the first official, and ill-fated, American expedition to the Arctic. Greely had been ordered by the U.S. government to establish a permanent base far north, which he did at Fort Conger, near the top of Ellesmere Island on Robeson Channel. Greely's twenty-six-man expedition then spent two years trying to find a route to the North Pole before turning back to Fort Conger. Expected resupply ships failed to reach Fort Conger, however, and Greely and his men headed southward in what became a horrific journey. Only seven of the expedition members were alive by the time they were found by the men of the *Thetis,* under the command of Winfield Scott Schley (who later became an admiral and played a role in the Great North Pole Controversy), at Cape Sabine.

Peary's obsession with Sverdrup had apparently been further fueled by a chance meeting in late October, when Peary stumbled upon the Norwegian's base camp while on a sledge journey. Sverdrup recounted that he had invited Peary to join his crew for breakfast, but that the American declined even to have a cup of coffee with him. Henson later told a biographer that Peary called him into his cabin when he returned from that sledge trip. Peary was very agitated, he said, and kept pacing around the room. "Sverdrup may at this minute be planning to beat me to Fort Conger," he told Henson. "I can't let him do it. . . . I'll get to Conger before Sverdrup if it kills me." And it almost did.

Once again, Peary's internal demons that were driving him to succeed caused him to act impulsively, and he paid dearly for it. Marching through the brutal cold and darkness, Peary spent seventeen days in December and January groping his way to Fort Conger and the cabin that had been empty since Greely abandoned it twenty years earlier. After he and Henson finally reached the cabin early in 1899, when Henson helped remove the forty-two-year-old explorer's boots, some of Peary's toes snapped off in his hands. In all, Peary lost eight of his toes to frostbite. He was dragged back upon a sledge to the *Windward,* where the expedition's surgeon, Dr. Thomas S. Dedrick, finished the amputations in mid-March, leaving only the little toe on each foot. The results of this reckless race with shadows—Sverdrup had no plans to go to Fort Conger—would hobble Peary for the rest of his days.

Meanwhile, some of Peary's staunchest backers had met in New

York and, under the leadership of Jesup, Bridgman, and several other financiers, formed the Peary Arctic Club, to give the explorer the firm monetary base he had been seeking throughout his career. What turned the tide was a letter from Peary, written in August from Etah, that focused on the purely imaginary contest he was running against Sverdrup and turned the entire affair into a game in which the United States could capture a prize, as if the quest for the North Pole was now a simple horse race with the Norwegians. This group of rich and powerful men would more than make up for the fact that the United States government at this time had no interest in providing financial backing to Peary's efforts, and it would eventually play a pivotal role in the great controversy that was to ensue.

When Peary sailed with the *Windward* back to Etah, two ships were riding at anchor: the *Diana,* a relief ship the Peary Arctic Club had sent, and Sverdrup's *Fram.* Peary refused to return home for medical treatment, as advised by Dr. Dedrick and Bridgman, who had come on the *Diana* to check on Peary. Sverdrup invited Peary—who had told one of the Norwegians in Sverdrup's crew that he had injured his feet in a hunting accident—to dinner, but Peary curtly refused, according to Sverdrup. Peary's bad behavior went a step further: He refused to let the *Diana* or the *Windward* carry word of Sverdrup's work back to civilization. Peary told Sverdrup that only Sverdrup's crew's personal letters that made no mention of his expedition would be taken south on his ships. Once again, Peary was guilty of a serious breach of ethics and good behavior.

It is noteworthy that Sverdrup really was not interested in pursuing the North Pole and spent all four years of his expedition doing just what he had said he was going to do: exploring the islands west of Greenland. Thus, Peary's hostility was unwarranted, and his recklessness was for naught.

The *Windward* sailed home, with most of the expedition's crew aboard, at the same time as the *Diana*—apparently because Peary had once again alienated his crew—leaving Peary with only Dedrick, Henson, and the Eskimos. Peary returned to Fort Conger in February 1900 and spent almost a year wandering around the region, mainly being carried about on his sledge.

The next spring, in April 1901, Peary, accompanied only by Henson and one Eskimo, departed Fort Conger for what he described as a "northern trip," not a run for the North Pole. Peary was hampered by the refusal of the other Eskimos to go northward with him. Henson broke the trail while Peary followed slowly behind on foot, in a painful exercise. Only forty-five miles from Fort Conger, they turned back; after another stay at Fort Conger, they headed south, and at Cape Sabine, on Ellesmere Island across Smith Sound from Etah, they were astonished to find the *Windward.* The ship had been frozen in the ice—with Peary's wife and daughter, now seven years old, aboard—since the fall.

By the end of 1900, the Peary Arctic Club's leaders were concerned. They had received no word from Peary since the *Diana* and *Windward* departed in 1899, nor had Mrs. Peary been heard from since the *Windward* returned north earlier that year. The club's members chartered another relief vessel, the *Erik,* and put Bridgman in charge of mounting a rescue effort. Needing a doctor, and one experienced in polar life, it was not surprising that Bridgman turned to Cook.

Cook was more than a little reluctant to go. In addition to the ill feeling remaining from their split after the earlier expedition, Cook was sure that Peary was safe and well. But Cook let Bridgman convince him to come along as second in command of the expedition. Cook not only went along as a volunteer, he agreed to pay his own expenses and to bring his own gear.

When they arrived in summer 1901, the group found Peary and the *Windward* at Etah, and they quickly realized that Peary was less than delighted to see them. Dissatisfied with his progress over the past three years and looking ill, Peary reluctantly agreed even to let Cook examine him. Cook believed Peary was suffering from anemia and suggested that he return home for treatment of that illness and for further surgery on the stumps of his amputated toes. Peary vehemently refused to go, saying he intended to use all the remaining year of his leave from the navy in the Arctic.

But, Peary ordered the *Erik* to take Dedrick, who had resigned from the expedition after a series of arguments with Peary, back to the United States. Dedrick had, by that time, moved into a stone Eskimo hut. Although the cause of this latest rupture between Peary and a crew member was never fully explained, it is known that it was a fight over medical treatment that Dedrick insisted on providing to the Eskimos, over Peary's objection. Peary apparently believed the Eskimos were not seriously ill and that Dedrick's ministrations only encouraged them not to work.

But Dedrick refused to return to the United States because he had decided that his honor required that he remain in Greenland as long as Peary or any members of his expedition were there. Dedrick refused to budge, even after Bridgman revoked the $1,800 bonus he was owed and refused to leave him any food from the *Kite.* Cook and another *Kite* passenger provided Dedrick with canned goods, a rifle, ammunition, and furs.

The *Windward* then departed for the United States, while the *Kite* carried Peary, Henson, and their Eskimos across Smith Sound to Cape Sabine and dropped them there before departing for the south. Peary prepared the group for another northward expedition. A month later, after the waters had frozen, Dedrick learned that Peary's Eskimos were sick, and he immediately raced across Smith Sound.

Peary, however, refused to let Dedrick treat the Eskimos and ordered him away from Cape Sabine. Six of the Eskimos died, according to Peary, who never mentioned Dedrick's offer of medical assistance in his writings. After the epidemic, many of the Eskimos refused to work for Peary any longer, although some were convinced to stay for a while with promises of rich rewards. By the time Peary and Henson reached the ice of the Polar Sea at the top of Ellesmere Island, however, only four Eskimos remained with him.

After making little progress during fifteen days of storms and poor traveling conditions, Peary gave up in despair. "The game is off," he wrote in his diary. "My dream of 16 years is ended. . . . I have made the best fight I knew. . . . I cannot accomplish the impossible."

Soon after Peary and Henson's return to Cape Sabine, the *Windward* returned, with Mrs. Peary and daughter again aboard. Mrs.

Peary told Peary that Nansen's "farthest north" had been broken in 1900 by Captain Umberto Cagni of the Italian Abruzzi Expedition. Peary then turned to Henson and said, "Next time I'll smash that all to bits. Next time." And with that, Peary returned home on the *Windward* in late 1902.

Cook, in the meantime, had gone on with his life after the Belgian Antartic Expedition. He married Marie Fidele Hunt, a well-to-do widow of another doctor, on June 10, 1902, his thirty-seventh birthday. At the same time, he became a family man, since his new bride had a daughter from her previous marriage.

Cook had actually stood Marie up; they had agreed to go out together, when Cook was called by Bridgman to help rescue Peary. Cook wrote a note of explanation to Marie, but she never received it. He clearly made amends when he returned to Brooklyn.

The new Mrs. Cook, who had been left in solid financial condition by her first husband, was an enthusiastic supporter of the explorer's latest dream: scaling the recently discovered Mount McKinley in America's newly purchased Alaskan territory.

CHAPTER 6

Atop the Continent

At the close of the nineteenth century, the United States's largest possession, the Alaska Territory, was virtually unexplored. The climate and the terrain of much of its interior, combined with its inaccessibility, had prevented all but the hardiest from trying to unlock Alaska's secrets.

In 1902, Alfred H. Brooks, head of the U.S. Geological Survey's Alaska branch, led an expedition to explore a portion of the territory's most dramatic physical feature, Mount McKinley, and wrote a report on the group's findings, the first survey of the giant mountain. The very existence of Mount McKinley had, in fact, not even been known until five years earlier, even though the mountain soars above twenty thousand feet, the highest point in North America.

Cook obtained a copy of this report, and it stirred his desire to lead the first expedition to climb all the way to McKinley's summit. Spurred by the enthusiastic moral and financial support of his new wife, and with an advance from *Harper's Monthly* for an account of his journey, Cook set about organizing the first expedition of his exploration career soon after he returned from the unnecessary rescue mission to Peary's Greenland camp in 1902.

Cook's plans centered on adapting the techniques and equipment he had perfected in his Arctic and Antarctic expeditions to mountain climbing. The primary element of this trek—which was to be a hallmark in all his adventures—was the simplification of methods and equipment: There would be no caravans of porters scaling the mountain carrying enormous loads of material, as was the usual practice. And the climbers would not be burdened with weighty backpacks. The staple food on the climb would be pemmican, a mixture of mashed dried beef, raisins, and nuts, held together by tallow. This dish, modified from a mixture North American Indians made, was now being used by most modern explorers. Cook's lightweight tent, which he had tested in Antarctica, would serve as shelter on the expedition. And Cook had developed a fur sleeping bag that was also an overcoat, which weighed only five pounds.

Historically, the territory of Alaska had belonged to Russia. But, during a mid–nineteenth-century budget crisis, the Russian government, tired of spending great sums of money maintaining its far-flung colonies, decided to dispose of some of the least productive ones. Among the territories the Russians put at the top of the surplus list was the vast wasteland of Alaska, located across the narrow Bering Strait from Siberia. The most likely candidate to be foolhardy enough to want to take this perpetual money loser off its hands, the Russians knew, was the United States. The young country had begun to recover from its divisive Civil War and was looking to expand its borders as one way of turning the nation's focus away from its internal problems.

The Russians decided that the enormous hunk of mostly uninhabited real estate was worth $5 million, but their shrewd negotiator, Minister Edward de Stoeckl, was no beginner at horse trading. Instead of initiating negotiations with the United States through Secretary of State William H. Seward in Washington, de Stoeckl began a campaign among Seward's friends in New York that was designed to spark interest in buying the property by planting rumors about how lucrative it would be to the United States to annex this territory for its natural resources, namely fish and furs.

By the time de Stoeckl sat down with Seward in 1867, the American was primed; the Russian set the price at $7.2 million, to give himself plenty of negotiating room, but Seward immediately accepted the opening price, much to de Stoeckl's surprise. Seward was so worried that de Stoeckl would back out of the deal that he ordered U.S. government clerks to work through the night after the negotiating session to prepare the treaty to formalize the sale.

The deal quickly became known in the United States as "Seward's Folly," and Alaska was dubbed "Seward's Ice Box." Much of this criticism, however, was quickly mitigated when, only a few years later, the fisheries of Alaska earned back much of the purchase price. But the population of the mainland United States quickly lost interest in the new acquisition, little of which had been explored. One good indication of how little known this region was, was that it took thirty years to find Mount McKinley. A gold-mining prospector stumbled across the peak during his travels in south central Alaska and named it Mount McKinley in honor of the president. Its discoverer estimated that the mountain was twenty thousand feet high, and McKinley would turn out to be the highest peak in all North America. That same year, Alaska's second tallest mountain, Mount St. Elias, made news when it was climbed by a team led by the duke of Abruzzi, the Italian naval commander who three years later would lead the expedition that broke Nansen's "farthest north" mark in the Arctic.

Cook enlisted four men to join his expedition in 1903: Ralph Shainwald, a college student who had already been on an Arctic expedition, and Robert Dunn, a young man Cook had met in Alaska a few years earlier, both of whom made financial contributions to the adventure; photographer Walter Miller; and Fred Printz, a guide who had been on the Brooks expedition to Mount McKinley. Cook was thirty-eight years old when his expedition left its base camp at a trading post in a village named Tyonek, 150 air miles from Mount McKinley. Thanks to Cook's planning, each man would carry fifty pounds of material on his back when the actual climb began; each man would be self-sufficient for almost two weeks.

To carry their supplies to the base of the mountain, where they would establish their main camp, the expedition employed fourteen pack horses; they followed a route Brooks had explored on his earlier trek, which brought them to Mount McKinley's western slopes through Simpson Pass between peaks of the Alaska Range of mountains, of which Mount McKinley is a part. In all, it took them fifty-four days on "a tortuous course of 500 miles through swamps and forests, over glacial streams, up and down mountain sides." From the base of the mountain, they first explored a ridge on the southwest side and got to about eight thousand feet before meeting an impassable obstruction. They moved twenty-five miles to the northeast and tried again, this time on the northwest face. At eleven thousand feet, they encountered a series of sheer granite cliffs that Cook estimated ran for four thousand feet. This was not the way to the top, he decided.

It was now September 1, too late to continue the quest that year before winter arrived. The men had to move fast if they were to get back to Tyonek before the snows began to fall. Because the ground had already frozen over their original route, which meant there would be no food for the seven horses that remained with them, Cook decided to cross to the eastern side of the Alaska Range and raft down a series of rivers—one of which he named after Bridgman, by now a leading force in the Peary Arctic Club, although he had supported Cook's Alaska efforts in his newspaper—to Cook Inlet (which was not named after Cook) and their headquarters camp.

After rafting a few miles down the Chulitna River, the expedition encountered two large glaciers, which Cook named the Fidele, after his wife, and the Ruth, after his stepdaughter. Cook quickly explored the first glacier to an elevation of six thousand feet, in an attempt to determine if it offered a route to the summit. He could see, at about ten thousand feet, that three spurs ran off the glacier, which might offer an avenue to the top. But there was no time for more exploration that year, so they continued homeward, arriving in Tyonek on September 26. Writing of his expedition, Cook said that the eventual conqueror of McKinley would be suitably rewarded, but that he "must be prepared to withstand the tortures of the torrids, the discomforts of the North Pole seeker, combined with the hardships of the Matterhorn ascents multiplied many times."

Although Cook failed to attain his goal—the summit of Mount

McKinley—he certainly enhanced his reputation within the exploration community. Brooks, who clearly dreamed of scaling to the top of the mountain himself, said Cook's return route, down the eastern side of the Alaska Range around Mount McKinley and down the rivers, was almost as important an achievement as reaching McKinley's summit would have been.

Cook gave his first formal talk about the details of the expedition at the dinner marking the tenth anniversary of the birth of the Arctic Club of America, which had been formed in the wake of the travails of Cook's bad-luck-plagued *Miranda* excursion to Greenland.

Despite Cook's increasing status as an explorer, his efforts to fund a new assault on McKinley's summit were at first no more successful than his previous attempts at fund-raising. In early 1906, however, Cook was introduced to Henry Disston, the son of a successful saw manufacturer whose company bore his name. Disston wanted to hunt big game in Alaska and offered Cook five thousand dollars if he would organize a hunting expedition to the foothills of Mount McKinley for him.

With this financial support, Cook organized his second McKinley expedition, signing up two veterans of his first expedition, photographer Miller and guide Printz; a topographer and Arctic veteran, R. W. Porter; S. P. Beecher, a cook; and three men who, along with Printz, would later play a role in the Great North Pole Controversy: a Columbia University physics professor, Herschel C. Parker, who agreed to contribute two thousand dollars; an artist and mountain climber, Belmore Browne; and Edward Barrill, a guide recruited from Montana.

The group gathered at Tyonek in late May 1906; Cook divided the party in two, one to travel with a train of pack horses, the other to take a boat he had designed and built especially for the fast and shallow rivers of the area. The parties converged forty miles up the Yantna River, about seventy air miles south of Mount McKinley. Only nine of the twenty horses made it to the rendezvous, six of them having been attacked and killed by Indian dogs, the others having been slain after being injured.

It was an even less pleasant trip from there. Their first route was impassable for the horses, so they doubled back and tried another avenue, only to be stymied again. "We had been over two months in the field," Cook wrote later, "fording and swimming glacial streams daily; with an almost continuous cold rain pouring over us, with boots daily filled with water and our garments pasted to the skin, we were not in humor to prolong the torment."

Browne, Beecher, Printz, and Miller were sent out to collect hunting trophies for museums, while Porter led a group to map the region south of McKinley. Cook scouted the mountain for several more days and decided that the northeast ridge offered the only likely path to the summit.

Before a climb could be attempted, however, Cook had to get back to Tyonek to pick up his wealthy client, Disston, so Disston could begin his hunt. It was a harrowing trip by boat, during which fifteen-foot-high waves churned by a storm almost sank the boat in Cook Inlet. Only Cook's heroic efforts saved them, according to his companions' later writings. But when they arrived at Tyonek, they discovered that Disston had decided not to come after all. Parker, however, chose to remain at Tyonek and to wait for a ship to take him home. In an article for *Harper's Magazine* about the trip, Cook politely reported that Parker "unfortunately was compelled to leave us to get to his college work in due time." Cook later would offer a much different, and more likely, version of Parker's departure.

Cook returned to the mountain with Barrill and a new member of the party, a prospector named Dokkin, who had joined the party at Tyonek. While the other expedition members were busy at their assigned tasks, Cook, with Barrill and Dokkin, took the boat back to Ruth Glacier. Cook claimed to have had no plans to climb the mountain at this time, intending only to survey possible routes with his companions. As always on Cook's forays, they were all traveling light, with each man carrying about fifty pounds of material in his backpack. Cook said this material was sufficient for each team member to supply himself for about ten days, but the supplies actually proved plentiful for thirteen days. In the course of their journey, Cook invented a biscuit that he said was particularly well suited for mountain climbing and polar exploration because it was easy to cook with a minimum of fuel in low-temperature surroundings.

On September 8, mindful of the fast-approaching winter, the three men set out on Ruth Glacier; Cook had set as their goal the top of the north ridge, which was at about twelve thousand feet. Dokkin quickly developed a fear of the deep crevasses that the three men were forced to jump across as they made their way up the mountain. Cook told Dokkin that he was free to leave them so he could prospect for gold in the lowlands, but asked Dokkin to cache supplies along the glacier on his return trek so that Cook and Barrill would be sure to have food upon their return.

Cook and Barrill found the early climbing easy and breathtakingly beautiful. "The scene changed every minute," Cook wrote as clouds swept by them. "The blue changed to purple, the purple to lilac, and at last a black veil of sadness dropped over this world of arctic flitter." That first night on the mountain, they settled into a model of the silk tent Cook had perfected in the Antarctic and managed to make a palatable meal out of some ptarmigan they killed.

By the end of their third day upon the glacier, they were at about eight thousand feet, and quite pleased with themselves and their progress. That third night, however, a storm struck and overturned their neat little world. "We thought we were at the gates of Hades. We were about ready to quit and seek a more congenial calling," Cook wrote. "But dawn brought its usual inspiration," and they continued upward. The next night, Cook put his Arctic experience to work again and built a snow house for himself and his companion, in which they spent a comfortable night.

During their next climb, the weather was again bad, and night overtook them as they were clinging precariously to a sixty-degree slope, too far from any safe spot to attempt a descent or to make a shelter. "As a duty to ourselves and to our families," Cook wrote, "we had no alternative but to dig into the icy side of the mountain and hold on for the night." They also vowed to give up the climb, if they managed to survive the night. Through the long and stormy evening, they literally clung to the mountain, as avalanches roared like passing trains down the steep slopes around them.

But with the light and security of the dawn came a change of heart: "Now our determination to retreat resolved into a resolution to go to the top," Cook wrote. They found the climbing easy the next day, but the bright sun also showed them how far they still had to go. Finally, above eighteen thousand feet, they got their first good look at the summit, which is always hidden from view at the base by clouds. And with that first look, they made their first discovery: "From below," Cook wrote, "the apex appears like a single peak, with gradual slopes. From the northern foothills we had previously discovered two distinct peaks. But now, from the upper slopes, we saw that there were several miniature ranges running up to two main peaks about two miles apart. To the west a ridge with a saddle, to the east a similar ridge, with one main peak to the southeast. This peak was the highest point, and to it we aimed to take our weary spirits."

Cook found the slopes from here "ridiculously easy," but found the work disproportionately difficult. Of course, they carried no oxygen, since it was not known at that time that the air was thin atop high peaks. "Our legs were of wood and our feet of stone," he said. The next morning they attacked the mountain again, struggling more against the thin air than against the snow. "Just below the summit we dropped over an icy shelf on the verge of collapse. . . . We edged up along a steep snowy ridge and over the heaven-scraped granite to the top. AT LAST!"

It was September 16, 1906; Cook reported that it was sixteen degrees below zero and that the summit of Mount McKinley was at 20,390 feet above sea level. They looked out at the panorama of the Pacific Ocean and the Arctic Circle laid out below them, and they tried to conserve their breath. Around them they noted a peculiar, never before noted, phenomenon. Cook wrote, "We were interested mostly not in the distance scenes, but in the very strange anomaly of our immediate surroundings. It was 10 o'clock in the morning, [but] the sky was as black as that of midnight. At our feet the snow glittered with a ghastly light. As the eye ran down we saw the upper clouds drawn out in long strings, and still farther down the big cumulus forms, and through the gap far below, seemingly in the interior of the Earth, bits of rugged landscape."

Thus, Frederick Albert Cook claimed his second big exploration prize, and one that earned him a great deal more publicity. Mount

McKinley was his first personal accomplishment, a far cry from his earlier achievement, in which he had been part of someone else's large expedition. While the Belgian Antartic Expedition had made its mark far from the United States, Mount McKinley was not only close to home, it was part of it. Accolades poured in when Cook returned to New York, and his life would never be the same again.

CHAPTER 7

Farther North

By the time Cook returned to New York in late November 1906 from his exploits on Mount McKinley, he had moved into the first rank of the world's explorers. That the virgin American territory was explored and conquered by a daring and resourceful native son again propelled Cook into headlines across the country, and proud countrymen showered him with praise and acclaim. Less than two weeks after his return, Cook was elected the second president of the Explorers Club, to succeed the retired explorer Adolphus W. Greely; during the meeting at which Cook was elected, he made his first presentation about his climb of Mount McKinley. This honor was quickly followed by appearances before large audiences at sessions sponsored by the American Alpine Club and the National Geographic Society.

There had been a brief flap shortly after Cook announced his feat, when Parker—who had actually resigned from the expedition in fear of his life after stating that the summit was unreachable, not because it was time for him to return to his classes—declared, while Cook was still in Alaska and he was in New York, that Cook could not possibly have climbed Mount McKinley. But when Cook reached New York, Parker immediately toned down his statements, saying only that Cook could not have accurately measured the mountain's height, since he did not bring the hypsometer with him for an accurate reading. (Cook's report that McKinley's main peak was 20,390 feet high was actually off by 70 feet; its summit is now reported to be 20,320 feet above sea level.)

But by the time of the American Alpine Club's dinner, any rift had apparently been mended, for the men were seen there together by newspaper reporters; Parker then represented Cook at another club function honoring the duke of Abruzzi for his climb of Mount St. Elias, Alaska's second-highest peak, and showed Cook's slides of the McKinley expedition.

Other words of doubt came from a frustrated would-be conqueror of the mountain, the Reverend Hudson Stuck, who was known as the Archdeacon of the Yukon. Stuck, who had once said, "I would rather climb that mountain than discover the richest gold mine in Alaska," refused to believe that anyone else could conquer it. In an exchange of letters with Alfred H. Brooks, the U.S. Geological Survey official who led the 1902 expedition to survey McKinley that had inspired Cook, Stuck wrote, "It is going to take a better man than he [Cook] to reach the top of that mountain"; presumably only Stuck fit that category of "better man." But Brooks replied in a letter, "I have gone over the matter in detail with Dr. Cook and am convinced he reached the summit of the mountain. I have heard him lecture on the subject, seen his photographs, and there is no doubt in my mind."

Cook's claim seems to have been accepted by almost everyone else, and the dinner given by the Washington-based National Geographic Society—which played a key role in Peary's career and would help lead the charge against Cook later—was an ironically noteworthy event, for it featured both Cook and Peary. In his introduction, the group's president, famed inventor Alexander Graham Bell, said, "We have had with us, and are glad to welcome, Commander Peary of the Arctic regions. But in Dr. Cook we have one of the few Americans, if not the only American, who has explored both extremes of the world, the Arctic and Antarctic regions. And now he has been to the top of the American continent, and therefore to the top of the world, and tonight I hope Dr. Cook will tell us something about Mount McKinley."

Peary's horror at that introduction was mitigated somewhat, no doubt, by President Theodore Roosevelt's lavish praise of Peary's efforts that night when he presented Peary with the National Geographic Society's first Gardiner Greene Hubbard gold medal. The award was named after the same Hubbard who had helped Mrs. Peary raise money for the relief expedition in 1895, which had sent the *Kite* to rescue the unsuccessful and dejected Peary from his Second North Greenland Expedition. In reply to Roosevelt, Peary said that reaching the Pole "is the thing which it is intended that I should do, and the thing that I must do. . . . And, God willing, I hope that your administration may yet see the Stars and Stripes planted at the Pole."

Cook returned to his medical practice in Brooklyn, but he had crossed a critical personal bridge: "After my Alaskan expeditions, the routine of my Brooklyn office work seemed like the confinement of prison. I fretted and chafed at the thought. Let me have a chance, and I would succeed. This thought filled my mind. I convinced myself that in some way the attainment of one of the Poles— the effort on which I had spent 16 years—would become possible."

Cook's desire to return to Greenland was building into an obsession. But he was again stymied by a lack of funds when he tried to outfit an expedition to the north. In March 1907, John R. Bradley, a wealthy gambling-casino owner and big-game hunter, asked Cook to lead an expedition to Greenland so Bradley could obtain some new trophies for his walls. "My immediate purpose was to return again to the frozen north," Cook wrote. "The least the journey would give me was an opportunity to complete the study of the Eskimos which I had started in 1891."

The arrangement, Bradley later wrote, was that "he was to photograph Eskimos, and I was to shoot walrus and polar bear." Although Cook, in *My Attainment of the Pole,* a book about his quest that was published during the controversy, downplayed his prior intent to make a run for the North Pole, such a plan was clearly in his mind from the earliest planning stages of the Bradley-sponsored trip.

After buying a Gloucester fishing schooner with Bradley's

money and refitting it for the icy conditions of the north by having heavy oak boards added over the ship's original hull, Cook had the ship, which he named after his benefactor, loaded with enough supplies for two years, in case the schooner should get locked in the ice like so many ships before it. He and Bradley had lunch in New York City in June at which Cook's ulterior motive was apparently first officially addressed.

As Bradley—who owned casinos in Palm Beach, Florida; New Orleans; and Texas—later recalled, they were eating at the Holland House when Cook said, "You and I could make it, John, with two Eskimos."

"Make what?" Bradley replied.

"Why not try for the Pole?"

"Not I. Would you like to try for it?" Bradley responded. "He said, 'There is nothing I would rather do. It's the ambition of my life.' "

Cook had devised a plan for a new route to the North Pole. While the so-called American Route, which was followed by Peary, called for traveling north through Smith Sound along the east coast of Ellesmere Island to the top of it, if possible, and then moving out on the ice of the Polar Sea, Cook believed he had a better route. He planned to take advantage of the work of two explorers who had preceded him in the area, Sverdrup and Nansen, and to cross Ellesmere and travel up its west coast to Nansen Sound. He believed that the ice conditions would be better there, partly on the basis of his study of data Nansen had obtained from the drifting voyage of the *Fram* and partly from Nansen's unsuccessful run for the North Pole that covered the same area. And both Nansen and Sverdrup had reported abundant supplies of game, with which Cook and his companions could restock their larder.

Although Bradley was not interested in pursuing Cook's plan to attain the Pole, he agreed that if Cook decided to make the dash to the Pole, he would not insist that Cook accompany the ship back to the United States. In addition, Bradley agreed to help furnish Cook with extra supplies from the ship if he remained in Greenland to try and attain his dream.

Within a month, using all the money he could get his hands on,

Cook acquired the gear he would need, as well as hickory for new sledges, a collapsible boat for crossing open water, and one thousand pounds of canned pemmican. To this material, he added all the material he had acquired during his earlier trips to the Arctic and Antarctic. Bradley spent about $50,000 outfitting his hunting trip and, it is estimated, he supplied Cook with $8,000 to $10,000 worth of material for the trek from his own ship's stores.

Peary, meanwhile, had also been hard at work. After his return to the United States in 1902, following the failure of his expeditions, he had purchased a seventeen-acre estate, called Eagle Island. The estate was located far enough off the coast of Maine to protect his privacy from the public. Although Peary grew up with little money, owing to his father's early death, Peary's wealthy backers made sure he no longer wanted for any material things. He was also, by now, collecting book and magazine royalties and, when he was healthy, was conducting a busy round of paid lectures.

After recovering on his new estate from professional surgery to minimize the discomfort caused by the field amputation of his toes, Peary began what had become his usual two-pronged prelude to a journey: fund-raising and a campaign to get additional leave from the U.S. Navy he seemed never to serve.

In a letter to rich past and potential supporters, urging them to join his Peary Arctic Club, Peary said he would go north again only if he had truly "first-class" equipment. Few expeditions in history had been better equipped than had Peary's last effort, but Peary needed things upon which to place the blame of failure. Central to his plan was his insistence on building a new ship designed especially for his efforts and to his specifications, which he estimated would cost one hundred thousand dollars, a princely sum in 1902. Fund-raising went slowly once again, since Peary's poor track record cost the campaign a good deal of its enthusiasm among potential donors. But the central core of men behind the Peary Arctic Club kicked up their efforts in early 1904, around the time they legally incorporated their little organization.

The group had two short-term goals, wrote Fitzhugh Green, one biographer of Peary. First was "the altering of public opinion so that existing prejudice against Arctic work would be lessened." This new antipathy was apparently not so much to "Arctic work" in general as to Peary's efforts. Peary was the only American who was launching expeditions to the North Pole at this time, and his continuing failures increased skepticism among potential donors. The group's second goal, of course, was to raise enough new money to build Peary's exclusive ship.

In an omen of important events to come, the publicity campaign, under the direction of Bridgman, was a smashing success. "Within a month of the new charter [in April 1904], magazine and newspaper articles were appearing all over the country, putting the new Arctic plans in the most favorable light possible," Green wrote. "This work of propaganda was done with the greatest amount of finesse."

But as the August 1 deadline for the receipt of fifty thousand dollars approached, which the builder insisted upon receiving before he would begin actual construction, the Peary Arctic Club was far short of funds. If work did not begin soon, the ship would never be ready in time for Peary's planned 1905 expedition. The ever-present and ever-generous Jesup agreed to provide twenty-five thousand dollars if the club found other donors to match his new gift. The group managed to meet this challenge grant, barely. Later, a friend of Jesup's anted up the rest of the other fifty thousand dollars needed to pay off the shipbuilder in full. When completed, the *Roosevelt* was surely the finest ship that had ever been built for Arctic travel. She was 184 feet long and had a hull specially designed to rise over ice and not to sit deep in the water, like most traditional ships, where it could be crushed by the immense mass of icebergs. This hull also helped the ship smash through the pack ice by rising over its edges and mounting it, so the ship's weight could help crush the thick ice pack.

Peary's new leave of absence from the navy was granted; it was an easy task now that President Roosevelt and his colonialist administration was in control. In return for the latest favor, Peary named the new ship after the president when she was launched in May 1905.

Although he now had his fancy ship, Peary wanted still more money before launching his new expedition, for such things as supplies and related necessities. At least another sixty thousand dollars was raised, making this expedition the most expensive one launched up to that time. Part of the need for these unparalleled amounts of money was Peary's new strategy for his quest: He was going to abandon his former policy of making a quick, lightly provisioned dash with only two or three companions, in favor of a large expedition carrying great quantities of supplies in relay. The idea was to free Peary of the burden of carrying all the heavy supplies that were necessary to make the trip to the Pole. These support teams would also break the trail over the ice and snow for Peary and his companions, which would make their traveling much easier and faster.

But some of the money Peary demanded before starting on his new expedition was strictly for creature comforts, as evidenced by his cabin on the *Roosevelt*—which featured a player piano—and to pay the salaries and expenses of four helpers he wanted to take along to minister to him: Henson, now called his "personal attendant"; a steward; a secretary; and a doctor.

Peary joined the *Roosevelt* in Nova Scotia, and the ship departed on July 26, 1905, on the journey that Peary was sure would take him to the North Pole. He had the ship and the crew he wanted and enough time and money to reach his elusive goal. Indeed, he was so sure of success that he made it clear to his closest assistants, Henson and the master of the ship, Captain Robert A. Bartlett, that this was to be his last Arctic expedition.

The *Roosevelt,* as Peary had hoped, was able to plow through the ice of Smith Sound, and it effortlessly delivered the expedition members to the waters off Cape Sheridan, some sixty miles north of Fort Conger. Peary sent three parties out at intervals to cache supplies and break the trail and then departed northward with his last group. But some three weeks later, he came upon all three advance parties, which had been stymied by a large trough of open water. This obstruction, since named the Big Lead, was a permanent obstacle to those who sought the North Pole. The Big Lead was located at the border between the northern limit of the ice that was attached to the land of Ellesmere Island and the southern limit of the sea's pack ice. Portions of the gap would temporarily freeze when climatic conditions were right, making the passage precarious for travelers. At the Big Lead, Peary sent two of the parties back to camp, leaving only Henson's group with his own.

Here, the seeds of what would evolve into the Great North Pole Controversy began to draw their first nourishment. As Peary pondered his future while waiting at what he labeled "the Hudson River" to freeze over, he was faced with some unpleasant facts: The weather "window" for making a dash to the Pole was fast closing, and another failure would likely end his career as an Arctic explorer. He was presently about 315 miles from the North Pole; the return journey from the Pole to land would require an additional 415 miles of sledge travel, and he had about thirty days left. To complete a round-trip to the Pole would thus require an average daily speed of about 25 miles over ever-changing terrain and in always-precarious weather, an unheard-of pace.

After a few days, the open trough froze enough for Peary and his companions to cross over to the northern shore of the Big Lead, and Peary decided to attempt the task despite the little time remaining to him. But now, without his other white companions, Peary's reported speed accelerated to all-time highs, as he must have literally zoomed over the ice. While he had averaged only about 3.5 miles a day as he struggled over poor ice conditions and in bad weather—and in the company of competent witnesses—to the Big Lead, on his first march after crossing it—and with only Henson as a witness—he managed to cover 30 miles. Henson could not use the tools that explorers routinely utilized to calculate distances traveled and thus was useless as a credible witness.

J. Gordon Hayes, who would write two important books dealing with the controversy in the years between the world wars, said, "It is remarkable that, immediately Peary leaves his white companions, his speed suddenly should become nearly 10 times as rapid as his previous average; that all the difficulties of the polar pack, which he himself had taught us were nearly insurmountable, should vanish like smoke."

Four days out from the Big Lead, a major storm beset the expedition, leaving its members immobilized for seven days, as the wind and snow lashed their igloo. While they were stalled, their supplies were dwindling and their time window was closing. All prospects of reaching the Pole now gone, Peary formulated a consolation prize for himself that would give him some public recognition and, he hoped, at least partially mollify his financial backers: He would aim for a new "farthest north" mark, beyond those of Nansen and Umberto Cagni. And on April 21, 1906, seven marches out from what they labeled Storm Camp—where they spent the days waiting out the roaring blizzard—Peary claimed a new northern mark at 87 degrees, 6 minutes north. At last, Peary had a prize for his wealthy backers and his supportive president.

Despite the incredible speeds Peary claimed to have traveled in reaching his record and despite the obvious inconsistencies in his story between what happened when in the company of others and what happened when he was alone, no one was interested in examining Peary's records too closely. America wanted its heroes, the Peary Arctic Club wanted its laurels, and there was no competing interest to challenge the claims. Besides, the world had Peary's word on it, and an explorer's word was his bond.

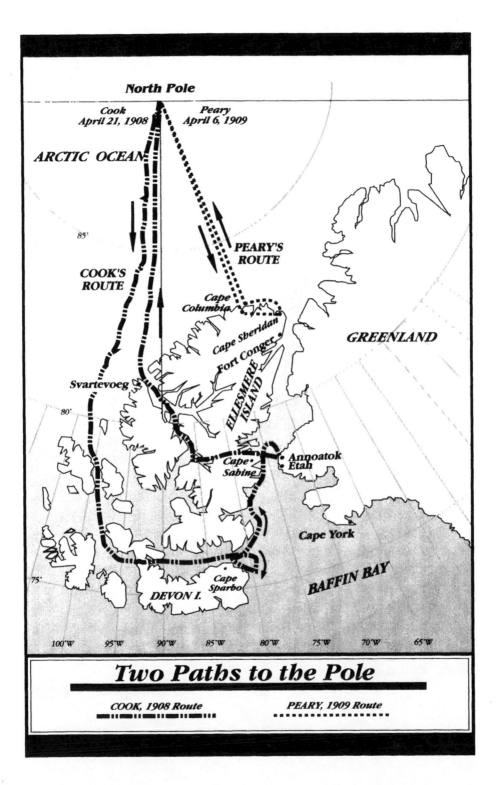

North Pole

Cook
April 21, 1908

Peary
April 6, 1909

ARCTIC OCEAN

85°

COOK'S
ROUTE

PEARY'S
ROUTE

Cape
Columbia

Cape Sheridan

Fort Conger

GREENLAND

Svartevoeg

ELLESMERE ISLAND

80°

Cape
Sabine

Annoatok
Etah

Cape York

75°

Cape
Sparbo

DEVON I.

BAFFIN BAY

| 100°W | 95°W | 90°W | 85°W | 80°W | 75°W | 70°W | 65°W |

Two Paths to the Pole

COOK, 1908 Route ■■■■■■■■■■■■■■■

PEARY, 1909 Route ·····················

LEFT: Frederick A. Cook, in a studio photograph, wearing Arctic gear sitting on a sledge and holding a sextant *(Library of Congress)*.

BELOW: Cook, circa 1906, in Greenland *(Cook Collection, Library of Congress)*.

Cook, circa 1901, in Greenland
(Cook Collection, Library of Congress).

Robert E. Peary, circa 1901,
taken in Greenland by Cook
(Cook Collection, Library of Congress).

Cook and Roald Amundsen used their imprisonment in the Antarctic during the winter of 1898–'99 to test Cook's design for a small silk tent that could be deployed quickly under Arctic conditions, and a lightweight sledge *(Cook Collection, Library of Congress)*.

◆

Henryk Arctowski, the Belgica's geologist and oceanographer, and Executive Officer Georges Lecointe drinking tea in the ship's galley *(Cook Collection, Library of Congress)*.

◆

Josephine and Marie Peary plus Robert Bartlett who captained Peary's ships on most of his voyages. Photo was taken on the coast of Greenland in, apparently, 1901 *(Cook Collection, Library of Congress)*.

Peary on the Roosevelt *(Library of Congress)*.

RIGHT: Roald Amundsen who would later become the first man to reach the South Pole. The photograph was probably taken during the Belgica's trip to the Antarctic in 1898–'99 *(Cook Collection, Library of Congress)*.

BELOW: Matthew Henson aboard the relief ship Eric in 1901. Cook was second in command of the expedition, sent to assist Peary *(Cook Collection, Library of Congress)*.

Cook's moonlight photograph of the Belgica, frozen in the ice of Antarctica *(Cook Collection, Library of Congress)*.

♦

PART TWO

CHAPTER 8

"Something Keeps Calling, Calling . . . "

"Often and often I have asked myself, what are the pleasures of the polar seas?" Cook told an interviewer in 1909. "Privation, cold, hunger, peril of frostbite and of death, solitude, unceasing and sustained exertion—these are manifest enough. In themselves they are not very fascinating. You sometimes recoil from them and wonder why you ever pushed into the great wilderness of ice. You escape, vowing never to return. But after a time, something revives in you. Your mind dwells more and more on the indefinable delights of the Arctic. Something keeps calling, calling, night and day, until at last you can stand it no more, and you return, spell-drawn, by the magic of the North."

It was surely the "calling, calling," that drew him to the deck of the schooner *Bradley* on July 3, 1907, as it left Gloucester, Massachusetts, with his wife; daughter Ruth; and baby daughter Helene, who had just turned two; benefactor John R. Bradley; and the ship's crew. The ship stopped at Cape Breton Island to let Cook's family off; the plan was for them to remain in Nova Scotia until the *Bradley* returned in the fall. If Cook, then one month into his forty-second year, had decided to return with the ship, they would accompany him back to New York on the *Bradley.*

Cook was on his way back to Greenland some eight months after Peary had returned from his latest expedition. Once again, Cook was suspending his medical practice and his family life to pursue the elusive brass ring, the quest of which occupied an increasingly larger amount of his attention.

Some of the men who left their indelible footprints in the snow and ice of the Arctic and Antarctic regions—such as Cook's rival Robert E. Peary—believed they were born to a destiny that compelled them to do so. These men made their quests in the name of patriotism, seeking possessions for the homeland or the fabled Northwest Passage, a long-sought shortcut to the Orient.

For Frederick Cook, however, it is clear that the polar regions were definitely an acquired taste. But once he had taken his first bite, as is evident in his own comments, he was as addicted to the pursuit of their fruits as any man has ever been. That Cook came to Arctic exploration purely for the adventure was not a surprising turn of interest in light of his upbringing.

Cook's father, Dr. Theodore A. Koch, had left Hanover, Germany, soon after he received his medical degree; German government authorities were probably not far behind him when he left. An adherent of the ideas of liberal politician Carl Schurz, Koch followed his mentor to the New World in 1850 in search of more political freedom, in the wake of a crackdown on Schurz's group by the German government. Schurz would have a successful career in his adoptive land, including service as a general for the Union forces in the Civil War.

Along with other followers of Schurz, Dr. Koch settled in Sullivan County, New York, then a rural section of the state in the heart of what would become the region's premier summer-resort area. The countryside of insulated hills and mountains was a good place for people of unpopular beliefs, for there was enough room between neighbors for residents to maintain their privacy. Epidemics of cholera and yellow fever in New York City the next year sparked a panicked exodus, which paralyzed all public transportation in the region as families sought the perceived safety of rural areas. As a result, many German families who had settled around New York City fled to upstate Sullivan County, to join their resettled countrymen.

Among the new wave of German refugees to go northward was Frederick Long, a successful cigar manufacturer in New York City, who abandoned his enterprise to take his wife and daughter, Magdalena, to safety. The Longs, with several friends, built a sturdy raft on which to make their escape up the Hudson River after the city's transportation system broke down under the wave of refugees. The Longs settled in a small town near young Dr. Koch's home.

Romance blossomed between Magdalena Long and Theodore Koch, and they married and moved into a tiny five-room house the hard-working doctor built on the Delaware River in the small town of Hortonville. By the time their fifth child, Frederick, was born on June 10, 1865, the family name had been altered. While Dr. Koch was serving in the Union Army examining new recruits—no doubt at least partially inspired by his mentor Schurz's service in the army—his name was entered in official records under the English spelling, Cook. There is some question whether it was an accidental mistake by a sloppy army clerk or whether Dr. Koch, tired of the mispronunciation of his name, took advantage of the opportunity to change it so he would blend in more smoothly in his adoptive land.

Although Cook Senior's medical practice thrived when he returned to private service, he, like many of his country colleagues, was chronically cash poor, since many of his patients paid him with the fruits of their labors: produce and meat. When he died suddenly of pneumonia five years after Frederick was born, the family's financial condition was tenuous. The family struggled on in their house for a while, although there was no money for frills, such as sleds with which to take advantage of the abundant snowfall around their home. But Frederick and his brothers were said to have built the best sleds in the region by hand, out of wood from the hickory trees that grew on their property.

In later years, however, Frederick could recall no extraordinary fondness for the snow and the cold, although like most of his peers, he enjoyed romping in it. "I remember no stirrings of the explorer in me when I went to school," he said many years later. "If I was born with it, it was so latent that I never perceived it. None of the other members of my family have it."

In need of more money with which to raise her brood of five,

Magdalena moved, when Frederick was thirteen, to Port Jervis, New York, where she thought jobs would be plentiful in that railroading center. Frederick showed a ready willingness to work hard to earn money, and he became a major financial contributor to the family while still a teenager. His three brothers found jobs with the thriving railroads, but Frederick was too young for such work, so he found a job in a glass factory. His next job was as a lamplighter: He would extinguish the naptha street lights on his way to classes in public school in the morning, and would fill and light them on his way home after his lessons.

After the family moved to Brooklyn in 1879, Frederick took a job selling vegetables at the Fulton Street Market, across the East River at the bottom of Manhattan, which opened at 2 A.M. and closed well after the start of his school day. He bought a used printing press and ran a second profitable business in his spare time between his full-time job and his schedule of classes at Public School 37.

At the same time, he struggled to keep relatively current with his schoolwork; although he was only partially successful, his lack of time for his studies did not diminish his interest in them. He had by now decided that he would like to become a doctor like his father. To pay for his higher education, Frederick established a milk-delivery business in his neighborhood. With his brother Theodore, he soon had a profitable home-delivery route, at a time when this service was just coming into vogue in the United States, after years of success in Europe. Frederick had several wagons in operation by 1887, when he started classes at the College of Physicians and Surgeons at Columbia Unviersity. When the college moved across town the next year, he transferred to the more convenient medical school at New York University.

When the huge Blizzard of 1888—which paralyzed much of the eastern United States for many days—interrupted both the milk-delivery business and medical school, Frederick and his brother Will found a practical solution to the problem of obtaining a load of coal to replenish the family's dwindling stockpile. The boys put sledge runners on a boat Theodore had built to use at the beach the next summer and filled it with coal at a local fuel-dealer's yard. On their way back home, they were offered premium prices for the precious coal by snowbound, and less inventive, homeowners. For a week, both night and day, Frederick and brother Will were in the profitable, if temporary, emergency coal-delivery business.

Frederick also somehow found time between his classes and his money-making enterprises to fall in love and marry. In early 1889 he wed Libby Forbes, but it was to be a short romance. The next year, Libby died of peritonitis one week after delivering a child who lived only a few hours.

When he graduated from medical school the next year, Frederick sold his interest in the milk-delivery business to Will and moved with his mother and sister into a house in Manhattan, where he hung out his shingle. Now, he was an adult with a profession, not just an industrious boy trying to help his mother make ends meet. But much to his chagrin, patients did not flock to his waiting room. During his first six months of practice, he later recalled, he had three patients.

Although this lack of business made him worry about his ability to earn a good living, it also left him, perhaps for the first time in his life, large blocks of leisure time. While he waited for patients, he devoured true-life adventure stories, tales of intrepid men who braved the mysterious far reaches of the world in search of adventure and fame, and perhaps a little fortune.

His favorite authors, Cook said later, were two of the first, and most daring, Americans to take up the call of the North Pole region in the mid-1800s, Elisha Kent Kane and Charles Francis Hall.

In 1850, Kane made his first trip north of the Arctic Circle as the doctor on a polar expedition that was searching for Sir John Franklin and his party. The ill-fated Franklin Expedition had left England in 1845 in what had been billed as the final search for the long-sought Northwest Passage, a shortcut to facilitate trade with the Orient. It took years to find any clue to the fate of Franklin and his 128 companions; then for thirty years, various explorers found bodies and remnants of the clothing of the expedition members. The company had frozen to death as they vainly sought a path to safety. Kane was among the crew of two small American ships that had been frozen in the ice when the Arctic winter descended upon them faster than they had expected. Kane's book on the voyage is still exciting reading, for it records phenomena that had rarely been seen before, and, in most cases, never written of before.

Charles Francis Hall died in 1873 during his Polaris Expedition, soon after breaking Kane's "farthest north" mark. Almost a hundred years later, a researcher would have Hall's body exhumed for an autopsy to try and determine how he died. The researcher, Chauncey Loomis, Jr., theorized that Hall died of arsenic poisoning committed by crew members who wanted to return home, and believes the autopsy supported that theory.

While the British explorers of this time were more motivated by the quest to feed the British Empire with new conquests and by the desire to find the elusive Northwest Passage, both these American explorers had clearly set their sights on reaching the North Pole. The two Americans also abandoned the dominant British approach of trying to sail through the Barrier Ice all the way to the Pole, in favor of a strategy of leaving their ships wherever the ice blocked them and then making their way over the frozen land and water on sledges.

While engrossed in these recent true tales of adventure about the frigid north one gloomy winter morning, Cook saw a story in the *New York Herald* about a planned expedition to Greenland that was being prepared by Robert E. Peary, an American civil engineer who was attached to the navy. Struck by the coincidence of the notice in the newspaper and his new and growing interest in the North Pole, Cook sent a letter to Peary, applying for the post of surgeon, even though he was not sure what a surgeon was to do on an expedition.

It was two months before Cook received an acknowledgment of his letter, in the form of an invitation to Philadelphia for an interview with Peary. When Cook arrived, he recalled during interviews forty years later, Peary was wearing his elaborate navy uniform, and presented a striking appearance with his large red mustache that ended in twisted points; his blue eyes; and large, sharp nose. Cook was wearing his brown hair combed straight back and had on a black suit, a starched white shirt with a stiff collar, and a tie around his neck.

While Peary was already a well-traveled, sophisticated man of thirty-five, the train trip to Philadelphia was the twenty-six-year-old Cook's first journey outside New York State. Peary had by then explored Central America and had attempted an expedition across the Greenland ice cap, while Cook had no such experience.

But Peary was also obviously taken with Cook and his fresh, untested interest in the North. He explained to Cook that Elisha Kent Kane's writings on the Arctic had been one of the primary inspirations for his own interest in exploring the region. Coincidentally, both men had also lost their fathers when they were young: Cook when he was five, Peary when he was three.

At the time, Peary was proposing a second journey to Greenland and was seeking a crew to accompany him. While his wife watched, Peary explained his Arctic plans to Cook. By all accounts, it was a successful visit, and Cook told a biographer during a series of interviews in the 1930s that he had liked Peary and his wife from the start. Before he returned home, Cook signed a contract to be the Peary expedition's surgeon and ethnologist and thus became the first member of the crew. In return for the right to this unpaid position, Cook agreed in the contract not to trade with the Eskimos, not to write books or magazine or newspaper articles, and not to give lectures about the journey without Peary's permission. Peary signed all crew members to a similar pledge, to ensure that he had a monopoly in the purchase of goods from the Eskimos and for his own writings and lectures.

Cook was obviously excited about his new adventure, but he did not expect it to be much more than a temporary diversion, a source of stories to tell his children and a productive way to spend his time. "There was no money in it," he later told an interviewer, "but there was a living, honor, and—what I did not expect to find—a new and absorbing passion, which ever since dominated my life."

CHAPTER 9

The Race Begins

As the *Bradley* continued its voyage northward, Cook brushed up on his use of the sextant by guiding the ship and comparing his calculations with those of the ship's master, Moses Bartlett. Moses was a cousin of Robert A. Bartlett, who captained Peary's ship and was one of Peary's closest assistants.

The *Bradley* sailed across North Star Bay, the present-day site of the large American Air Force Base, Thule, named after the Latin expression *Ultima Thule,* meaning the northernmost edge of the inhabited world. When they arrived, a group of Eskimos, led by explorer Knud Rasmussen, came out in their kayaks to greet them. Rasmussen, who became a founding father of modern Greenland by encouraging the Danes to stake a claim on the northern half of the island, was half Eskimo. He was living at the village of Uummannaq to study the culture of the local residents.

Cook invited Rasmussen to dine aboard his ship, but because Rasmussen was also living like an Eskimo, with the Eskimos' standards of grooming and cleanliness or, more accurately, lack of them, Bradley refused to let Rasmussen eat with him. Cook was embarrassed because he was forced to ask Rasmussen to eat with the crew, a slight that Rasmussen long remembered and blamed on Cook.

Cook was pleased with the signs of prosperity he saw among the

Eskimos, which meant that the recent hunting had obviously been good for them. The Eskimos looked well fed, and packs of dogs were everywhere. This abundance increased his prospects of remaining behind and launching his expedition, for he counted on there being a large crop of sledge dogs available and enough food for the villagers to be able to provide for his needs, in addition to their own. While Cook visited the Eskimo settlements along the coast as the ship sailed slowly northward toward Etah, Bradley hunted for his trophies.

After scouting around, and recalling his earlier days in the same area, Cook led the party to a tiny village, Annoatok, twenty-five miles north of Etah and some seven hundred miles from the North Pole, where he decided to make his winter headquarters. Annoatok, which means "windy place," is set in a sheltered cove between the sparklingly clean water and a rock ledge that protects it from some of the winter winds and has a breathtaking panoramic view of Ellesmere Island. Although Ellesmere appears to be near the shore of Annoatok, it is across Smith Sound, a world away, except when the sea is frozen in winter. Cook described Annoatok as the "northernmost settlement of the globe, a place beyond which even the hardy Eskimos attempt nothing but brief hunting excursions."

All the best hunters of the tribe of Eskimos that had settled in the Etah region were in the general vicinity of Annoatok at the time, there were scores of healthy dogs, and the villagers had already filled their larders with meat. "Nothing could have been more ideal," Cook wrote. "With all conditions in my favor, might I not, by one powerful effort, achieve the thing that had haunted me for years?" If he didn't try now, he wondered, "it was a question if an opportunity should ever again come to me." All he would need, in addition to the healthy Eskimos, plentiful dogs, and supplies, was good weather and his own continued good health. "The expenditure of a million dollars could not have placed an expedition at a better advantage. The opportunity was too good to be lost."

Cook sought one volunteer from among the *Bradley*'s crew to remain with him; several crew members immediately asked to be chosen, including Captain Moses Bartlett, but Cook believed the captain was necessary to get the *Bradley* home safely. Cook chose Rudolph Francke, John R. Bradley's steward and chef, because, he said, Francke was young and healthy and seemed to have quickly adapted well to life in the Arctic.

On August 26, all the Eskimos of Etah were put on the *Bradley* and enlisted to help land Cook's supplies at his headquarters. There was no harbor at Annoatok, so the material was lowered into all the small boats that could be rounded up and towed near the shore. Because there was a heavy sea, the supplies were thrown up on the beach or on rocks, wherever the little boats were able to come near the shore. The material Cook had purchased and brought with him, coupled with the supplies Bradley gave him from the ship's stores, was more than sufficient, Cook believed, to get him through the coming winter and to take along on his dash to the Pole.

Cook's supplies included 10,000 boxes of matches; thousands of cans of food; 150 gallons of alcohol for fuel; barrel after barrel of flour and rice; crates of biscuits; 150 feet of stovepipe for the cabin he planned to build; and tons of myriad odds and ends, ranging from cooking utensils to beads and trinkets, to use in trade with the Eskimos.

On September 3, the ship departed, leaving Cook and Francke strictly to the company of the village's Eskimos for at least the approaching long winter. Bradley had offered to send the ship back to pick them up the next summer, but Cook declined, saying they would sledge to southern Greenland and board a ship to Denmark. Bradley later wrote how impressed with Cook he became during the trip: "Cook never complains, never swears, doesn't care whether his hair is long or short, doesn't care whether his shoes are tied or not, but just keeps plodding along."

When the *Bradley* departed, Cook was left in Greenland with only one man who spoke his native language, far from his family and friends. But he knew he would be too busy in the next six months to be melancholy: There was hunting to be done, meat to dry, and skins to be prepared into clothing to outfit the expedition. In addition he wrote, "A wild thrill stirred my heart. The hour of my opportunity had come." It was the realization of his dream to perform an "unprecedented feat—a feat of brain and muscle in which I should, if successful, signally surpass other men." He compared his quest for achievement with those who seek to excel at sports. "At the time, any applause which the world might give, should I succeed, did not concern me; I knew that this might come, but it did not enter into my speculations."

Cook, with the full cooperation of the Eskimos, began arduous preparations for his journey. But his preplanning and organization served him well. All his supplies were packed in wooden crates of similar size; by putting them together, tops inward, he was able to erect his sturdy little house quickly without having had to bring along extra material. And he also had ready access to all the supplies that were contained in the boxes, and the box lids became roof shingles. The house had interior dimensions of thirteen feet by sixteen feet, Cook reported, and was built on that first day in Annoatok. The boxes were held together by small strips of wood, and paper was pasted between the cracks. In the best Eskimo tradition, a layer of sod was put around the outside of the boxes, which insulated the house, but allowed some air to circulate through it.

A table was built around a pole in the center of the house that supported the roof, and the bunks were convertible into workbenches. Owing to the sharp temperature differences within the hut, Cook devised a system of storing perishables near the floor, where it was coldest; hides, which had to remain moist so they could be worked, were stored in the center to take advantage of constant freezing and thawing; at the roof level, where it was warm, Cook dried meat for the coming expedition.

Cook and Francke set about building Cook's refined-design sledges, and the Eskimos began making fur clothing for the spring trek. To test the sledges and to sharpen his skills driving a dog team, Cook spent a good deal of time roaming Greenland's west coast. At one point, he visited Rasmussen in North Star Bay by sledge, a 250-mile round-trip.

The Eskimos seemed delighted with the diversion their outlander guests presented and as interested in the white man's peculiar habits as Cook was in theirs. Soon after settling in, Cook and Francke established a routine of breaking for tea around four o'-clock each afternoon. Noticing this practice, the Eskimos of Annoatok began arriving at the packing-crate house every afternoon, right on time. "Fortunately," Cook wrote, "tea was one of the supplies of which I had brought a good deal for the sake of pleasing the natives, and it was not long before I had a very large and gossipy afternoon tea party every day, in this northernmost human settlement of the globe."

While only tea was brewing in Cook's pot, a tempest was gathering steam down south. Cook had sent back with Bradley a letter to Bridgman revealing his intention to reach the North Pole. The letter was dated August 26, but since Bradley could not mail it until the ship returned to Nova Scotia, Bridgmen did not receive it until October 1. It immediately sent Peary and his growing cadre of supporters into a full-scale tizzy. The letter told Bridgman, "I have hit upon a new route to the North Pole and will stay to try it. By way of Buchanan Bay and Ellesmere Land and northward through Nansen Strait over the Polar sea seems to me to be a very good route. There will be game to the 82nd degree, and here are natives and dogs for the task. Kind regards to all."

Peary was outraged when he learned that Cook was in Greenland. He had originally intended to return to the Arctic for still another "final" attempt at the North Pole that summer. But, beset by financial worries and, some historians believe, torn by a desire to remain with his wife and their two children (a son, Robert E., Jr., had been born to the Pearys in 1903), he was still in the United States when Cook's letter arrived.

When Cook's plans became widely known, newspaper editorial writers expressed confidence in his ability to attain the goal, which only fed Peary's rage and his inability to do anything about what he thought of as Cook's poaching in his preserve. It was already far too late in the year to do anything about Cook in 1907. Peary ordered an all-out effort to raise the funds necessary to return to Greenland the next spring, but then Jesup, the longtime mainstay of Peary's money-raising efforts, died. In June 1908, when Peary was scheduled to set sail, the expedition was fifty thousand dollars short of its goal, and there was speculation that the *Roosevelt* was about to be seized for nonpayment of Peary's outstanding bills.

But the fates would once again smile kindly upon Peary. In the nick of time, Peary was saved by several of his die-hard supporters, led by Jesup's widow, General Thomas H. Hubbard—who had contributed to his last expedition—and others. Jesup was replaced as president of the Peary Arctic Club by Hubbard who, although far less rich than Jesup, was a powerful man with many friends and proved as loyal to Peary as his predecessor had been. Hubbard, Mrs. Jesup, and Zenas Crane, a wealthy paper manufacturer, wrote him checks in June to cover the fifty-thousand-dollar shortfall and pave the way for the new expedition to chase after Cook.

At that same time, Peary signed what was to become an essential part of this tale, an exclusive contract with the *New York Times* for the rights to his story of the expedition for four thousand dollars. Of late, the *Times* had begun to challenge its larger rival, the *New York Herald,* for news about explorations. The genesis of this rivalry stemmed from a desire for revenge by William C. Reick, who had quit the *Herald* after a dispute with owner James Gordon Bennett and joined the *Times's* staff in 1906. Reick had suggested to *Times* publisher Adolph Ochs that they sign Peary up as "their" explorer. Before signing the contract with Peary, the *Times* had treated Cook fairly and had been supportive of his bid for the North Pole. In an editorial in October 1907, soon after Cook's intentions were made known publicly, the *Times* said, "We have more faith in him than we have in the vociferous explorers who would fly to the Pole and back. . . . It is to men of this sort, who prepare to encounter the obstacles of the Arctic in a reasonable way, that we must look for any further knowledge of the geography of the Far North. Dr. Cook knows his business."

But after the signing of the contract with Peary, it was to be forever the *Herald*'s candidate, Cook, against the *Times*'s man, Peary.

Peary began his campaign to defile Cook immediately after learning that he would attempt to get to the North Pole and to plant the seeds of doubt about any eventual claim by Cook to the North Pole, many months before Cook was to make one. When asked to succeed Cook as president of the Explorers Club, Peary accused Cook of having breached etiquette by not having informed the Explorers Club in advance of his plans. Peary said "he did not care to serve

unless the club would give him the assurance that, in the event of
Dr. Cook returning and claiming to have found the North Pole,
proper proofs would be demanded of him. . . . Mr. Peary was
prevailed upon to accept the presidency, the club acquiescing to the
demands he made concerning proofs from Dr. Cook."

This was an astonishing and unprecedented demand. That the
Explorers Club acceded to Peary's petty, arrogant conditions is a
strong indication that it was, by now, fully dominated by Peary's
supporters, men who were willing to bend the rules of exploration
and fair play to aid their hero.

Peary sent a similar letter accusing Cook of poaching in his
private domain to the International Polar Commission before Cook
had even left Annoatok and imploring the commission to demand
similar proof, if Cook were to claim that he had reached the North
Pole.

But Peary's nastiest attack was sent to his new mouthpiece, the
Times. In a long letter to the editor—which, interestingly enough,
the *Times* published not then, but in the middle of the Great North
Pole Controversy two years later—Peary accused Cook of "appro-
priating" "my" Eskimos and dogs at "my" depot of Etah. He even
made the astonishing claim that the Eskimos were no doubt using
their knowledge of where the best game was to be found—which
he had the audacity to say that he had taught them—to help feed
and clothe Cook. "I wish to say that I regard Dr. Cook's action in
going north 'sub rosa' . . . for the admitted purpose of forestalling
me as one of which no man possessing a sense of honor would be
guilty."

Thus, Cook was now part of an unholy, if mighty, triumverate
of top-flight explorers—the others being Nansen and Sverdrup—
who were "forestalling" Peary, preventing him from accomplishing the goal he believed God had put him, and him alone, on Earth
to achieve.

The clear implication of Peary's claims was that anyone who
sought to explore the Arctic, or, heaven forbid, to try to reach the
North Pole, was guilty of "sub rosa" conduct and of "forestalling"
the great Peary. In all, Peary's claims would have been laughable
if they were not later taken seriously as a wave of hysteria, induced

by the Peary Arctic Club, the National Geographic Society, and the *New York Times,* changed the writing of history.

The extent of Peary's growing clique was crowned after the *Roosevelt* left New York on July 6, 1908, on what was one of the hottest days New York had seen in years. The ship made a stop at Oyster Bay, on New York's Long Island, for its passengers to lunch with President and Mrs. Roosevelt and to allow the Roosevelts and their three sons to inspect the ship and to bid Peary bon voyage. "Mr. President, I shall put into this effort everything there is in me—physical, mental and moral," Peary said he told the president as the Roosevelts were departing. And the president responded, " 'I believe in you, Peary, and I believe in your success—if it is within the possibility of man.' "

CHAPTER 10

To the Pole

The sky over Annoatok went dark on October 24, 1907, as the sun slipped below the horizon, where it would remain for four months until the first glimmers of dawn returned in late February. By now, Cook was employing "every man and woman, and most of the children, of this tribe of 250" Eskimos in preparing his food and clothing, boots, lines, and dog harnesses. "There was much to do," Cook wrote, "and with the earliest dawn of the morning of the next year we must be ready to start for the Pole."

Cook, Francke, and the Eskimos had quickly settled into a productive routine, which was necessary to ensure that everything would be ready for the expedition's departure in the spring. About the only break the industrious Eskimos took came late in October. As the sun was setting, a sadness settled over the village, a general pervasive feeling that would last all 118 days of the winter darkness. On the actual day the sun disappeared, Cook discovered that the Eskimos began a formal holiday of melancholia, a time during which they reflected on the deaths and mishaps that had beset the tribe during the past year of light.

"I shall never forget that long, sad evening, which lasted many normal days," wrote Cook.

> Sitting in the box-house, I was startled suddenly by a sound that made my flesh for an instant creep. I walked to the door and threw

it open. Over the bluish, snow-covered land, formed by the inden-
tures and hollows, stretched dark-purplish shapes—Titan shadows,
sepulchral and ominous, some with shrouded heads, others with
spectral arms threateningly upraised. . . . Out of the sombre, heavy
air began to issue a sound as of many women sobbing. From the
indistinct distance came moaning, crooning voices. Sometimes hys-
terical wails of anguish rent the air, and now and then frantic cho-
ruses shrieked some heart-aching despair. . . . Here was a scene that
perhaps a Dante might adequately write about. I cannot.

Puzzled over what had happened to inspire such sadness, Cook
walked quietly around the village. He found several clusters of
women, sobbing together, praying, he later learned, for children
who had fallen into the icy waters to their deaths and for husbands
who had not returned from hunting trips. The men of the village,
meanwhile, remained inside their igloos, chanting and dancing to
mark the events of the past year and working themselves into fits
of crying and laughter.

The Eskimos believed that when the sun disappeared, it took
their souls with it, since those spirits were contained in their shadows. This belief apparently led to the period of mourning that
coincided with the setting of the sun. And when this heartrending,
tearful period of mourning was over, Cook reported, his neighbors
returned to work, happy to be busy through the long winter's night.

Early on February 19, 1908, the day the first slice of the sun
could be seen at Annoatok, Cook and his party began their journey
toward the North Pole. With Cook were Francke and nine Eskimos, each of them guiding a loaded sledge. Although Cook reported that nearly all the Eskimos of the region had volunteered to
accompany him, he chose the hardiest among them.

The villagers had done all that Cook had asked of them, and all
the expedition members left Annoatok well dressed against the
elements and loaded down with food and supplies. The 103 dogs
Cook had amassed for the expedition were pulling a load that
amounted to four thousand pounds of supplies, including biscuits
and pemmican, and two thousand pounds of walrus fat and skin,

which was to feed the men and the dogs until they crossed Smith Sound and found game on Ellesmere Island.

Cook had based much of his strategy on obtaining fresh meat and fat during the early stages of the journey, which would allow the expedition members to save the pemmican for farther north, where there would surely be no game. It was this need for food that had contributed to Cook's westerly route, through areas that Sverdrup and the Eskimos had reported were abundantly supplied with musk oxen, hares, birds, and polar bears—the staples of the Arctic's food chain.

But when the advance party Cook had sent out to get fresh meat for the expedition met them on the other side of Smith Sound, they reported they had found little game. Once again, the Arctic was proving to be an unreliable theater for exploration. The advance team turned over to Cook the one musk ox and eleven hares they had managed to find. Cook, now worried that the journey might have to be put off until the next year because of the inadequate food supply, sent Francke and most of the Eskimos back to Annoatok, to conserve supplies. Francke was also sent back to guard what supplies were still stored at Annoatok, in case Cook gave up his quest and turned back, for then he would need the supplies for a new expedition the next year.

Cook, having kept the best Eskimo drivers, sledges, and dogs from among his group, pushed on. Several days later, as he began to think that his expedition might be doomed from the outset, their fortunes changed. From there to their planned jumping-off point from land, Cape Svartevoeg on the northern tip of Axel Heiberg Island, they captured more than 100 musk oxen, 150 hares, and 5 bears. What they did not eat or feed to the dogs was cached for use on their return trip, when, Cook knew, they would be hungry and low on supplies.

On March 16, at Svartevoeg, which was so named by Sverdrup but was later renamed Cape Thomas Hubbard by Peary, Cook made the final preparations for the "dash" over the remaining 520 miles to the Pole. In line with his earlier practices, he trimmed the expedition to its smallest possible number of travelers and supplies.

One sledge was to be left at Svartevoeg, as an emergency spare for the return trip. Cook decided that two Eskimos would accompany him, and the three of them would take two sledges pulled by 26 dogs and carrying 805 pounds of beef pemmican, 130 pounds of walrus pemmican, 50 pounds of musk-ox tenderloin, and small amounts of other foodstuffs. As the sledge loads lightened, Cook expected to feed the weaker dogs to the others; eventually, he calculated, they would get down to six dogs before the journey—which he expected would take eighty days—was concluded. This would provide about one pound of food a day for the men and dogs with a little to spare.

The thought that went into each item Cook chose to take with him is evident from the inventory of the expedition, down to three aluminum teaspoons, one tablespoon, one pound of coffee, two pounds of tea, and a pound of matches. "Every possible article of equipment was made to do double service," Cook explained; "not an ounce of dead weight was carried which could be dispensed with."

Cook's sledges were a perfect example of his planning. Rather than the Eskimo-designed cumbersome, heavy sledges that had solid wooden beams for runners—that all other explorers of the day used—Cook employed lightweight struts and crossbars, all made from the seasoned hickory he had brought with him to Greenland and mounted a sheet of thin iron on the light wooden runners. Cook's sledges weighed fifty-two pounds, half the weight of most traditional models. They were designed for easy repairs, and when a part could not be fixed, the sledge could be cut down into a smaller vehicle. A further improvement was that Cook built into the sledge the frame of a vital collapsible boat they would need to cross open leads, and the canvas boat covering was put to various uses, including service as a ground cover under their tent.

Cook's instruments included a French surveyor's sextant and various attachments, including terrestrial and astronomical telescopes; a liquid compass, aluminum compass, and pocket compass; field glasses; an artifical horizon; pocket chronometers; a pedometer; thermometers; and an aneroid barometer. Cook also took a camera with which to record the journey.

As human company, Cook wrote that he "had carefully watched

and studied every one of my party and had already selected E-tuk-i-shook* and Ah-we-lah, two young Eskimos, each about 20 years old, as best fitted to be my sole companions in the long run of destiny.'' These two Eskimos were unmarried and had no others who were dependent upon them for survival, which also was a factor in Cook's selection. During his 1891 trip to Greenland with Peary, Cook had met his companions' parents, and them, when they were young boys.

On March 18, Cook and four Eskimos mounted the Polar Sea ice and began the march. Koo-loo-ting-wah—who had been the "lead man" on two of Peary's earlier expeditions—and In-u-gi-to had volunteered to accompany Cook over the severely broken ice at the sea's edge; Cook could only hope that his theory that the ice would smooth out away from the pressure line caused by the sea ice pushing up against the land was correct; otherwise, they had no chance of making it all the way to the Pole before the spring thaw began and broke up the ice pack or before their food ran out.

They made good progress as this last phase of the northward journey began, and on the third day, sixty-three miles from Svartevoeg, Cook sent Koolootingwah and Inugito home. Cook explained that to take them any farther would have depleted his supplies and posed a greater danger to their safe return to land. Now fully committed to making his trek, he sent a note to Francke with the returning Eskimos, telling him that if Cook had not returned by June 5, Francke was to seek passage home on any ship that called at Etah and to leave Koolootingwah in charge of the supplies at Annoatok. The two departing Eskimos declined to take any supplies for themselves or their dogs, intending to make a twenty-four-hour dash to reach land and food. "There were no formalities in our parting on the desolate ice," Cook reported. "Yet, as the three of us who were left alone gazed after our depart-

---

*The hyphenations are from Cook's book, *My Attainment of the Pole,* and are designed to help readers understand the pronunciations of these difficult names. Throughout, Eskimo names will include Cook's punctuations the first time they are used.

ing companions, we felt a poignant pang in our hearts. About us was a cheerless waste of crushed wind-and-water-driven ice."

Two days later, Cook got his first sight of the Big Lead, the area of open water that Peary had faced two years earlier. "My hopes sank within me," he said. The giant gash in the ice twisted snakelike through the ice fields. "The wind, blowing with a vengeful wickedness, laughed sardonically in my ears," as he contemplated what to do here, still four hundred miles short of his goal.

It was forty-eight degrees below zero, too cold to use the canvas boat, and Cook lay awake most of the "night" trying to come up with a solution. The next morning, he found that thin, young ice had formed over a stretch of the Big Lead; but Cook did not know if it could be trusted to bear their weight. Twice during his time in Greenland, he had fallen through such ice and had been saved only by quick tugs by his companions on his lifeline. But there was no choice, he decided. "I knew delay was fatal, for at any time a very light wind or a change in the drift might break the new ice and delay us long enough to set the doom of failure upon our entire venture." Time and their ever-depleting store of supplies was continually working against them.

The dogs were unhitched from the sledges, and lifelines were run between the explorers and the sledges. "With bated breath and my heart thumping," Cook was the first to venture onto the thin ice. "I knew as I gently placed my foot upon the thin, yellowish surface, that at any moment I might sink into an icy grave. . . . A dangerous cracking sound pealed in every direction under my feet. The Eskimos followed. With every tread the thin sheet ice perceptibly sank under me, and waved, in small billows, like a sheet of rubber. Stealthily . . . we crept forward. . . ." Finally, they were across, and intoxicated with their success.

Next, Cook was faced with a seemingly endless field of massive pressure ridges, huge obstructions that the travelers had to climb over or cut through. Then Cook was confronted with an even more disturbing potential obstacle: His young companions were becoming uneasy about being in this unknown place, so far from land. Cook recalled a comment one of the Eskimos had made when the company split up a few days earlier. Before departing, either

Koolootingwah or Inugito "had pointed to a low-lying cloud to the north of us. 'Noona' (land), he said, nodding to the others. The thought occurred to me that, on our trip, I could take advantage of the mirages and low clouds on the horizon and encourage a belief in a constant nearness to land, thus maintaining their courage and cheer." This is exactly what he did now, and with great success. All around them, low-lying clouds far in the distance appeared to be the shores of faraway lands in what was actually a barren waste-land built exclusively of ice.

In fact, Cook later wrote that he also regularly saw mirages in the distance, even though he knew they were mirages. More than fifty years later, when the U.S. military forces were building an incredible city deep under Greenland's ice cap to study how best to fight a war under Arctic conditions, their personnel had similar experiences. "One of the problems faced by engineers . . . [as they transported supplies and men across the ice cap using large tractors] involved a tendency to see mirages, some of which appeared on the horizon as medium-sized Midwestern cities," according to one account. "Men have mentioned observing buildings, churches, etc., as well as a false horizon. . . ."

Increasingly, Cook was becoming a father figure to his young companions, who leaned heavily upon him for assurance that all was well. To them, he was *Doto,* presumably derived from *Doctor,* and he called them *Etuk* and *Wela.* He learned the sharp differences between the personalities of his companions: Ahwelah was exuberant and emotional, while Etukishook was sullen, thoughtful, and reliable.

Onward they marched, slowed often by swirling storms and great hummocks of ice. After grueling marches, the group on most "nights" would quickly build a snow house, secure and feed the dogs, and collapse inside their shelter. The alcohol stove would be lighted to melt water from the ice, and they would make a soup by melting a rock-hard brick of pemmican in the water. Or, if they did not have the patience to cook this soup, they would simply let the water soften the pemmican and then chew it.

Mile after mile they traveled, with Cook feeling "the ever-constant presence of those who had died in trying to reach the goal before me. There were times when I felt a startling nearness to them—a sense like that one has of the proximity of living beings in an adjoining room. . . . I felt their unfailing determination revive me when I was tempted to turn back. . . . I felt that I, the last man to essay this goal, must for them justify humanity; that I must crown three centuries of human effort with success."

And one night, Cook almost got closer still to this line of departed explorers. He was awakened from a deep sleep by loud explosions under his head. "It seemed as though bombs were torn asunder in the depths of the cold sea beneath me." But when he looked around the igloo the three travelers had built for the night, nothing seemed out of place, except that the two Eskimos were staring at him and obviously frightened. He looked out through a peephole they had cut in the igloo, but everything appeared normal, so he went back to sleep. The next time he woke up, he was floundering in the frigid ocean, still wrapped in his sleeping bag. "I think I was about to swoon," Cook said, "when I felt hands beneath my armpits and heard laughter in my ears. With an adroitness such as only these natives possess," he was lifted out of the water. He watched helplessly as his companions gathered all their possessions, which had joined Cook in the sea when the crevasse suddenly opened up beneath their igloo. They had all been saved by luck, he said. "Had we slept a few seconds longer we should all have disappeared in the opening crevasse. The hungry Northland would again have claimed its human sacrifice."

On March 30, eight days after crossing the Big Lead, Cook spotted and photographed what he believed to be a new body of land, which he named Bradley Land, after his wealthy benefactor. He noted it when he was at 84 degrees, 50 minutes of latitude and 95 degrees, 30 minutes of longitude; it was ice-sheathed and off to the west. There was no time to inspect this new land, he reported, and they never even got a good look at it because of a veil of mist that enshrouded it, but he did bring a photograph of it home with him. He made plans to visit the land on their return trip. Cook also reported that he found no evidence of the land Peary had said he had spotted during his 1906 expedition and named Crocker Land, although Cook did at one point note what he said could have been a band of land-enveloping mist in the general vicinity of Peary's reported finding.

By now, some three hundred miles from Svartevoeg and two hundred miles from the North Pole, they had passed all traces of animal life. "We were alone—alone in a lifeless world," Cook said. "We had come to this blank space of the Earth by slow but progressive stages." They were becoming numb from fatigue, driven only by Cook's vision of reaching the Pole. "In the Ultima Thule of the aborigines, we reverted to a prehistoric plane of living," struggling forward, eating the rocklike frozen pemmican bricks without even trying to melt them because it took too long and required too much effort. Besides, they were nearly out of fuel for the stove.

On April 11, Cook's daily observations showed that they had reach 87 degrees, 20 minutes of latitude on longitude 95 degrees, 19 minutes. Thus, the three weary travelers had already exceeded Peary's claimed "farthest north" of 87 degrees, 6 minutes from the 1906 expedition. And they were still some 160 miles from their goal.

They had entered an upside-down world, where the touch of a knife on a bare hand left a painful burn, where ice-cold water felt hot to their fingers. "In our dreams," said Cook, "heaven was hot, the other place was cold. All nature was false; we seemed to be nearing the chilled flame of a new Hades."

Two days later, Cook faced another critical moment. His companions, dispirited by a violent westerly wind that had dogged them for days, adding bone-chilling cold to their hunger and weariness, asked him to return home.

"It is well to die," Ahwelah wailed to him. "Beyond is impossible; beyond is impossible." Cook looked at Ahwelah, who had tears running down his face; Etukishook stood nearby, grim faced and looking southward, toward home. He tried to cheer them up and told them it was only "five sleeps" to *Tigi-su,* the Big Nail in the top of the world.

His companions were disturbed by the fact that their shadows rarely seemed to change as the days wore on; at 90 degrees of latitude, of course, shadows would remain the same height throughout the day. Cook continued to talk soothingly to the Eskimos, to promise them that they would all be home at Annoatok in "two moons." Their hope restored by Cook's assurances, his companions' spirits rose, and the three of them resumed their trek with new vigor.

Finally, on April 21, 1908, a few days behind the schedule he had given his companions, Cook wrote words that men had struggled in vain for so many years to write: "At last we step over colored fields of sparkle, climbing walls of purple and gold—finally, under skies of crystal blue, with flaming clouds of glory, we touch the mark! The soul awakens to a definite triumph; there is sunrise within us, and all the world of night-darkened trouble fades. We are at the top of the world! The flag is flung to the frigid breezes of the North Pole!"

CHAPTER 11

Lost in the Gray Mist

Cook wasted little time in celebration, now that he had reached the long-sought top of the world. Or, as he put it, "My mental intoxication did not interfere with the routine work which was now necessary." His first order of business was to confirm that he and his companions were indeed at the North Pole.

Cook had been taking readings throughout his journey, both to mark his progress and to ensure that they were moving in the right direction, since there were no landmarks on which to take bearings. He now began a detailed set of new observations, using the sextant, artificial horizon, pocket chronometer, and other instruments. He knew that pinpoint accuracy was impossible. The refraction of the sun's rays distorted the sextant readings, making a precise reading impossible, and the compasses were unreliable at this latitude, since they were far above the magnetic North Pole. So, he knew that all his readings would be only approximations, although they would be helpful to mark his general position.

His first observations answered one major question that had been raging among scientists: Was the North Pole a land mass, similar to what scientists believed made up the South Pole; was it merely a floating pack of ice; or was the Pole covered only by the open Polar Sea?

The ice cap he saw ended the theory held by some scientists that the Polar Sea was unfrozen. Cook then dug a hole in the ice and solved the next mystery: He found water. Thus, he realized, the cover over the North Pole was continually shifting, as the ice drifted, since it was not anchored to land. To several historians, Cook's accurate description of what is now known to exist at the North Pole is the best evidence that he did, indeed, make it to, or close to, the North Pole.

Next, Cook tied a broken axe to a long lifeline and lowered it through a newly formed crack in the ice cover; he found that the water's drift at the Pole was toward Greenland. While other explorers had speculated on the current's direction, Cook was the first to report it was so. This movement is today known as the Trans-Polar Drift.

Cook also noted, during the later stages of the trip, that the ice pack seemed to have flattened out, with no pressure ridges or hummocks to climb. Later travelers confirmed that the pack ice does indeed flatten out above 88 degrees north, and Cook was the first man to note it.

Further examination of the pack at one point led him to believe it was glacial ice, not sea ice, although the barometer showed they were at sea level. He melted some of the ice over the alcohol stove and found that, indeed, the resulting water was not salty. "I am inclined . . . to put this down as ice on low or submerged land," Cook decided. This finding could prove to be a significant bit of evidence in the attempt to verify Cook's claim. Cook had apparently discovered what today would be called a glacial ice island, a huge, floating chunk of ice that had broken off from a glacier. Similar islands were discovered in the late 1940s and today scientists plot the movement of several of them. Such islands of freshwater ice were unknown in Cook's time.

Cook came onto the North Pole on the 97th meridian west. His first observation at the Pole—taken at noon on April 21—put him at 89 degrees, 59 minutes, 45 seconds north latitude. After completing his set of observations, Cook moved the group four miles to the south, toward the magnetic North Pole, to confirm his readings and their location. At this new spot, observations were taken every six hours, from noon on April 21 until midnight of April 22, while he and his companions set their furs out to dry and they all tried to regain their strength for what was sure to be a grueling return march.

Because "the uncertainties of error by refraction and ice-drift do not permit" complete accuracy, Cook said, he was creating as much data as possible "not to establish the pinpoint accuracy of our position, but to show that we had approximately reached a spot where the sun, throughout the 24 hours, circled the heavens in a line nearly parallel to the horizon."

In a less scientific, but more colorful, test, Cook also buttressed his claim through a homemade testing device. Beginning at midnight on April 22, Cook marked a spot on the ice and positioned Etukishook upon it. At the end of the shadow Etukishook cast, Cook drove a hole in the ice. Every hour until noon Etukishook stood on the spot, and Cook marked a similar hole at the top of the Eskimo's shadow. And when they were done, Cook said, a perfect circle had been formed. This "was an important observation placing me with fair accuracy at the Pole," Cook said, "for only about the Pole . . . could all shadows be of equal length."

While taking the observations, the three travelers got as much rest as they could and indulged in relative luxury by having a hot meal and—what Cook said they had missed even more than hot food—unlimited amounts of water. Cook reported that although they could melt snow in their mouths while they were on the march, that ice-cold liquid failed to satisfy their basic desire to consume water to make up for the fluids they were losing through exertion and to the bone-dry air of the Arctic.

Cook's last order of business was to leave a mark of their accomplishment. While he knew any symbol he left would be unlikely to be recovered, since, as he had already discovered, they were on an ever-moving ice cap, he deposited a note into a metal tube, along with a small American flag. "We are in good health," he wrote, "and have food for 40 days. This, with the meat of the dogs to be sacrificed, will keep us alive for 50 or 60 days." And he concluded the note by asking its finder to send it to the "International Bureau of Polar Research" in Belgium.

Now, an immense irony hit Cook. "Although the Pole was discovered, it was not essentially discovered . . . in the eyes of the world unless we could return to civilization and tell what we had done." And Cook knew the return trip would probably be even more perilous than was their journey north, since they would face new perils as they headed south because the warming temperatures would have already begun the annual breakup of the pack ice. On midnight of April 22, 1908, Cook and his party, the first men to have walked on the top of the Earth, left the North Pole, bound for the place where they had departed from land, Cape Svartevoeg.

The first days of the return journey were uneventful, and the travel was easy. Cook set a course along the one hundredth meridian to make up for the easterly drift of the pack and, he hoped, to allow them to explore Bradley Land and to see more of the previously uncharted terrain of the Arctic.

By April 30, he reported, they had traveled 121 miles from the Pole, but found that the eastward drift of the ice was getting stronger; so he set them a course that was even farther west to compensate for it. On May 2, a thick fog suddenly descended upon them, accompanied by a biting west wind. Fatigue quickly returned to their weary, undernourished bodies, as they plodded ahead, step by step, driven onward only by the promise of their return home. Too tired to build igloos, they survived the nights by pitching Cook's silk tent wherever they stopped. And, with no sun available with which to take readings because of the fog, Cook did not know where they were. Their food supply was dwindling, yet they could tell they were still far north of the lands where they would find game. By mid-May, they were reduced to half-rations, that is, eight ounces of frozen pemmican a day for each of them. The surviving dogs received even less.

Finally, on May 24, the sun broke through the fog long enough for a reading, and Cook found they were at about 84 degrees of latitude near the ninety-seventh parallel, 162 miles from Svartevoeg. They had been averaging fewer than 12 miles a day, compared with their northward pace of around 16 miles a day. When they neared the latitude of Bradley Land, which they had discovered on their way north, the area was still obscured by the mist. Cook decided that spending the time trying to find and explore the island, since it was unlikely to house game this early in the spring, could be fatal. In their present condition, he reckoned, they would be unlikely now to exceed 10 miles a day of progress. He set their new course a bit more westerly, and they resumed their march, as the fog again enclosed them in a cloud of gray cotton.

They had to make their way around a huge lead in the ice, and the wind shifted and came at them from the east. "The following days were days of desperation," he wrote later. "The food for man and dog was reduced" again, and they were again traveling blind. "A gray mystery enshrouded us. Terror followed in our wake. Beneath us the sea moved—whither it was carrying us I did not know. That we were ourselves journeying toward an illimitable, hopeless sea, where we should die of slow, lingering starvation, I knew was a dreadful probability."

On June 13 the skies again cleared long enough for Cook to take a reading. To his horror, he discovered that they were in Crown Prince Gustav Sea, one hundred miles south of Svartevoeg and fifty miles west of Axel Heiberg Island, on which Svartevoeg sits. And between them and Axel Heiberg—and its abundant game and their bountiful and waiting caches of food—was a sea filled with broken, impassable ice. Cook, it was later determined, had unwittingly made another discovery that buttresses his claim: He and his companions had become caught in a then-unknown clockwise current, which moves the ice in a southwesterly direction where they encountered it. This is now known as the southeastern segment of the Western Arctic Gyre.

After finding himself far west of where he expected to be, Cook must have struggled to retain his composure in front of his two emotionally fragile companions. In his field notes, however, he accurately described their plight: "Heiberg Island is impossible to us. What is our fate? Food and fuel is about exhausted, though we still have 10 bony dogs. Upon these and our little pemmican we can possibly survive for 20 days. In the meantime we must go somewhere. To the south is our only hope."

This was the last entry contained in the records that Cook was able to bring home with him. His other records were lost to history, owing to peculiar circumstances that were beyond his control, which would later complicate his claim to having reached the North Pole.

During this time of despair, the sun broke through the fog on June 14, as the hungry and exhausted group of men and dogs resumed their march in search of food. And at six o'clock the next morning, Cook wrote, "We were awakened by a strange sound. Our surprised eyes turned from side to side. Not a word was uttered. Another sound came—a series of soft, silvery notes—the song of a creature that might have come from heaven. I listened with rapture." This seemingly heaven-sent sound was actually the sound of a snow bunting. "We were back to life! Tears of joy rolled down our emaciated faces." And as hungry as they were, Cook said, they gave no thought to killing this missionary of hope, preferring to share this sound of life than to temporarily quell their chronic hunger pangs.

Later that day, after climbing a high ridge, they set foot on land for the first time in more than three months. Their resting place was a bleak, barren island, an appropriate setting for the ragged, bone-thin, and unkempt group. After pitching their tent, all the survivors—men and dogs—ate one of the dogs that had been ailing. Cook said that while their stomachs were "conscienceless," they were not, and they knew that they were eating the flesh of a creature who had been faithful to them. But their own bones were sticking through their skins, and so they ate, their feelings of having betrayed a companion a lesser evil than the pain in their empty stomachs.

The next day, they managed to kill a bear with one of the few remaining rifle cartridges, and the men and the dogs devoured it raw. And other bears, attracted by the smell of carrion, came to their camp in a steady parade, which provided an abundant food supply for the hungry explorers in exchange for just a few more cartridges.

Fed to bulging finally, and with full sledges of bear meat, they headed southward, bound for Wellington Channel and, eventually, Lancaster Sound. They hoped that a passing whaler might find them during the summer hunting season and take them across Baffin Bay to Greenland and home and family.

As Cook and his companions were making their way southward, Cook's note to Francke, which he wrote in mid-March, was given to Francke by Koolootingwah and Inugito upon their return to Annoatok. When Cook had not arrived by late May, Francke followed Cook's instructions and began to travel with several of the Annoatok Eskimos by sledge south the hundred miles to North Star Bay. Francke was carrying Cook's store of narwahl horns and hundreds of blue-fox and musk-ox skins; Cook valued the lot at ten thousand dollars.

Francke injured his leg during the run, however; he stashed the skins and tusks and returned to Annoatok. He reported that the pain subsided eventually, and he and the Eskimos again ventured toward North Star Bay, this time in a boat. But there were no whalers in the bay when they arrived, so Francke left a note asking for any passing vessel to pick him up and sailed back toward Annoatok. It was a gruesome journey; his leg again pained him, while violent storms delayed their progress. Francke was also apparently suffering from a growing case of scurvy. After a full week of being drenched by rain and sea, and days after they ran out of food, the group made it back near home. As they rounded the far point of the bay at Etah on August 10, on the way to Annoatok, Francke saw what he must have thought was a heaven-sent savior, Peary's *Roosevelt* lying at anchor.

He sped toward the ship, ecstatic to see white men and a way home. But once again, Peary's peculiar version of hospitality was displayed, this time by the *Roosevelt*'s crew. According to Ross G. Marvin, Peary's secretary, Francke first asked for Peary, but was told that he was on his other ship, the *Erik,* which had brought additional supplies for the expedition and was not at Etah at the time. Francke then asked for the assistance of the *Roosevelt*'s doctor to treat his leg, but was refused the aid. In the words of one of the other crewmen, who was interviewed by a magazine writer after Peary's ships returned to New York, "The man [Francke] could hardly walk, but I would like to tell you, sir, that the steward on board would not give him a drop of coffee or anything to eat. So he went on shore to sleep with the Eskimos."

Francke was clearly in poor shape physically and emotionally. He was afraid that Peary would deny him passage home, that he would have to spend another dark winter surrounded only by Eskimos speaking their strange tongue, and that he would have to survive on Eskimo food for many more months.

The next morning, Captain Robert A. Bartlett went ashore and found Francke. He apologized for the treatment Francke had received and invited Francke out to the ship so he could be fed. Actually, Bartlett's primary motive was to get Francke to tell him all about Cook's adventures in the Arctic. With a full stomach of familiar food, Francke was delighted to tell Bartlett and Marvin what he knew of Cook's activities and of Cook's departure for the Pole in the spring. Of course, he could not tell them if Cook had been successful, or even if Cook was still alive. After relating his tale, Francke asked Bartlett for permission to return to America on the *Erik,* but the *Roosevelt*'s captain said that only Peary could make that decision.

When Peary arrived at Etah, he agreed that Francke could travel on the *Erik,* but only if he turned over all Cook's property—furs and horns, which Cook had valued at ten thousand dollars, and all Cook's supplies that remained at Annoatok, along with the hut, all of which Cook said was worth another thirty-five thousand dollars. Furthermore, Francke was told he had to write Peary a letter authorizing the transfer of the goods. This was a most unusual and outrageous demand to make for passage home on a ship, especially on a ship that would be making the voyage in any event. Bradley was later presented with a bill for one hundred dollars for Francke's passage. Mrs. Cook, enraged at Peary's unconscionable behavior, personally repaid the fifty dollars Peary had given to Francke to cover his travel expenses to New York from Newfoundland, where the *Erik* had docked.

Francke's first, short note turning Cook's invaluable possessions (since there was no way of replacing the supplies from home) to Peary was apparently unacceptable to Peary, so another, more detailed one was prepared. Francke, who was German but spoke English relatively well, then wrote to Peary, "I leave you all the stuff laying at Atha [Etah] and Annoatok to take of them because I can't do it. I am in crippled condition. . . ." Peary was finally satisfied, and the *Erik* sailed for home on August 21, apparently with Cook's furs and ivory aboard. It is believed that the narwhal tusk that Peary later presented to President Roosevelt as his primary gift to the president from this expedition was actually one of the tusks he stole from Cook.

Peary's next move was still another egregious violation of ethics without precedent in exploration. He had a notice posted on the outside of Cook's hut that read: "This house belongs to Dr. F. A. Cook, but Dr. Cook is long ago dead and there is no use to search for him. Therefore, I, Commander Robert E. Peary, install my boatswain in this deserted house." There was no reason to presume that Cook was dead; besides, barring an emergency of his own, Peary had no justification for expropriating the supplies of another explorer.

In Cook's hut, Peary installed his boatswain, John Murphy, an illiterate bully whom Cook later described as "a rough Newfoundland bruiser"; cabin boy William Pritchard, who had been ordered to read Peary's order to Murphy periodically, since Murphy could not do so himself; and Harry Whitney, scion of a wealthy New Haven family, who had paid Peary two thousand dollars to sail on the *Erik* to hunt in the Arctic and then persuaded the explorer to let him remain in Annoatok so he could resume his pastime in the spring.

According to Cook, Whitney later told him that even Bartlett "quivered with indignation at the blushing audacity of this steal" of Cook's hut and supplies. "The stores were said to be abandoned. The men, with Peary's orders, went to Koolootingwah and forced from him the key with which to open the carefully guarded stores," Cook wrote. Cook also later charged that Peary ordered Koolootingwah not to mount a rescue mission for him and his companions, claiming it would be useless.

On August 18, Peary—unsure of Cook's fate—set sail on the *Roosevelt* to reach a northern roost at which he and his men would sit out the winter, poised to launch their own dash for the North Pole as soon as spring settled upon the Arctic.

Meanwhile, Mrs. Cook, who was rightly concerned about her husband's safety, sent relief supplies northward aboard the ship, the *Arctic*. When the relief ship docked at Annoatok in August, Murphy became threatening and abusive to the *Arctic*'s captain, Joseph E. Bernier. To avoid a confrontation, Bernier cached the relief supplies on the rocky coast a little south of Etah and left them in Whitney's care.

CHAPTER 12

A North Pole Faker

Cook and his Eskimo companions were successful in obtaining food as they happily made their way southward in June 1908, consuming what they killed as they traveled after finishing the bear meat they had loaded upon their sledge. However, when they neared Devon Island, they saw that a southerly wind had jammed their intended route to Lancaster Sound with huge chunks of broken ice, over which they could not possibly sledge. Travel overland across the island was also impossible, since Eskimo lore held that there was no game in the interior of Devon Island and they had no food in reserve to last them on a journey across the island.

Cook decided they would cross into Jones Sound, between Devon Island and the southern part of Ellesmere Island, where the ice was still relatively solid. Along this route, they were able, using some of their precious and dwindling supply of rifle ammunition, to kill some ducks for their own food supply. But the travelers found no large game with which to feed the dogs, and they did not have enough cartridges to kill a sufficient number of ducks to feed the ever-ravenous dogs.

On July 7, as they stood facing a large area of open water, Cook had to deal with what he called "the saddest incident of a long run of trouble": They would have to travel across the water in the canvas boat they had carried all the way from Annoatok, and that meant leaving the surviving dogs behind. There were wolves in the area, and Cook said two of the dogs had already run off to join them. His hope was that the rest of the dogs would do the same in order to survive. When they departed in their boat, after taking one of their sledges apart and stowing it aboard, Cook reported, "The dogs howled like crying children; we still heard them when five miles off shore."

For two weeks they struggled in the 12-foot-long canvas boat, dodging icebergs and bad weather in the 190-mile-long, 40-mile-wide Jones Sound, as they slowly made their way eastward toward Baffin Bay and Greenland. They averaged about 10 miles a day of progress toward the east. Actually, Cook estimated, they were traveling about 30 miles a day, but in a circuitous route as they paddled around many obstructions. By now, they were almost completely out of food; four cans of pemmican, which Cook was saving for the last, was all that remained. And he had only four cartridges for the rifle, three of which—unknown to his companions—Cook intended to save for their own deaths, if things became too awful to bear.

While looking for a place to change course toward the north, and home, they were caught in a large, fast-developing storm. As the sea churned about their fragile craft and seemed about to swamp it, one of the Eskimos said that he smelled land, and they paddled furiously toward the scent. They reached shore just before the storm's full fury hit them. After the squall passed and the trio resumed their journey, Cook soon made an improvement on his sledge design.

Since they had no dogs, the men were now tediously dragging the sledge when they were on the ice; when they reached water, they had to stop and put everything in the boat. Cook had the idea to lash the boat to the top of the sledge upside down. When they reached open water, they turned the contraption over, climbed into the boat, and paddled across with the sledge attached below.

In early August, they were twenty-five miles east of Cape Sparbo, on Devon Island's northern shore. For the first time since their return to the area, they found evidence of old Eskimo settlements. This was a heartening sign because it indicated there was likely to be game in the area, since the Eskimos would not have settled in a barren place. Indeed, the travelers soon found and killed an enormous seal and stopped to patch their boat and their clothes with the seal's skin and to rest their weary bones. Then they continued on.

Near the end of August, it was clear to them that they had no chance of making it across the sea to Greenland before winter set in. Sadly, they turned their attention to finding a suitable place to spend the dark, cold—and gameless—months ahead. They all agreed that the only logical choice was to return the way they had come and make for Cape Sparbo, which seemed to offer the most likely haven.

As the dispirited group paddled the boat back toward Sparbo, Mother Nature was not content with her victory. "Suddenly something white and glittering pierced the bottom of the boat!" Cook wrote. "It was the tusk of a walrus, gleaming and dangerous. Before we could grasp the situation he had disappeared, and water gushed into our craft." Walrus can grow to enormous size and can be very aggressive, as these seasoned travelers knew. Instinctively, they took off after the walrus, as Ahwelah rammed his knee into the hole to slow the inrushing water. When they realized they could not catch up to the walrus, they made for a drifting iceberg, where they patched the boat with a piece of boot.

Later, the hungry trio came upon a herd of ten sleeping walruses. They crept slowly and silently over the ice toward the herd, their improvised harpoon (a knife nailed to a wooden shaft) at the ready. Then they spied a huge polar bear, which was also stalking the herd, paying no attention to the humans, which were apparently no gastronomic match for a meal of walrus. They watched as the bear sneaked up on the herd, "envious anger welling up within us. Our position was helpless. His long neck reached out, the glistening fangs closed, and a young walrus struggled in the air. With dismay and rage, the walruses sank into the water, and the bear slunk off to a safe distance, where he sat down to a comfortable meal. We were not of sufficient importance to interest either the bear or the disturbed herd of giants."

The three men settled for some tiny fish they found around rocks near the shoreline that they were able to catch with their bare hands. They devoured them raw, thinking all the while longingly of the bear's superior menu.

The next day, however, after an incredible fifteen-hour battle with a giant walrus, Cook and his Eskimos devoured their first full-scale meal in weeks. Cook estimated that the walrus weighed three thousand pounds, and they made a large fire with the animal's blubber and began cooking pot after pot of the meat. After gorging themselves into a stupor and stashing the rest of the meat under rocks, they slept for about fifteen hours. When they awoke, they discovered that bears had broken into their cache and stolen the rest of the walrus, which they had expected to live off for many days to come. They were heartsick over this latest loss and frustrated by their inability to protect their hard-earned spoils.

By mid-September, they had made their way back to Cape Sparbo—which is approximately three hundred air miles from Annoatok—and settled into a small cave they located during a search for a likely winter home. While cleaning out debris in the cave, they were delighted to find that the cave had obviously been occupied by humans previously, since they found within it a traditional Eskimo platform for their beds. Cook speculated the cave had been prepared for a small family, and it required little alteration to suit their needs. But while they were excavating the cave to give themselves an additional foot of headroom, Cook wrote, "I suddenly experienced a heart-depressing chill when, lifting some debris, I saw staring at me from the black earth a hollow-eyed human skull. The message of death which the weird thing leeringly conveyed was singularly unpleasant; the omen was not good."

What they needed most to do next was to fill their larder for the winter. They spotted herds of musk oxen, but they were unable to kill them. There were no cartridges for the rifles, and the skins of the oxen were too thick for their improvised spears and harpoons to penetrate. They tried stoning the oxen, to no avail. But Cook and the Eskimos again proved the domination of intelligence over brawn. By throwing stones and rushing at the herd, the hunters managed to separate three oxen from the main herd. They advanced on them, throwing stones and making loud, aggressive noises. The oxen continued to back up slowly, step by step, as they kept their eyes fixed upon their attackers. At last, one of them stepped too far and tumbled down the steep cliff where the hunters had steered them. After scaring the others over the edge, the men ran down the cliff and butchered the oxen.

Cook and the Eskimos next devised traps to snare the oxen; then they could advance on them and kill them with well-aimed thrusts from lances they made out of their pocketknives. The trio quickly gathered enough meat to last them through the winter.

Now that their formerly all-consuming drive for food was relieved, Cook began to appreciate everything around him. He studied the plants, animals, and birds that he saw and marveled at the interdependence that allowed life to continue on those shores, no doubt some of the most desolate and barren land on Earth.

But as the sun slipped lower and lower in the skies, Cook found his freedom of movement shrinking; bears were everywhere, and they were all in a frenzy to find food to fill their bellies to get them through the winter.

By November, "days now came and went in short order. . . . The moon and stars appeared at noon. The usual partition of time disappeared. All was night."

They kept six-hour watches now, tending their ever-burning fire to keep the bears at bay, reluctant to leave their outdoor camp and settle into their underground haven. In these days, they thought of home and family. "We knew that we were believed to be dead," Cook wrote. "Our friends in Greenland would not ascribe to us the luck which came after our run of abject misfortune"—luck that had left them with a cave for the winter and an ample supply of food. "This thought inflicted perhaps the greatest pain of the queer prolongation of life which was permitted us. . . . We could not have been more thoroughly isolated if we had been transported to the surface of the moon."

And here they spent the long winter of 1908–09, a forty-three-year-old physician from New York City and his two young Eskimo companions, telling and retelling tales in the language of Greenland, speculating about their future, and dreaming privately of what was to come.

Meanwhile, Peary and his party spent the winter comfortably lounging aboard the *Roosevelt,* locked in the ice off Cape Sheridan, where they had anchored on September 5, 1908. Peary's plan was again to use the large support parties to move supplies northward, to break the trail for him to travel, and to build igloos for him to sleep in. As in the 1906 expedition, he announced that he would attempt to follow a meridian, this time the seventieth, all the way to the North Pole.

Peary was not a well man. He was fifty-two years old and hobbled about on his toeless feet; the leg he had broken in 1891, which Cook had set, was throbbing, bothering him, Peary said, for the first time since it had healed. After all his cries of wolf, this was surely the last chance he had to reach the North Pole. The night before the expedition was to begin, Peary wrote, "This was my final chance to realize the one dream of my life. . . . [It was] the drawing of the string to launch the last arrow in my quiver."

Robert A. Bartlett, the captain of the *Roosevelt,* led the first advance party from the ship to the jumping-off point of Cape Columbia on February 15, 1909. A week later, Peary made the ninety-mile trip and immediately invoked "the Peary discipline," the "iron hand ungloved," in the words of Matthew Henson. "He commenced to shout and issue orders, and by the time he had calmed down," both Bartlett and expedition member George Borup had loaded their sledges and headed northward.

Peary followed on March 1 and was able to make 10 miles headway on his first day out. Three days later he met up with his advance parties, which were again stopped at the south shore of the Big Lead, which had delayed them on the last expedition. This time they spent a week waiting for ice to cover the open water. After they finally made it across, Peary outlined his plan: He would reach the North Pole in fifteen marches in which he would cover the remaining 250 miles; at various points, the others would be sent back until only he, Henson, and four Eskimos, with five sledges, were still on the trail.

The most disappointed member of the expedition was Bartlett, who maintained that Peary had told him he would be accompanying him all the way to the Pole. Under the new plan, Bartlett's supporting party was to be the last to return to the ship. When that time came, on April 1, Bartlett took off with his dogs for the north, rather than southward toward the ship, contemplating, he said later, making the dash over the remaining 150 statute miles by himself. But after a few miles, he thought better of it and turned around.

Here in earnest begins the double-talking and ever-shifting versions of events by Peary and his closest associates that have left the true story of who did what and when unclear even to this day.

Soon after his return from the Arctic, Peary told reporters that he had sent Bartlett back because he wanted his honors not to be clouded by the presence of another white man at the historic event: reaching the North Pole. In the backward racial climate of the day, Henson's credibility was low, on a par with that of the Eskimos; thus, Peary would be the only "real person" history would note if the group actually got to the Pole. Also, Henson could not use the sextant, so he could not verify Peary's location. In later testimony before a subcommittee of the House of Representatives, Peary repeated the sentiments about Bartlett, saying, "I did not feel ... I was called upon to divide with a man who, no matter how able and deserving he might be, was a young man and had put in only a few years of that kind of work, and who had frankly, as I believed, not the right to it that I had."

In his book on the expedition, however, Peary offered another, more politic scenario. He said the first reason he took Henson all the way was because of Henson's skills with the sledge and the Eskimos. His second reason was that Henson "would not have been so competent as the white members of the expedition in getting himself and his party back to land. . . . While faithful to me, and when WITH ME [Peary's emphasis] more effective in covering distance with a sledge than any of the others, he had not, as a racial inheritance, the daring and initiative of" the four white men who had headed the accompanying support parties. "I owed it to him not to subject him to dangers and responsibilities which he was temperamentally unfit to face."

Although Peary's comments do need to be considered in light of the era in which they were made, they clearly ignored the pivotal role Henson had played in nearly all Peary's earlier expeditions. A more reasonable answer to Peary's choice of Henson as a companion can be found by studying the records.

First, sending Bartlett back meant that Peary was the only member of the expedition left who could read a sextant. Although this action was to taint his claims forever, there was no one left on the trip who could challenge his readings. Another important motive is that Peary was clearly exhausted, and, if we are to believe Henson's first accounts of what occurred following Bartlett's departure, Peary spent most of the rest of the journey toward the Pole and back being carried like baggage on a sledge, hardly the image of the conquering hero. A servant could be expected to carry Peary uncomplainingly; a colleague might not have been so inclined.

Up to the day of Bartlett's forced departure, the Peary expedition had averaged 14.4 miles a day from the point they joined up, a speedy but not unusual pace for that time and in line with Cook's reported daily advances. But as had occurred during the 1906 "farthest-north" march, as soon as all the other white witnesses were gone, Peary's sledges seemed to sprout jet engines, and their speed nearly doubled. The first day, the group traveled twenty-five miles, according to Peary; that distance would actually prove to be below the astonishing average of twenty-six miles a day that Peary reported for the five marches he said brought the group to the North Pole.

With Bartlett, who had been breaking a trail for Peary, gone, Peary wrote, "Now I took my proper place in the lead. Though I held myself in check, I felt the keenest exhilaration, and even exultation, as I climbed over the pressure ridge and breasted the keen air sweeping over the mighty ice, pure and straight from the Pole itself."

Henson's version was quite different, however. In 1910, he told a newspaper reporter, "Because of his crippled feet [Peary] had ridden on the sledges the greater part of the journey up. . . . He was heavy for the dogs to haul. We knew he could walk but little on rough ice. . . . Much of my work was ahead, breaking the trail and caring for advance things."

Peary said he took no observations from the time Bartlett left on April 1 until April 5, when he discovered he was only thirty-five miles from the Pole. In addition, Peary said he never took a longitudinal reading because he found them to be a waste of time. This was an astonishing comment. As one of his biographers reported,

"Peary was lost as soon as he left his meridian. He had no means of knowing where he was. If he assumed he was on the meridian, when he was east or west of it, his compass bearings would lead him farther astray; and not knowing his longitude [since he was taking no longitudinal bearings] he could not correct his bearings."

On April 6, Peary reported, he miraculously found the group to be at 89 degrees, 57 minutes, about 3½ miles from the goal of his life. To have come this near an imaginary spot in a frigid, ice-littered, and blinding environment by dead reckoning made Peary either the greatest navigator in history (which no one has ever praised him for being) or the luckiest man in the world. And now, supposedly on the verge of accomplishing his life's work, Peary reported, he was too tired to go on and reach the Pole. Incredibly, he wrote, he went to sleep while he was almost in sight of the Big Nail.

Then, after a night's sleep, on April 6, 1909, he wrote—on a piece of loose paper that was later inserted into his bound diary—"The Pole at last. The prize of three centuries. My dream and goal for 25 years. Mine at last! I cannot bring myself to realize it. It seems all so simple and commonplace."

Peary's group left the Pole on April 7, apparently reenergized, since they set an all-time record for sledge travel that day: 61 statute miles, thus covering in one day what Peary said had taken two days of unparalleled speed on the way up. The next night, he said, they reached the camp from which Bartlett had been sent back. "Thus he covered 150 statute miles (not to mention extra distance caused by detours around ridges and other obstructions) in 56 hours, with time out for rest and sleep," wrote Frederick J. Pohl in the introduction to a book written by Cook about his return journey from the Pole and published after Cook's death. "He either traveled 75 statute miles a day for two days or he never came near the Pole," concluded Pohl.

By comparison, Cook claimed twenty-nine miles as his record on the trek to the Pole and back; Fridtjof Nansen, who had a reputation as an expert dog driver, reported that his own best day on level ice was twenty-five miles and at that, the dogs had shown serious wear by day's end. Ironically, Cook's claimed rate of travel had raised some eyebrows soon after his return; Peary's claims made Cook's certainly pale by comparison.

There is no way that Peary and his companions covered the distances he claimed. Add to that Henson's observations on Peary's physical condition—"Already the strain of the hard upward journey was beginning to tell, and after the first two marches back he was practically a dead weight"—and the conclusion is unavoidable: Peary had not traveled 150 miles from the camp in the first place and thus had not reached the North Pole.

Because the story of Peary's journey had to be written backward, since it was clear to Peary that he had to account for the 150 miles, plus detours, to the Pole and the 415 or so miles back to the ship, the tale is replete with scores of inconsistencies and omissions, which several historical and geographical writers have taken great pains to pinpoint over the intervening eighty years. Somehow, the denials and corrections have never received much publicity, and Peary's fraudulent claim has remained intact, although the winds of change now seem to be stirring anew over the Big Nail.

Three other events involving Peary's return trip give further strong weight to the theory that Peary, Henson, and the Eskimos never made it to the Pole.

• Despite his weakened physical condition, Peary and his group made it back to the *Roosevelt* on April 23, meaning that it took them twenty-two days less to come home than it had taken to go north. In fact, they came back so fast that they almost beat Bartlett to the ship, even though they said they had traveled at least 300 miles farther than Bartlett. This is precisely what happened during Peary's 1906 expedition, when he claimed his "farthest north" mark. In 1906, despite allegedly traveling some 230 statute miles farther than a support team he had ordered back to the ship, Peary arrived back at the *Roosevelt* at almost the same hour as the support party.

This time, Peary arrived at the *Roosevelt* three days after Bartlett, but only after having spent two days resting at Cape Columbia before starting out for the *Roosevelt*. Peary's apologists explained the 1906 matter by claiming that the support party was led by an inexperienced sledge driver. No such claim could be made about Bartlett, who was an excellent dog handler and ice traveler.

• Partially to account for his unprecedented speed, Peary explained that they had zoomed down the seventieth parallel—it is interesting that he could even find the seventieth parallel, since he took no longitudinal readings—and stayed in each of the igloos they had built on the northward trek. And that explanation would indeed account for some of their speed, were it not for the fact that the entire ice pack was continually drifting eastward. Thus, the igloos would no longer have been at the seventieth parallel when he got there. If, however, Peary had followed the line of march they had taken north—assuming he could find it, with the storms and poor weather conditions that prevail there—he would never have made it back to Cape Columbia, but would have instead made landfall far to the east, upon the shores of northern Greenland.

• As a final important point of evidence, when Peary arrived back at the *Roosevelt,* his life's dream supposedly accomplished, and faced all the men who had made it possible, he said nothing and made no claim to have reached the North Pole. He later said he told Bartlett of his accomplishment when he got back, after Bartlett had guessed that he had made it. To expect a crew that had sacrificed as much and worked as hard as these men had not to have been rewarded with the knowledge of his, and thus their, success is beyond the pale. If the men accepted Peary's silence, it seems reasonable to believe that it is because they were all aware of his failure.

CHAPTER 13

Back to Civilization

Cook, Etukishook, and Ahwelah, meanwhile, had spent a restless winter cooped up in their tiny cave. There was barely room for the three of them, and they took turns occupying the one spot in the cave where they could stand fully erect. Although they remained friends over the dark months and exchanged tales about themselves and their dreams, Cook longed for an involved conversation with people who shared his native tongue and his background.

Their desperation for new company is obvious from one story Cook related about the adventure. Soon after they had reluctantly retreated to the cave, the three men began to hear noises inside it—scraping, scratching sounds. They wondered what the noises could be and mounted a thorough search. They found nothing, but "when all was quiet at the time which we chose to call midnight, a little blue rat came out and began to tear the bark from our willow lamp trimmer. I was on watch, awake, and punched Etukishook without moving my head," Cook wrote. "His eyes opened with surprise on the busy rodent, and Ahwelah was kicked. He turned over and the thing jumped into a rock crevasse."

The next day, they risked running into the still-marauding bears and went outside to gather some willow roots for their new, and welcome, companion. They arranged the roots they had gathered in a row near the back of the den, and soon the rat came and ate them, "but he permitted no familiarity," Cook said.

Two days later, they were rewarded for their efforts by the appearance of not only the rat, but its mate. After some testing of the men's intentions, the rats quickly settled into the routine of the underground camp. They became important friends for the weary, bored travelers. "They were beautiful little creatures, but little larger than mice," Cook explained. "They had soft, fluffy fur of a pearl blue color, with pink eyes. They had no tails. Their dainty little feet were furred to the claw tips with silky hair."

After assuring themselves that the men intended them no harm, the rats took up residence in the open, above Cook's berth. "They were good, clean, orderly camp fellows, always kept in their places and never disturbed our bed furs, nor did they disturb our eatables. With a keen sense of justice, and an aristocratic air, they passed our plates of carnivorous foods without venturing a taste, and went to their herbivorous piles of sod delicacies."

But then the rats deserted them, to begin their nocturnal hibernation, joining most of the rest of the animal world in a deep winter's sleep. The three men were now alone, the only living, awake creatures for hundreds of miles around their den.

Cook compared his existence to that of a Stone Age man: huddled in a damp, cold, dark cave, sleeping on a platform of rocks. There was only a single spot in the cave where one of them at a time could stand up straight; their primary food was raw meat, eaten frozen. During these long months, Cook worked on his diaries, which would form the bulk of his two books, several magazine articles, and a multipart newspaper series on the adventure. When he ran out of paper, he wrote between the lines of his previous writings, printing in tiny letters with the stub of a pencil he kept very sharp. He devised a series of abbreviations and symbols to help him conserve the precious paper, to get more words into the finite space.

Finally, as sunrise approached, the first stirrings of life began. The rats awoke and rejoined them. The smaller surface animals— the plentiful hares and foxes—began to roam the land. Then the bears emerged from their winter's sleep, many of them with cubs in tow. After taking stock and deciding that they had more than enough food for themselves, the three men began leaving piles of meat for the bears. They would delight in watching the bears devour the musk ox and seal meat while they viewed them through the peephole they had cut through the wall of their den.

On February 18, 1909, seven days after the sun returned to their sky, Cook and the Eskimos loaded up a sledge they had reconstructed over the winter and resumed their trek to Annoatok, which Cook reckoned was about three hundred miles away, in a straight line, but many more miles distant over the route they would have to follow.

The journey was difficult, and they found no game. By the thirty-fifty day out from Cape Sparbo, they were out of food and still one hundred miles from Cape Sabine. And, because of the circuituous route they were forced to take by the melting ice, by Cook's reckoning they were still as much as two hundred miles from Annoatok.

By now, they were reduced to eating walrus hides they had saved to repair their clothing. Cook lost his front teeth to this culinary delight. Next they actually ate their shoelaces before they came across a rotted seal that had been cached for them by Pan-ic-pa, Etukishook's father, at Cape Sabine. Cook said it smelled like Limburger cheese and tasted odd, but they were in no condition to be choosy, so they devoured it all. Then they headed out to cross Smith Sound to Greenland, thirty miles away and a perilous journey, since the ice was broken by much open water. Cook knew that this last leg would be made even more difficult by the fact that they were unlikely to find anything to eat as they crossed the dissolving ice pack.

Indeed, by the time they made their way across Smith Sound, they were reduced to eating their boots and were very close to death. "So weak that we had to climb on hands and knees," Cook wrote, "we reached the top of an iceberg, and from there saw Annoatok. Natives, who had thought us long dead, rushed out to greet us."

It was April 15, 1909, when they were carried back by jubilant villagers to Annoatok, fourteen months after their departure for the Pole. In that time, the three voyagers had covered some two thousand miles by sledge and boat and survived one of exploration's greatest adventures, capped by the attainment of the greatest remaining geographic prize on Earth. Even if they had not reached the North Pole, their return journey around Ellesmere Island and Devon Island and back to Annoatok would rank as one of exploration's greatest sledge journeys.

Cook was astonished to meet an American upon his return, the hunter Whitney, whom Peary had brought to Greenland. Whitney had accompanied the Eskimos who spotted the men crawling on the ice and rushed out from Annoatok to rescue them. Whitney took Cook to his cabin, which Peary had expropriated, and together with cabin boy Pritchard, bathed and fed Cook, and then bathed him and fed him again. Cook recalled that he ate all night, stopping only to rest his jaws. Whitney told Cook that he was the dirtiest man he had ever met.

As he recovered his strength, Cook asked about Peary's taking over of his supplies and his cabin and learned all about Peary's arrival in Etah, his mistreatment of Francke, and his departure for the Pole. Cook was furious about Peary's actions, he said, not because he needed the supplies—he said Peary would have been welcome to them if he had a real need for them—but that the theft of his material for Peary's trading purposes was a serious breach of ethical conduct.

Cook took an immediate liking to Whitney and to Pritchard, but then these were the first men from "home" he had seen and talked to in more than a year and a half. "In due time," Cook wrote, "I told Whitney: 'I have reached the Pole.' Uttering this for the first time in English, it came upon me that I was saying a remarkable thing. Yet Mr. Whitney showed no great surprise, and his quiet congratulation confirmed what was in my mind—that I had accomplished no extraordinary or unbelievable thing."

Cook now realized that he was in a race with Peary for the honors of claiming the North Pole. After an amazingly quick recovery from his long ordeal, three days later he was ready to leave Annoatok. He seemed to have little doubt that Peary would also reach the mark, and rather than wait for a chance passing ship, Cook decided to sledge down to Upernavik, after pledging Whitney, Pritchard, Etukishook, and Ahwelah to secrecy. Cook did not want Peary to know that he had made it all the way to the Big Nail until he could tell the world.

Whitney tried to persuade Cook to wait for the ship that Whitney's family was supposed to send to bring him home, but Cook was sure that he would be better off making the dangerous three-hundred-mile sledge trip than risking Peary's speedy return. From Upernavik, he hoped to be able to catch a coastal ship that would take him farther south, where he believed he would find a boat to take him to Copenhagen.

Cook did agree to let Whitney carry back to the United States a trunk containing his instruments—which would be checked for accuracy when he returned to prove the veracity of his readings—and most of his original field notes and the American flag he had flown over the North Pole. He also left with Whitney a box filled with clothing, supplies, and furs, along with scientific specimens he had collected during his days in Greenland.

Cook said he left all these things with Whitney because he was afraid of what would happen to them—especially his instruments and his original records—on his perilous, overland journey in search of a ship to take him to Denmark.

On his trip southward, Cook, alone with his thoughts for the first time since his safe return to Annoatok, felt the first stirrings of the public acclaim that he speculated he might receive for his accomplishment in American exploration and geographic circles. But he said, "In the wildest flights of my imagination I never dreamed of any world-wide interest in the Pole."

Late in May, Cook finally arrived in Upernavik and headed directly for the house of the Danish governor of the region, a man named Kraul. The tall, fifty-year-old bachelor took his first look at Cook, dirty and unkempt and wearing old, worn clothing, and asked a single question: "Have you any lice on you?" After being convinced that Cook did not have any unsavory travelers on him, Governor Kraul opened his home to Cook, where he remained until around June 20, when the *Godthaab,* a Danish supply ship, stopped at Upernavik.

Cook rode on the *Godthaab* to Eggedesminde, where the first dinner in his honor was held. About twenty-five people, including explorer Knud Rasmussen, feted Cook in the dining room of the King's Guest House, which was reportedly the only hotel in all Greenland at the time. At that celebration were Henning

Schoubye, captain of the *Hans Egede,* a Danish blubber ship that regularly traveled between Greenland and Denmark; Jens Daug-aard-Jensen, Denmark's inspector of North Greenland; and several Danish reporters and scientists, including ethnologist Dr. Hans P. Steensby, who happened to be traveling on the *Hans Egede.*

Captain Schoubye told the group that he had been present when Rasmussen, the explorer and writer, had questioned at least thirty-five Eskimos in the North Star Bay area about Cook's journey. He said the natives told Rasmussen that Cook had "jumped and danced like an angacock [witch doctor] when he had looked at his 'sun glass' and seen that they were only a day's journey from the 'Great Nail.' " Dr. Steensby added that Cook's forced stay at Cape Sparbo would turn out to be a good thing because when the account was published, "one will see what an excellent polar Eskimo Cook had become, and one will not be surprised that this man was able to reach the Pole."

Cook was now hoping to catch a ride to Labrador on an idle walrus schooner—which would allow him to stake his claim at home, in the United States—but he eventually decided he could save time by going to Copenhagen on the *Hans Egede,* a blubber ship that also carried passengers. He would thus be able to present his North Pole claims in person to the Danish government, which then had complete control over Greenland and over the North Pole.

In conversations with the scientists and newspaper correspondents who happened to be among the *Hans Egede's* passengers, Cook began to get an inkling that his accomplishment might have some good financial possibilities. At the time, he had only forty or fifty dollars in his pockets, he said, not even enough to cover his passage on the ship to Denmark.

While Cook had apparently planned to arrive quietly in Copenhagen and look up the proper government officials so he could stake his claim to the North Pole, at the urging of his fellow passengers, and with the cooperation of the ship's captain, the *Hans Egede* stopped at Lerwick in the Shetland Islands. It was from this tiny telegraph station that Cook informed the world of his accomplishment and from which his first story, a two-thousand-word piece he had already composed since his return to Annoatok, was sent to the *New York Herald* for the small sum of three thousand dollars.

Two days later, on September 3, 1909, Cook arrived in Copenhagen.

While Cook was slowly making his way back to civilization, Peary was even more slowly preparing to bring his expedition home. He returned to the *Roosevelt,* which was still anchored off Cape Sheridan awaiting him, in late April. But for no known reason, he and the ship remained there for five weeks, instead of rushing southward, as would be expected, so he could get home and tell the world that his life's work had been completed. And Peary, of course, had no way of knowing what had become of Cook and what, if any, claims Cook was making. The *Roosevelt* finally left Cape Sheridan on July 18.

Peary first heard of Cook's reported journey to the North Pole, or at least that Cook had returned safely from a journey to the far north, at a small Eskimo village near Etah. When they arrived at Annoatok, Peary—in an incident that several historians called unprecedented in the history of exploration—ordered that the two Eskimos who had accompanied Cook be interrogated. Courtesy among colleagues should have prevented such interference; indeed, Rasmussen later asked Cook for his permission before attempting to talk with his two Eskimo traveling companions.

Etukishook and Ahwelah, true to their word to Cook, told Peary's people [Peary was not conversant enough in the language to participate] that they had gone only a little way north and, in line with Cook's use of the distant cloud formations to calm his companions, told Peary's men that they had never lost sight of land. It is unclear whether Peary was yet aware that Cook was claiming to have gone all the way to the North Pole. Although the two Eskimos were apparently never specifically asked if the Pole had been reached during the journey with Cook, it is hard to imagine that no one in Peary's crew would have picked up murmurings from the villagers.

In a magazine article late in 1909, Whitney—who had remained in Annoatok after Cook's departure—said that Cook's Eskimos came to him after their first interrogation by Peary's people to ask "what Peary's men were trying to get them to say." Whitney said the two told him that Peary's aides had shown them some papers, but "the Eskimos declared that they did not understand the papers."

Whitney and Pritchard also kept their word to Cook. Thus, Peary surely knew that Cook had been far north, had spent fourteen months on the ice, had returned alive, and was already on his way home, although he may not have realized that Cook would claim the grand prize.

As the *Roosevelt* prepared to sail, the ship Whitney's family was supposed to send to retrieve him had still not arrived. Afraid that he would be left behind, alone, for another long winter, he asked permission to sail on the *Roosevelt* when it departed. Peary agreed, but when he learned that Whitney intended to bring Cook's belongings, instruments, and notes along with him as he had promised Cook, Peary told Whitney the material could not be brought aboard.

Just as Peary had refused Sverdrup similar assistance nine years earlier, he was now adamant about not helping Cook by bringing any of his material back to the United States.

Whitney revealed later that he had tried to sneak the box containing Cook's field notes aboard the *Roosevelt* despite Peary's orders, but Peary somehow found out about his attempt. "When I said I did not want anything belonging to Dr. Cook aboard this ship, I meant I did not want a single thing he had," Whitney said Peary told him. And he placed Whitney on his "word of honor as a gentleman" not to bring any such material along.

So Whitney, with Bartlett's assistance (which Bartlett later denied), took all Cook's belongings, including his precious field notes and instruments, tossed them into a stone circle of rocks on the shore at Etah, and placed a canvas top over them.

Not all Whitney's later actions were as commendable as his attempt to smuggle Cook's records on board the *Roosevelt*, however. Soon after Peary's ship sailed, it met up with the *Jeanie*, which had been sent for Whitney. After Whitney transferred to the ship and told his story to Sam Bartlett, the master of the *Jeanie* and a cousin of the men who captained both Peary's *Roosevelt* and Cook's *Bradley,* the captain suggested that they return to Etah and recover Cook's records.

Whitney refused the request, however, saying he wanted to resume his hunting and that returning to Annoatok would cut into his time for fun by a day or two. This thoughtless decision by Whitney would become a historic blunder, which greatly added to the muddle. Throughout the controversy, Whitney vacillated between bravely supporting Cook, even at times when it was unpopular to do so, and seeming to support the Peary cabal surreptitiously.

The next startling example of Whitney's ambivalent role came less than a year later, when Whitney returned to the Arctic on a supposed hunting trip with Peary's close friend, Captain Robert A. Bartlett, and another wealthy sportsman, Paul J. Rainey. In a magazine article that is so full of contradictions and misstatements as to be laughable, Rainey wrote that the group was up in the Arctic only to hunt game. Yet they stopped at Cape Sparbo and located Cook's winter den; visited Annoatok; and, most important, went to where Whitney and Bartlett had cached Cook's material at Etah.

Despite their claims that they had "refrained from touching or opening" the cache of Cook's material, pictures Rainey took and provided for the article showed that they had clearly disturbed it. Rainey even had the audacity to state, "It seems peculiar . . . that an explorer, returning from the Pole and reaching a point where he could have obtained plenty of help from the Eskimos, should have left valuable records in a place so unprotected." Of course, it was Rainey's traveling companions who had—unknown to Cook— stashed Cook's material, a fact that is not included in Rainey's article. It is highly unlikely that they did not take the material on board their ship. Yet if they did take it, it is also strange that Whitney participated or never admitted that they had done so, since he later backed Cook on several key points when questioned by reporters and signed a public statement that he believed Cook had reached the North Pole.

Even if Rainey, Whitney, and Bartlett had only looked at Cook's notes and instruments, one of the camp followers Peary attracted,

Donald MacMillan, a gym teacher from Worcester, Massachusetts, surely would have taken care of them for his hero. MacMillan spent a great deal of time in the Arctic in the years after the controversy erupted, in his attempts to prove Peary's claims. He based himself at Etah, so if the records were still there when he arrived, it is a sure bet they were not there when he left in 1914.*

In any event, Peary's refusal to bring the records back on the *Roosevelt* severely damaged Cook's claim to the North Pole, but it also prevented Peary and his army of supporters from using the records to prove that Cook had not reached it. But at the time, it no doubt seemed to Peary to be his only alternative. By then, Peary had apparently already decided to fake his own claim to the Pole, which is a strong indication that he might well have known that Cook would stake a similar claim. With few of Cook's original records available for comparison, he knew his records, spotty as they were, would look better to the world.

Finally, on August 20, 1909, Peary and the *Roosevelt* departed the shores of Greenland, offering Peary what would be his last glimpse of his "promised land." Peary was now definitely informed of Cook's claim to have reached the North Pole, and he ordered the *Roosevelt*'s crew to load up her boilers and race back to Newfoundland and the wireless station from which he could stake his own claim.

*Despite Cook's early attempts to launch an expedition to retrieve his material, there is no record of anyone else ever looking for them. During a visit to Etah in August 1987, I was unable to find any trace of the cache, although locating the remains of the old village of Etah was not difficult. The ruins of old Etah sit at the mouth of a picturesque natural harbor that is protected from the winds and has a curving coastline that offers suitable anchorage for large ships. A stream—water runoff from the glacier that runs all the way up to the ridge behind the village—still gurgles today, just as Cook described it in his book some eighty years ago. Over the years, there have been scattered reports that one of Cook's instruments or notebooks has been located, but none of the reports has ever been verified.

CHAPTER 14

Acclaim

The news spread out in dots and dashes from the tiny telegraph station in the Shetland Islands, off the northern coast of Europe, and like a tidal wave, grew in magnitude until it hit distant shores with a deafening roar: The North Pole had been conquered at last!

Instantly, the name Frederick Albert Cook was etched into the world's consciousness on that Wednesday, September 1, 1909, when his two brief wireless telegraph messages forever changed history. To his long-abandoned wife he wired: "Successful. Well. Address Copenhagen." And to the International Polar Commission in Brussels, he wrote: "Reached North Pole April 21, 1908. Discovered land far north. Return to Copenhagen by steamer 'Hans Egede.' "

And as simply as that, the forty-four-year-old Brooklyn physician and self-taught, part-time explorer, who had long been presumed dead, seemingly put an end to a quest that had become an obsession for adventurers who heard the dying call of the vanishing wild.

Two days later, on a sunny Friday morning in Copenhagen, the *Hans Egede* reached the dock. The first glimpses of the conquering hero must have been disappointing for most of the thousands of Danes and hundreds of journalists from around the world, who elbowed each other for room on the banks of the city's port to bear witness to history.

After nearly two years away from the United States and all the trappings of civilization, Cook was a slim, shy man, who hardly made an inspiring appearance. He wore a shiny, ill-fitting, rumpled suit that could more accurately be said to have surrounded his slender, five-feet, ten-inch frame than to have been worn on it. Atop his head, covering his brown hair, was a sailor's cap, from beneath which his bright blue eyes and large mustache were visible. Rounding out his peculiar wardrobe were a pair of Eskimo mocassins on his feet. Photographs of his arrival showed an awe-struck, almost fearful-seeming man surrounded by great throngs of smiling well-wishers.

But despite his humble appearance, Cook was eloquent when he later took pen and paper and described the events and his feelings. As the *Hans Egede,* the small Danish blubber ship, approached the city, "Like a bolt from the blue, there burst about me the clamor of Copenhagen's ovation," he wrote.

> I was utterly bewildered by it. I found no reason in my mind for it. About the North Pole I had never felt such exultation.
>
> When I went on deck, as we approached the city, I saw far in the distance flags flying. Like a darting army of water bugs, innumerable craft of all kind were leaping toward us on the sunlit water. Tugs and motors, rowboats and sailboats, soon surrounded and followed us. The flags of all nations dangled on the decorated craft. People shouted, it seemed, in every tongue. Wave after wave of cheering rolled over the water. Horns blew, there was the sound of music, guns exploded. All about, balancing on unsteady craft, their heads hooded in black, were the omnipresent moving-picture-machine operators at work. All this passed as a moving picture itself, I standing there, dazed, simply dazed.

Cook's astonishment soon led to well-founded trepidation. After being officially welcomed to Denmark by King Frederick's son, Crown Prince Christian, American Ambassador Maurice F. Egan, and a pier full of dignitaries, Cook—along with a phalanx of journalists, Ambassador Egan, and others—attempted to reach a carriage to take him to a hotel. As soon as security was relaxed when the prince left, the crowd surged across the police barricades and surrounded the group, nearly crushing them all in their attempts to get a closer look at the conquering hero. Cook lost his welcoming bouquet, his cuff links, and then his cuffs as he was patted and pawed and as the cheering Danes tried to grab souvenirs. Several attempts were made to hoist Cook up on the shoulders of well-wishers, but his welcoming committee managed to extricate him each time. Cook and his hosts finally escaped from the mob after several close calls that seriously threatened their safety.

Later that day, Cook, after having lunch with Ambassador Egan and paying his respects to elderly King Frederick, returned to the hotel and found a large assembly of the world's journalists waiting to question him. For an hour he was grilled by the reporters, who asked question after question. The questions "came like shots, in many tongues, and only now and then did familiar English words strike me and quiver in my brain cells," Cook said.

The questions that were fired at him ranged from the curious to the skeptical to the accusatory. And by nearly all accounts, Cook handled himself exceedingly well, winning many converts among the professional doubters in the course of this press conference, with his humble, straightforward responses to their aggressive, skeptical probes.

"Doctor, would you say you really think, so far as you are able to judge, that you have discovered the North Pole?" he was asked.

"I think so," he replied.

"You have set foot right on it?"

"Oh, I couldn't say that. I got to where there wasn't any longitude."

"What does the Pole look like?"

"Ice."

"You made a dash to the Pole?"

"It was simply that—a dash. We did not try to carry all the heavy instruments that others carry. Therefore, there is nothing so scientific about the achievement. We traveled as lightly as possible, and made 15 miles a day."

Wrote one journalist later, "It is afterward that the simplicity of his manner, his pleasant directness, the probability of what he says, come back to mind and make it harder to believe that he lies than that he tells the truth."

Another journalist, a correspondent for the United Press, wrote, "After a day strenuous enough to tire a Roosevelt and distressing enough to wreck the patience of a Job, Dr. Cook, in the face of discouraging skepticisms which would have snatched away his laurels almost before they were bestowed, was called upon to clear away an international incredulity which seemingly barred his entrance to the Hall of Fame. He succeeded in the effort. . . . Dr. Cook modestly met every inquiry with a directness and frankness that quickly won all of his hearers."

Within days, fellow explorers Amundsen and Otto Sverdrup traveled to Copenhagen to give Cook their congratulations in person. At that time, Cook later reported, he advised Amundsen to set his sights on discovering the South Pole.

Reaching the top of the world had fascinated—and eluded—man from at least the start of recorded history, which helps explain why the world stopped and took such notice of Cook and his claim. All manner of men had tried every conceivable route and method up to now, and to no avail. Tired, disheartened men returned from their efforts—when they did return—with tales of incredible hardship from the cold and unforgiving environment and spoke of the unique pain inflicted by a frozen desert in which few could survive, let alone journey across mountains of ice and around yawning crevasses to a mythical point on the top of the globe, all for the glory of claiming to be the first to get there.

Thus, it was little wonder that by the time Cook had settled into his hotel room in Copenhagen, he had a mound of cabled financial offers to consider that had poured in from around the world. There was hardly a publication or a publisher in the United States that did not want to own the rights to Cook's story, and all the major foreign publications were joining the quest as well. Newspapers, magazines, and book publishers proposed ever-higher inducements, in fear that they would lose the bidding to their competitors. William Randolph Hearst made a blanket offer to double anything proposed by anyone else. His offer would have meant at least $400,000, since Cook had received a $200,000 offer, although an unnamed European syndicate was reported by American newspapers to have offered $500,000. Instead, Cook chose to give the *New York Herald* his exclusive story for only $20,000 because the *Herald* had helped him before and he thought it only proper to repay the newspaper.

William T. Stead, a noted British journalist and editor who quickly became the unofficial chairman of the press corps trailing Cook in Copenhagen, could hardly contain himself, saying that Cook "in business affairs is almost as innocent as a child. . . . It is enough to make one weep! But, as he used to say plaintively, 'I am not out for money.' He certainly is about the last man whom any business firm would send out for money. Any American newsboy could give him points in the art of looking after himself."

But Cook believed that loyalty required that he stay with the *Herald*. James Gordon Bennett, who owned the *New York Herald,* the *New York Evening Telegram,* and the *Paris Herald,* was locked in a fierce circulation battle with the growing *New York Times,* and the *Times* was a major sponsor of Peary's latest attempt to reach the North Pole. While Cook's relations with Bennett and his newspapers would remain good, this fateful decision would cost Cook dearly, and he would later wonder how different history might have been had he signed on with the powerful, and combative, Hearst.

By Monday, September 6, Cook was exhausted. The endless schedule of public appearances, coupled with his desire to return home to his family, led him to decline an invitation to address a dinner to be hosted by the Danish newspaper *Politiken* for the many foreign correspondents who were still in town to cover Cook's every move for their publications. Cook had already made a presentation that day to the Danish Geographical Society and had been interviewed by several of the journalists. "Tired to death and exhausted with want of sleep," Cook said, he wished most of all to leave Denmark for New York to be with his family and friends.

However, the *Politiken*'s management insisted that he come for at least a brief appearance and promised the weary traveler that he would not be subjected to any attempts to interview him. Cook, ever the good guest, relented, and by all accounts, enjoyed himself. The tension and suspicion of the first days in Denmark had largely dissipated, and Cook and the reporters shared good cheer. He was presented with a large garland of flowers when he arrived at the Tivoli for the banquet, which he gamely wore around his neck as a pack of photographers snapped away.

While the correspondent for the French newspaper *Matin* was speaking, someone—Stead would later claim it was he—handed Cook a note and then read it aloud: "Stars and Stripes nailed to the Pole." It was Peary's first message since leaving for Greenland the summer before, sent by telegraph from Indian Harbor, Labrador.

"My first feeling, as I read it, was of spontaneous belief. Well, I thought, he got there! On my right and left men were arguing about it. It was declared a hoax. I recognized the characteristic phrasing as Peary's. I knew that the [telegraph] operators along the Labrador coast knew Peary and that it would be almost impossible to perpetrate a joke. I told this to the dinner party. The speeches continued," Cook wrote.

Cook was asked to respond by the journalists, who were suddenly back on duty, just as they, too, were preparing to leave for home and the next big story. "I am proud that a fellow American has reached the Pole. As Rear Admiral [Winfield Scott] Schley said at [the battle of] Santiago, 'There is glory enough for us all.' He [Peary] is a brave man, and I am confident that if the reports are true, his observations will confirm mine and set at rest all doubts."

Cook cabled his congratulations for Peary to the *New York Herald,* saying graciously, "I am glad he has won, as two records are better than one. His work over a new route has an added value. It will clear another large unknown space [from maps of the north] and add one epoch-making contribution to the annals of polar exploration."

But Peary, fully living up to his reputation, immediately made it clear that he was not going to settle for any consolation prize. After he had been read Cook's congratulatory telegram by a reporter for the *Herald,* Peary replied, "I am the only white man who has ever reached the Pole." In a telegram to the Associated Press, Peary went even further. Saying he had interviewed the Eskimos who had accompanied Cook, Peary charged: "Cook's story should not be taken too seriously. . . . He did not get out of sight of land. . . . Cook has simply handed the public a gold brick."

Cook was flabbergasted. Once again, his naiveté made the situation almost humorous, since he seemed incapable of believing that a rival would make such unfounded and undocumented charges. He later wrote, "That Peary would contest my claim never entered my head. It did seem, and still seems [in 1911], in itself too inconsequential a thing to make such a fuss about." He said that while many of his supporters and trailing journalists advised him to issue an angry reply of his own, he said, "This I did not do; did not feel like doing."

Instead, Cook canceled plans to stop in Brussels on the way home to New York and booked passage on the steamship *Oscar II,* setting the stage for a world-size controversy.

CHAPTER 15

A Prize Long Sought

There was amazingly widespread interest throughout the world in the continuing struggle against nature to reach the North Pole, amounting to a full-fledged international obsession, one that generated the kind of fervor and passion and hype that comes today from a World Cup soccer championship or a professional football Super Bowl contest.

The quest for the Pole appealed to many sides of human nature: Man's desire to best Mother Nature was no less keen in those days, and national pride within the several nations that fielded "players" in the race was extremely high, especially in the United States, which was the homeland of both the primary finalists in this high-profile contest. The race also entertained and amused the populace with tales of strange human and animal life in the Arctic, in an age long before commercial television and prepackaged imagery.

This fascination with the North Pole was not one that began in those heady days at the end of the 1800s and early this century, as the Industrial Revolution was forever altering life throughout all of the "civilized" world. According to one newspaper's tally in the wake of Cook's claim, 743 men were known to have died in pursuit of the North Pole, beginning with a British expedition in 1553 under the direction of Hugh Willoughby; that attempt ended with the death of all 62 participants near Lapland during Queen Mary I's reign.

A Greek explorer, Pytheas, made the first known journey to the Far North in the fourth century B.C., during the age of Aristotle, when Greek adventurers were exploring much of the world for nations to conquer and treasures to bring home. Sailing from what is now Marseilles on France's Mediterranean coast, Pytheas traveled around the British Isles and got as far north as the southern edge of the Arctic ice pack. On that journey, he became the first outsider known to have crossed the Arctic Circle and to see the midnight sun, the perpetual daylight that envelops the Far North from the beginning of the region's fleeting spring through its short summer.

Hunters and treasure seekers may well have touched Greenland's shores before Pytheas, but their efforts are lost to time. Greenland's permanent inhabitants are believed to be descended from the same tribes of Eskimos that today inhabit Alaska and northern Canada. During harsh winters, some portions of the tribes apparently crossed over the frozen Arctic waters that usually separated North America from Greenland, in search of game. These seminomads eventually built their winter homes along the west coast of Greenland; in the summers, they moved to homes near the main supplies of food, along the migration routes of the animals they hunted.

According to history, it was 1,000 years after Pytheas's journey before the next European voyagers, the Vikings from Norway, sailed the Arctic waters. The Vikings explored the northern reaches of America and then colonized western Greenland, going almost as high as the seventy-sixth parallel, a "farthest north" mark for man that they were to hold for more than 250 years.

While the traditional explanation given for man's desire to explore the north centers on finding ways of improving commerce, a closer examination calls this commercial rationale into question and fails to explain the fervor of most of the contestants. Despite occasional tales about fabulous hidden wealth said to lurk behind the ice curtain that shrouded the north land, most who chose to hunt for what the Eskimos call *Tigi-su*, the Big Nail, were clearly driven by a compelling combination of curiosity, a desire to etch their names into history's pages, and the thrill of adventure.

Exploration of the Far North began in earnest late in the sixteenth century, as the British ranged far and wide around the globe. The English adventures in the north began with Martin Frobisher, who believed he could find a shortcut to China by going north and over the top of the globe, through the "Northwest Passage" he was sure existed. Frobisher was stopped by the Arctic's permanent mantle of ice, which was named the Great Barrier Ice. A few years later, John Davys followed up on Frobisher's efforts and was similarly stymied. The next known effort to reach the North Pole along the way from Europe to Asia was an expedition led by John Phipps in 1773. Phipps, too, was eventually stopped by the Great Barrier Ice.

By that time, there were all manner of theories about what would be found in the Far North, if only the ice could be surmounted. Some of the more imaginative scenarios featured visions of a temperate climate at the top of the globe, which could be reached only by somehow piercing the Great Barrier Ice. Another popular theory was that the Earth was hollow and that the first man to get to the North Pole would find the passageway to the center of the planet.

The theory that the Great Barrier Ice was really a ring protecting the perpetually open waters of a temperate polar sea gained adherents early in the nineteenth century, when an unusually large number of icebergs were seen floating southward into the shipping lanes between Europe and the New World. Scientists are still unsure what led to this upheaval in the ice pack, but its immediate impact was unquestionable: major renewed interest in finding a path through the barrier.

The British launched two expeditions in 1818 that led to further mapping of the northern reaches, but they failed to locate any passageway through the ice. However, these expeditions also brought to the north men who would later be instrumental in exploring the area.

A key turning point came in 1845, when Britain's Royal Society decided to launch a "final" expedition to locate the long-sought Northwest Passage. Sir John Franklin, a sixty-year-old retired navy admiral, was chosen to command the expedition's ships, the *Erebus* and the *Terror*. The two ships were last seen in July 1845, in Baffin Bay near Lancaster Sound. After several years passed with no word from Franklin, rescue teams were dispatched from England and the United States; these searches for the Franklin Expedition developed their own lore, as several near-tragedies beset the would-be rescuers.

Eventually, it was learned that Franklin and all his 128 crewmen perished from starvation, scurvy, and exposure. But Franklin's expedition actually contributed more to Arctic exploration than the eventual discovery of the Northwest Passage ever did because the search for him led to the greatest surge in the exploration of the Arctic in history.

And those men—Franklin and his would-be rescuers—fired the imaginations of Cook and Peary, which, in turn, set the stage for this new drama, almost one hundred years later.

For inexplicable reasons, Peary now chose to hide out aboard the *Roosevelt,* after he arrived at Indian Harbor, Labrador, on September 5, 1909, at 10 P.M., while Cook was still being toasted in Copenhagen. He waited to send his first message claiming the North Pole as his prize until the next day, once again choosing sleep over history, just as he had done when he claimed he was only steps from the North Pole. On September 6, Peary wired the Associated Press: "Stars and Stripes Nailed to the Pole." Ironically, Josephine Peary received her first telegram from him at the same telegraph station in Harpswell, Maine, where Marie Cook had gotten her first word from her husband upon his return from the Arctic.

By September 8, Peary had still not published an account of his journey, even though he had been back in North America for three days. Instead, his efforts were directed to firing the first underhanded shot at Cook and Cook's claim. This was a peculiar order of priority for a longtime explorer recently returned from accomplishing his only major goal in life.

As Cook prepared to return to the United States and take his case directly to the American people, the Danes rushed to his aid. One newspaper reporter wrote, "Those who remember how Peary behaved when years ago he saw Sverdrup as his competitor in Smith

Sound will be certain that Peary would be an uncompromising enemy of anybody having the audacity to rival him in the run for the Pole, and would employ all possible methods to defeat a competitor, but that Peary would use perfidious means nobody had imagined." Sverdrup and Amundsen also came to Cook's defense, Amundsen even traveling from Oslo to greet his old friend publicly.

Finally, on September 9, after he had had a chance to study Cook's story in the *Herald,* Peary presented the tale of his expedition's claimed journey to the North Pole. The Great North Pole Controversy, as it was quickly named by American newspapers, had begun.

The long delay between the start of the Great North Pole Controversy and the entrance of both the claimants only fired the confrontation. Journalist and author Lincoln Steffens wrote, "The situation is as wonderful as the Pole. And whatever they found there, those explorers have left there a story as great as a continent. The Pole discovery is peopled with human romance: it is part of the epic of man. It is great. I am as excited about it as I haven't been about anything for years."

The controversy seemed tailor-made for the new status of the United States: that of an emerging world power. Two Americans vying for the grand prize of world exploration well illustrated the New World's rise, as the reins of global leadership were shifting westward across the Atlantic Ocean from the crown of the British Empire, which seemed incapable of retaining them.

Indeed, Britain's last major exploration claim—just over two years later—was for a near miss, the failure of Royal Navy Captain Robert Falcon Scott to be the first man to reach the South Pole. Scott, who followed the time-honored exploration methods of his forefathers, lost the contest to Cook's friend and companion, Norwegian explorer Roald Amundsen, who paid close attention to improvements others had made in methods and equipment, especially those of Cook. Scott's failure was celebrated as an unfortunate unhappy ending to a heroic journey. However, his incompetence and his embracing of the old methods of exploration that held it unmanly to use dogs to pull sledges had doomed the expedition to failure and many of its participants, including Scott, to slow deaths by starvation and scurvy.

Great Britain was losing its grasp on its empire at the end of the twentieth century's first decade, while the United States was beginning to feel its oats. The former colony had, by virtue of the Spanish-American War, taken its first war booty and become a colonial power; Teddy Roosevelt was extolling his countrymen to take risks for national glory; and for the first time in its short history, the United States was looking outward.

It is not surprising, then, that Roosevelt had become one of Peary's most vocal boosters. To Roosevelt, Peary represented just the sort of bold, brash man, willing to risk all for fame and glory, who epitomized his vision of America's future. To one of Peary's biographers, at least, the president and the explorer "almost seemed cut form the same mold. . . . Both men made enemies quickly and easily because of their abruptness."

The country's big newspapers were happily beating the drum for Roosevelt's vision of America's new world role, and they merrily stoked the flames of controversy that surrounded the North Pole dispute, for it was a purely American dispute. While Cook was sailing across the Atlantic to conduct his fight from home and Peary mysteriously remained anchored off the coast of Newfoundland, in virtual self-imposed quarantine, the newspapers trumpeted every little scrap of new information—or every restatement of old information—about the conflicting claims.

The nation was well primed for what was sure to be a great spectacle, the tussle for the right to be called the discoverer of the North Pole. The growing rivalry between James Gordon Bennett and his *New York Herald* and Adolph Ochs and his *New York Times* clearly intensified the dispute, among their own newspapers' readers and in the many other newspapers around the nation that reprinted the dispatches from the two big-city dailies.

The battle between the newspapers attracted legions of commercial quick-buck artists. "The centuries-old struggle for the Pole had been turned into a veritable orgy of public disputation," one historian wrote. Overnight, books appeared on newsstands, most of them simply reprints of newspaper accounts. Home atlases bearing the endorsement of Peary were for sale in a matter of weeks, as was a soap powder whose manufacturer advertised that it was the very brand that Cook had used in the Arctic.

Finally, on exactly the same day—September 21, 1909—Cook arrived in New York and Peary came ashore at Sydney, Newfoundland, setting the stage for a titanic struggle.

Marie Fidele Hunt Cook holding daughter Helene. Mrs. Cook's daughter from her previous marriage, Ruth Hunt, is next to them *(Cook Collection, Library of Congress)*.

♦

Cook's photograph of Ahwelah and Etukishook at the North Pole on April 21, 1908 *(Frederick A. Cook)*.

Eskimo women alongside a typical summer tent near the village of Uummannaq along the west coast of Greenland *(Cook Collection, Library of Congress)*.

Cook's photograph showing Edward M. Barrill standing at the summit of Mount McKinley on September 16, 1906 *(Frederick A. Cook)*.

LEFT: Lillian E. Kiel, the *Hampton's* Magazine stenographer who revealed that the publication's editors had manufactured Cook's "confession" that he had not reached the North Pole *(Photo supplied by Janet Vetter)*.

BELOW: Roald Amundsen, left, and Engebret Knudsen work on Cook's plan to free the Belgica by cutting a channel to open water. The ship can be seen beyond Amundsen *(Cook Collection, Library of Congress)*.

The Belgica crew had brought an explosive called tonite with them in place of dynamite. It proved unsuitable for the cold weather. Here the men try to use it to help clear the channel *(Cook Collection, Library of Congress)*.

◆

RIGHT: Cook's ethnographic studies of the Eskimos include nude photographs of men and women. This photograph is of a young woman named Ahnini *(Cook Collection, Library of Congress)*.

BELOW: Peary with his dogs aboard ship in Greenland *(National Archives)*.

The remains of Cook's hut at Annoatok where he wintered before embarking on his fateful journey to the North Pole. These are the first known photographs of the hut since the one Cook included in his book about the trek *(Howard S. Abramson)*.

The harbor at Etah. The now-abandoned village was a crucial weigh station for Cook and Peary's polar explorations *(Credit: Howard Abramson)*.

♦

PART THREE

CHAPTER 16

Showdown in America

Cook had his first respite from the unceasing demands of the press and the public, and from the growing questions and accusations, when the *Oscar II* steamed beyond the range of the wireless equipment of that age. Finally, he had a chance to get some sleep, to have time alone for contemplation in his cabin, and to stroll along the decks of the Danish ocean liner as it steamed through the Atlantic's green waters. With the aid of his secretary, Walter Lonsdale, he polished up his manuscript for the *New York Herald.* This multipart, detailed series would be the basis for his first book on his exploits in the north, which was eventually titled *My Attainment of the Pole.*

But as soon as the *Oscar II* came in range of the wireless station in Newfoundland, the battle began anew, and word of Peary's escalating charges against Cook was received. "At this time," Cook wrote later, "every vestige of pleasure in the thought of the thing I had accomplished left me. Since then, and to this day, I almost view all my efforts with regret. I doubt if any man ever lived in the belief of an accomplishment and got so little pleasure, and so much bitterness, from it."

Peary had made his accusations against Cook's claims and then quickly retreated from view again, first on board the *Roosevelt,* and later on his island home in Maine. Many days passed before he offered his version of the trek to the North Pole and back to land.

It seemed that Peary was not going to say anything about the North Pole until Cook had printed his version: Peary's supporters said it was for his protection, so Cook could not mimic Peary's statements; Cook's supporters believed it was so that Peary could copy Cook's words, without fear of contradiction.

Cook, in line with journalist William Stead's writings about Cook's childlike naïveté, seemed to think that all he had to do was make his claims to the American people and press, and all would be well. His countrymen would see the truth of his statements, he believed, and he could collect whatever laurels were his and go on with his life.

Cook was looking forward most to being reunited with his family—his wife, her daughter, and their young daughter. Although he expected he would be greeted with a small reception, he was sure he would not be faced with a spectacle similar to the mob scene that had greeted his arrival in Copenhagen. He attributed the first incredible welcome to the Danes' overriding interest in the Arctic, while he was sure New York "was too big, too unemotional, too much interested in bigger matters to bother much about the North Pole."

But he soon received word that worried him anew. The *Oscar II*'s owners, in an attempt to help their honored guest, had burned tons of extra coal in the ship's boilers to get him across the Atlantic to New York an entire day faster than normal. But when they arrived off the coast, city officials begged the captain to stay out of the harbor, for the welcoming reception was set for the following day, Tuesday, September 21.

The *Oscar II* spent the night anchored off Shelter Island, at the harbor's entrance, and the crew worked to keep a flotilla of little boats away, most of them carrying journalists. Now Cook knew it was not to be a quiet little welcome-home ceremony with his family on the morrow.

Indeed, the next morning, when the *Oscar II* pulled into the quarantine station in the harbor, it was surrounded by at least a score of boats full of reporters, photographers, and cameramen, all recording the homecoming of the American hero. The flotilla included a tug that he could see carried his wife Marie and the children, Ruth and Helene. The family's reunion was held in the privacy of the tug, and then they were all transferred to the *Grand Republic,* an excursion steamer that was based in New York and had been chartered for the occasion by some of Cook's welcomers.

As the *Grand Republic* took the Cooks on a water tour of the New York bay, the returning explorer was greeted with the same kind of thunderous applause and hoopla that he had received in Copenhagen. "I remember standing in the pilot house of the Grand Republic, my little ones by me," Cook wrote, "and watching thousands of men along the wharves of the East River, going mad. The world seemed engaged in some frantic revel. Factories became vocal and screamed hideously; boats became hoarse with shrieking; the megaphone cry was maddening. Drawing up to a gayly decorated pier, a thunder of voices assailed me. I felt crushed by the unearthly din."

According to one newspaper reporter who was on hand, "When the Grand Republic . . . [reached] her dock at South Fifth Street, Brooklyn, the biggest noise of the day began. . . . Every whistle let loose until all the noises in the world were merged into one ear-splitting shriek. You could sit next to the main deck band with your head down in the bell of the bass horn and never hear an oom-pah."

Cook found himself shoved into an open touring car, in which he was driven through the streets of Brooklyn; on his ride he passed mobs of cheering New Yorkers. At a reception in his honor, hundreds more well-wishers greeted him, although by this time they were forbidden to shake his hand, which had been worn raw during the long day of welcome. Finally, after midnight, he forced his way through another large crowd that was waiting for a glimpse of him in the lobby of his hotel, the Waldorf-Astoria in Manhattan. Some minutes later, he and Marie were alone in their room at long last—for the first time since summer 1907 when they were on board the *Bradley* on the way to Newfoundland.

The next morning the tumult began all over again. The primary event of the day was a mass press conference (Cook termed it an "inquisition . . . [that] both interested and amused me") with the American press, in a replay of the session he had in Copenhagen. Again Cook was peppered with the same queries he had answered many times before as the correspondents in New York tried to decide for themselves the veracity of his claims.

Cook was asked a string of questions by a reporter from Peary's chief journalistic supporter, the *New York Times*. Someone had quietly slipped Cook a copy of the many telegrams that had been sent by Peary to the *Times,* including a long list of questions for the newspaper's reporters to ask Cook so they could trip him up. Therefore, when the *Times* reporter started on his list of twenty-six questions, Cook was prepared for him. When the reporter asked if he had taken any observations of the moon while he was at the North Pole, Cook replied, "I could not make any observations of the moon because it was daylight all the time." Next he was asked whether he had used stars to verify his position. Cook replied that there are no stars evident in the sky in the Arctic during the summer.

Cook again seemed to do very well with the assembled, naturally suspicious, reporters and with the American people. Several straw polls conducted by newspapers gave Cook huge leads in support over Peary, as readers utilized packets of cards that were quickly printed and distributed for sale at ten cards for twenty cents. The cards carried the legends, "Cook I believe in you" or "Peary I believe in you," left room for the voter's name and address, and were addressed to the local newspaper in whatever city in which they were being sold. According to a tally made by the *Pittsburgh Press* at the end of September, Cook was leading Peary 73,238 to 2,814.

Even though the Peary forces had begun their attack on Cook's story, Cook seemed to be doing well. And he seemed satisfied that he would prevail after a short, if nasty, battle with his rival. Unfortunately, his optimistic view was more a product of his naïveté than of a reasoned and insightful assessment of what lay in store for him.

Although Cook had quickly gained the support of most of the newspaper correspondents in Copenhagen after his first interviews with them early in September 1909, there were two notable exceptions: Philip Gibbs, a thirty-two-year-old feature writer for the *Lon-*

don Daily Chronicle, and Peter Freuchen, a writer for the Danish newspaper *Politiken,* who had some limited experience in the Arctic himself. Coincidentally, Freuchen's first journey into the Arctic had also been aboard the *Hans Egede,* the ship that brought Cook to Denmark. In 1906, Freuchen was a stoker on the ship, part of a team that was preparing a Danish expedition to northern Greenland.

Gibbs and Freuchen met in Copenhagen before the ship docked with Cook aboard. Soon after Freuchen and Gibbs met the returning explorer—if not before—they decided between themselves that Cook had not reached the North Pole, even though no one had yet heard his story of the expedition. The ambitious Gibbs was looking for a story that would make him a journalistic star, while Freuchen was apparently motivated by his belief that no one could reach the North Pole and return alive.

Thus, while most journalists wrote of Cook's triumphant arrival in Copenhagen in glowing terms, Gibbs wrote, "Dr. Cook, the hero, was hiding in his cabin. He . . . came out . . . with a livid look, almost green. I never saw guilt and fear more clearly written on any human face. He could hardly pull himself together when the Crown Prince of Denmark boarded his ship and offered the homage of Denmark to his glorious achievement." Either Gibbs had attended a different homecoming ceremony than did all the other journalists in Copenhagen or he had already decided on a plan to make himself famous, at Cook's expense.

This was the first, but far from the last, of Gibbs's dispatches that seemed to have been constructed from his fantasies. In his tales about Cook, he quoted imaginary people, he quoted people as having said the opposite of what other correspondents reported they said, and he interpreted events in the worst light for Cook on every occasion. In what must be considered less than a surprise or a coincidence, most of Gibbs's anti-Cook dispatches ended up on the front pages of the *New York Times.*

What Cook did not know was that he was facing the first shot in what would be one of the most dastardly media campaigns in history. Although Gibbs and Freuchen may have made their decision independently, they quickly became part of a conspiracy directed by Peary and his rich and powerful supporters to deny Cook the honor of having reached the North Pole first, so the laurels could be awarded to Peary.

Cook was examined by officials of the Royal Geographical Society of Denmark, who were weighing his claims to the North Pole. Professor Torp, rector of the University of Copenhagen, reported that after being interviewed by various committee members, including an astronomical scientist, "Dr. Cook stood the test perfectly, although the examination was of an intricate scientific nature. There was not a detail or question put to him which he failed to reply in the most satisfactory way. . . . I dare say, therefore, that there is no justification for anybody to throw the slightest doubt on his claim of having reached the North Pole." As a result, the University of Copenhagen recommended that Cook be awarded an honorary doctorate, and King Frederick, who was also the president of the university, decided to do so.

The Danish officials stated they were unable to conclude definitively that Cook had reached the North Pole because they had not seen his original notes; therefore, Cook agreed to send the original papers to Denmark as soon as he received them from Whitney, who was presumably carrying them to New York. Gibbs's story, however, focused on the lack of "proof" that Cook had been to the Pole. It was written to indicate that the Danes had serious doubts about Cook's claim because of this lack of data, when, according to Torp's comments, it was much more a matter of the papers representing the final proof.

In another story, Gibbs claimed to be quoting a letter that Rasmussen wrote to his wife in which he said Cook "was a knave and a liar." Mrs. Rasmussen later strongly denied the story, saying that the letter in question had actually voiced strong and unequivocal support for Cook. But as so often happens, the corrections and the denials of Gibbs's fantasies received far less ink than did his original stories that attacked Cook and Cook's claims.

Freuchen aided and encouraged Gibbs in his slanderous attacks on Cook and went on to become one of Peary's biggest idolaters, never missing an opportunity to disparage Cook and his claims in several books he later wrote. When Peary retired from exploration,

Freuchen attached himself to Knud Rasmussen and moved to the village on North Star Bay where Rasmussen then lived.

Gibbs, meanwhile, interviewed one of the passengers on the *Hans Egede* who had accompanied Cook from Greenland to Copenhagen, a Swiss scientist named Dr. de Quervain. According to Gibbs, Cook had promised to show de Quervain his instruments. "I suggested he should show me his observations, as of course, I had long experience in these matters," Gibbs quoted de Quervain as saying. But Cook did not show him the instruments, and when de Quervain later asked Cook to show him the observations, "he said he would prefer not to do so," de Quervain stated.

A few days later, another reporter interviewed Dr. de Quervain. In contrast to Gibbs's story, which created the clear impression that the scientist doubted Cook's veracity, the other reporter wrote: "Dr. de Quervain says that after having tested Dr. Cook's figures and statements . . . [while aboard the *Hans Egede*], he is convinced Dr. Cook reached the North Pole." That comment, somehow, did not make it into Gibbs's report or into the *New York Times*.

Gibbs's attacks on Cook ended only when Cook left Denmark for New York and the *London Daily Chronicle* chose to send a correspondent other than Gibbs to the United States to follow the Great North Pole Controversy.

With the luxury of hindsight, the concerted actions of the rich and powerful Peary forces are clear and easily definable, although no less incredible and unprecedented. Many painful lessons can be learned from studying the next few months in the evolution of the Great North Pole Controversy. And the fruits of the miscarriage of justice are still with us, firmly etched in the history books of the United States and most of the rest of the world.

When the first word of Cook's success reached the United States, many of the individuals and institutions that had supported Peary joined the chorus of praise for Cook's accomplishments. Cook's reaching the North Pole was so unexpected, since most people had thought that he had become the latest victim of the quest for the North Pole, that the news generated perhaps more instant acclaim than a similar announcement by Peary might have done. Besides, nothing had been heard from Peary at the time of Cook's claim.

But the core of Peary's supporters—the chief officers of the Peary Arctic Club and their friends—wasted no time in plotting to ruin Cook. Presumably, the campaign had been hatched when Herbert L. Bridgman—who would play a pivotal role in the scheme by orchestrating the press's attack on Cook—had received the letter from Cook revealing his plan to make a run for "Peary's" Pole.

The key conspirators appear to have been Bridgman, the publisher of the *Brooklyn Standard Union* and secretary of the Peary Arctic Club, who became the press agent for the effort; General Thomas H. Hubbard, a rich lawyer, with major holdings in railroad and newspaper properties, and the club's president, who kept the scheme well supplied with money and legal advice; and Gilbert H. Grosvenor, the editor of *National Geographic* magazine—a man whose fingerprints appear on many of the subplots and who apparently spent many hours trying to cover up the multitudinous flaws in Peary's claims and to search for gaps in Cook's story.

Early in the controversy, the Peary forces obviously realized that although Cook's claim had several flaws—the primary one being the lack of a credible, independent witness—Peary's claim, at best, suffered from similar problems. So a way had to be found to repudiate Cook's claim to the North Pole without drawing attention to the identical problems inherent in Peary's.

The conspirators quickly devised the plan they believed was most likely to succeed: Destroy Cook's claim by destroying his reputation as an explorer and as a man. Thus, the major focus would be on Cook's character. Besides, Cook had no resources with which to launch a counterattack on Peary and his less-than-sterling character, and, in any event, he had shown no inclination to do so.

CHAPTER 17

The Peary Cabal

From the beginning of the Peary cabal's press onslaught, Cook was on the defensive. He seemed unable to accept that his opponents were prepared to stop at nothing to deny him the claim to being the first man to have reached the North Pole.

By carefully timing the release of material—which included reams of innuendo, misleading information, outright lies, and forged data—the Peary forces began to chip away at Cook's reputation. And Cook's refusal to counterattack left him particularly vulnerable to the dastardly campaign.

Mount McKinley

Before Cook even made it back to New York, the Peary team began an assault on his claim to having been the first man to climb to the summit of Mount McKinley. Fred Printz, a guide and packer who had accompanied Cook and Edward N. Barrill part of the way up the mountain, was featured in a story in the *New York Sun* in which he alleged that Cook had not climbed McKinley.

The story—dated the same day Peary arrived in Newfoundland—quoted Printz as charging, in an interview, that "Barrim [Barrill] told me afterward that Cook offered to give him hush money. Dr. Cook agreed to pay me $150 and expenses on the trip, but he did not even pay me my expenses, and I had to borrow money to get home." How the *New York Sun* reporter happened to be in Butte, Montana, to interview Printz was not disclosed, but the deep involvement of General Hubbard, one of the three in the Peary cabal, soon surfaced.

Indeed, this story showed the underlying strategy of the entire campaign, when Printz allegedly said: "I am just as sure as I'm living that Dr. Cook never saw the North Pole. Any man who would make the representations he did as to his alleged ascent of Mount McKinley is capable of making statements credited to him in the press about the North Pole."

Word of what was afoot had obviously not been circulated to all parties. On the same day that Printz's charges appeared, Willis L. Moore, president of the ardently pro-Peary National Geographic Society, told the *New York Herald* that he regretted the drive "in some quarters . . . to revive the discrediting of his ascension of Mount McKinley [harking back to Herschel Parker's initial doubting of the accomplishment]. Our society had Dr. Cook lecture before it on the subject . . . and I assure you we would not have invited him if there had been the slightest doubt of his integrity, courage and ability."

Following Printz's accusations, Barrill defended Cook, telling the *New York Times* that Printz's comments were irrelevant, since only he and Cook "made the climb."

Two days after Printz made his statement, the McKinley expedition's cook and Parker—who had abandoned the trip in fear of his life and was convinced the mountain could not be climbed—both alleged that Cook had never climbed Mount McKinley. They were hardly witnesses to events, however: During the climb, the cook was, of course, back in camp and Parker was on his way to New York.

Cook later stated that Printz offered to write a counteraffidavit for him for $350; Printz is reported to have later written such a document, which he offered to a reporter for the pro-Cook *New York Herald* for $1,000.

On September 16, the *New York Herald* rushed to Cook's aid, quoting Dillon Wallace, an Arctic explorer and writer, as saying,

"I have reason to believe a conspiracy has been afoot to discredit Dr. Cook . . . that was born two years ago, when those who are responsible for it first heard that he was in the north prepared to attack the Pole. . . . These men were afraid of Cook because they knew well his courage, good judgment, determination, temperament, balance, experience, and general ability as an explorer. They gave him full credit . . . as an authority of high standing . . . until they learned that he was a dangerous rival of Mr. Peary for polar honors."

Next, James A. Ashton, a lawyer in Tacoma, Washington, whom Hubbard had hired, entered the controversy. When Cook learned of Ashton's connection to Hubbard, he belatedly realized that the effort to discredit him would not simply go away. He sent a wire to Barrill, asking him to come to New York for a press conference to refute the allegations. Instead, Barrill went to Seattle, accompanied by Printz and Walter Miller, the photographer who had accompanied Cook on both his expeditions on Mount McKinley and who, it turned out, was working for Ashton and the Peary forces.

Cook later revealed that a man from the Peary Arctic Club had offered Barrill one thousand dollars if he would provide any news that would be detrimental to Cook. The *New York Herald* sent a reporter to Montana, and the correspondent reported that Barrill was being pressured to sign an affidavit against Cook and that some unknown party had offered Barrill five thousand dollars in cash to do so.

In an affidavit, an associate of Barrill told the *Herald*'s reporter that Barrill had first told him that he and Cook had indeed climbed the mountain and refused the money, saying "he would have to sell his own soul" to testify against Cook.

But Barrill—known to his friends as "Big Ed"—had a change of heart after he returned from a trip into the Bitterroot Mountains of Montana to discover that Cook's climb of the mountain was suddenly big news again. "When he returned to his home in Darby, Montana, and caught up on the news of the world, he understood that for the first time in his forty-five years, he held the high cards. He smelled money," said Hugh Eames, a writer who investigated the affair.

Barrill had been known by many names during his lifetime—
which was testament either to his unremarkableness or his shifti-
ness—and had spent most of his adult years as a blacksmith and a
guide. But he was no rube. When Barrill realized what was going
on "and smelled money, a strange thing happened. He shut up,"
Eames reported. Long known for his loquaciousness, Barrill—after
reminding the press that he was the only one who was with Cook
and, therefore, the only other person who knew the whole story—
went silent in public. In private, he was hard at work trying to make
a deal.

Not content with the original offers he received for his story,
Barrill went to Seattle, where he reportedly told the editor of the
Seattle Times that he would give him an affidavit against Cook if he
was offered enough money to do so. Dissatisfied when no deal was
struck, he went to Tacoma to meet with lawyer Ashton. Cook later
stated that he had a witness who saw Barrill being handed $1,500
as part payment for his affidavit: "This money was paid in large bills,
and placed in Barrill's money-belt. There were other considera-
tions. . . . His soul was marketed at last. The infamous affidavit was
then prepared." Cook offered to produce the evidence, but no one
took him up on his offer.

Rather, Barrill's affidavit was unveiled in the *New York Globe*—
which was partly owned by Hubbard, the president of the Peary
Arctic Club—on October 15. The release was timed to coincide
with Cook's appearance before New York City's Board of Alder-
men, in order to embarrass him most, while he was being presented
with the key to the city in honor of his accomplishment. In the
affidavit, Barrill charged that Cook had gotten nowhere near the
summit of McKinley; he said that they had actually climbed an
eight-thousand-foot-high peak that was almost twenty miles away
and faked the photograph of Barrill holding the American flag over
the summit on this little hill.

It is clear that the Peary forces knew that Barrill would not make
a credible witness, so while his affidavit was well used, he himself
was kept hidden. Barrill came to New York, produced and signed
the affidavit, and left, without making a public appearance or answering a reporter's questions. That the press would accept such a

document solely on the word of the Peary forces was also convincing evidence of the reporters' lack of concern for evenhandedness in reporting the story.

Indeed, the press's performance was hardly professional throughout the controversy. For example one writer who examined the Cook-Peary confrontation some twenty years afterward, recounted how Bradley, the hunter who had bankrolled Cook's trip north, had inadvertently fostered an apocryphal tale that later haunted Cook. Bradley had finally agreed to grant a short interview to a particularly persistent reporter. "What do you want to know?" Bradley asked the reporter. "Well, Mr. Bradley, I thought maybe you could tell us how Dr. Cook got the Eskimos to help him with his expedition, if he didn't have a lot of goods to trade them." Bradley replied, jeeringly, "Damn it, son, I thought you knew Doc had a barrel of gumdrops with him, and it's a settled fact that an Eskimo will follow you to the devil for a few gumdrops."

From then on, the press sarcastically reported that Cook had claimed to have bribed the Eskimos with gumdrops; one enterprising entrepreneur even began marketing gumdrops with Cook's name on them.

When asked about Cook's charges that Barrill's affidavit had been purchased, Hubbard denied it was so and then proceeded to contradict himself. "Well, let him try to prove it. It is not so. The affidavit was obtained exactly as any other sort of affidavit is obtained. There was no bribing. It was a simple piece of business— that's all."

By now, the debate over Mount McKinley was almost as heated and widely reported as the Great North Pole Controversy, which is precisely what Peary's supporters had counted on. And Peary had retired from the debate—and the line of fire—to his private island in Maine, content to let his idolaters and investors chip away at Cook's reputation.

Svartevoeg

While Cook was reeling from the continuing accusations over his claims to Mount McKinley, Peary fired two shots from his Maine hideout—claims that contradicted each other—and then disappeared from sight again.

First, on September 28, Peary published a map that claimed to "prove" that Cook had never reached Svartevoeg, on the northern tip of Axel Heiberg Island, which Peary tried to rename Cape Thomas Hubbard, after one of his major benefactors. Today, this point is called Cape Stallworthy.

Peary, in charges that were featured in "his" *New York Times,* said that if Cook had been to Svartevoeg, he would have undoubtedly found Peary's cairn [stone trademark], which Peary said he left in 1906 on the expedition during which he made his "farthest north" claim.

"If he can show a record of mine which I placed in a cairn . . . the cairn being so conspicuous that no explorer could overlook it, the production of that record would be conclusive proof that he was there. It has always been the custom of explorers to take away such records and substitute their own."

In 1911, Cook wrote, "A great deal of careful search and study was prosecuted about Svartevoeg" in looking for the cache while he and his four Eskimos—the two who would accompany him to the North Pole and the two who turned back after several marches farther north—passed through the area, since Cook was aware of Peary's claim to having left a cairn there in 1906. "But no such cache was found, and I doubt very much if Peary ever reached this point, except through a field-glass at very long range," Cook wrote.

In fact, in 1914, when one of Peary's greatest sycophants, Donald B. MacMillan, went to Svartevoeg in his multiyear attempt to verify Peary's journey and to destroy Cook's claim, he actually ended up providing more evidence to buttress Cook's claims. After spending more than a full day looking for Peary's cairn, which was supposed to be located in a place "so conspicuous that no explorer could overlook it," according to Peary, MacMillan gave up and resumed his journey north over the sea ice, as he sought Peary's mythical Crocker Land.

However, as he continued his journey, he noticed a cairn on a low point much farther west and south than Svartevoeg. After a time-consuming and physically strenuous effort, MacMillan reported, he was finally able to retrieve the Peary record, far from where Peary said it was.

MacMillan's difficulties showed, among other things, that Cook could easily have passed through Svartevoeg and not seen Peary's cairn. But even more important, it showed how poor were Peary's sense of direction and use of instruments. If Peary could not locate the northern coast of Svartevoeg under good conditions, how could he find a spot on a floating ice mass some 520 hard and dangerous miles to the north?

In addition to verifying Cook's claim that Peary's cairn was not at Svartevoeg where Peary said it was, MacMillan's continued searches also uncovered two caches that Cook left for his return trip.

In an interesting reversal, just two weeks after Peary claimed that Cook could not have been at Svartevoeg because Cook had not found Peary's cairn, Peary alleged just the opposite: that Cook had indeed been at Svartevoeg, but that he had traveled only a little farther north from there before doubling back and traveling south to Cape Sparbo, where Peary then admitted that Cook spent the long winter of 1908–09, before returning to Annoatok.

Peary's change of story—which the press neither challenged, nor even noted, since it was clearly under Bridgman's influence, if not control, by now—was apparently caused by Peary's discovery that two other Eskimos (Koolootingwah and Inugito) had traveled north of Svartevoeg with Cook and the two other Eskimos for three days.

Peary and his followers simply abandoned one story and picked up the other, with no attempt to explain the change. And the press corps brought down one Peary banner and hoisted the other, with hardly a moment's hesitation. MacMillan's later finding of Cook's caches one hundred miles to the north surely put the lie to Peary's second story, but was little noticed by the press.

Eyebrows were not even raised when just a week later, the newspapers carried an astonishing report from Rasmussen, who had visited the Eskimos in the far north and then sent his findings in a letter to his wife, which was printed in several newspapers.

"To sum up," Rasmussen wrote,

the Eskimos think that Cook reached the goal, and that he during the voyage showed great nerve and energy. The Eskimos are very glad that the Pole has been discovered, as the many expeditions . . . took away the best men from the tribe. They are at the same time very proud of Etukishook and Ahwelah, as it is their conviction that Cook would never have reached the goal without them. The above facts must be looked upon as strong confirmation for Cook.

Personally, I want to express my unreserved admiration for Dr. Cook. A man who, with his bare hands, has passed a winter at Cape Sparbo, a man who on his feet has walked to Annoatok through deep snow, through twisting ice and utter darkness, that man certainly deserves to have been first at the Pole. His name is Frederick Cook. No one in the world can name him as a swindler.

Despite this astonishingly strong endorsement from one of the few independent men who had talked to the Eskimos in their own language and who knew the terrain well, the press campaign against Cook continued unabated.

Satisfied with their results up to this point, the Peary forces were now ready to take their man out of the closet. The National Geographic Society, which had been a major investor in Peary's last expedition and several earlier ones, now set itself up as the official judge of the North Pole claims, on the theory that since both contenders were Americans, it had the right to decide the legitimate claimant.

The National Geographic Society tried to get the Danes to waive their rights to weigh the conflicting claims and to send Cook's records to it for its review. When the Danes refused, Gilbert Grosvenor, then president of the society, and other members of the Peary cabal began a clandestine effort to get the U.S. State Department to intervene by putting pressure on the Danes. However, the government declined to get involved, fearful of touching off an international diplomatic dispute.

When the National Geographic Society made its demand directly to the Danes, even the *New York Times* reported that while the Danish investigating committee welcomed an American observer to its deliberations, it "resented strongly the suggestion of the National Geographic Society [that it] should be represented at the inquiry, on the ground that the society had no scientific standing whatsoever."

Cook also refused to participate in the National Geographic Society's examination, saying that the society was incapable of determining whose claim was valid because of its lack of expertise in scientific matters. Besides, he said, the society was hopelessly biased toward Peary. He was right on both counts, and the National Geographic Society went on to prove it.

As was revealed in later congressional testimony, a three-member committee of the society—all good friends of Peary's—held a perfunctory interview with Peary at a house in Washington, D.C., and then traveled to that city's railroad terminal where, in the semidarkness of the baggage room, they looked into a trunk that contained what Peary said were the instruments he had taken to the North Pole.

On the basis of their cursory examination of Peary and his tools, the National Geographic Society's committee declared, on November 3, that their own Robert E. Peary was not only the first man—but the only man—to have reached the North Pole.

Cook, meanwhile, had moved his family and secretary Walter Lonsdale from the Waldorf-Astoria in Manhattan to the Gramatan Inn in Bronxville, so he could prepare his new report for the University of Copenhagen's examining committee in private. Money was pouring in from his writings and speeches, but it seemed to pour out at least as fast as he tried to defend himself from the increasing avalanche of doubts.

Lonsdale, who was Cook's constant companion in this period, had come to Cook when the explorer had made an urgent plea to Maurice Egan, the U.S. ambassador in Copenhagen, after his return from the Arctic. Lonsdale had been part of Egan's staff. Although he apparently gained Cook's respect and trust, Lonsdale clearly alienated the press through his British affectations and dress and his penchant for keeping people waiting for appointments.

Cook seemed to believe that despite the loss of a portion of his original records because of Peary's underhanded actions, he could still somehow provide the Danes with enough data for them to remove the qualification of their support of his claim because of the lack of definitive proof.

Although Cook told few people where he had moved, a man named George H. Dunkle appeared at the Gramatan Inn one day and said he was an insurance broker who had been sent by Cook's Arctic benefactor, John R. Bradley. Cook had been looking for life insurance to protect his family in case he died, but several companies had turned him down because they said he was too great a risk, owing to his celebrity and his penchant for visiting dangerous places.

Dunkle was supposed to arrange for an insurance policy, but his actions seemed designed more to gain Cook's confidence than to obtain Cook's insurance business. One day in November, Dunkle presented a friend of his, August W. Loose, who said he worked as a statistician for the insurance company that was interested in insuring Cook.

Loose told Cook that he was an expert navigator and could help him recheck his calculations of his observations. "The idea seemed reasonable," Cook later explained; "anything that would help me was welcome. . . . He pointed out, what I myself had been thinking about, that all observations were subject to extreme inaccuracy. He suggested his working mine out backward to verify them," and Cook agreed.

Cook gave Loose $250, which Cook said was intended to cover the supplies and books Loose would need to do his work. Loose moved into the Gramatan Inn to work on the records, while Cook continued to work on his report for the Danes. It was not unusual for explorers to pay others to verify their work, and Peary also hired men to confirm his readings and calculations from his journey.

On November 22, after he had completed his report and was preparing to send it off, Cook visited Loose's room because he had to have the calculations then if they were going to be of any use to him. He found Loose and Dunkle there, and papers strewn all about the room. "I think we have this thing all fixed up," Loose told

Cook. "Now, Doctor, I want to advise you to put your observations aside," Dunkle said. "Send these to Copenhagen!"

"I looked up amazed, incredulous," Cook said. "I felt stunned for the moment, and said little. I then took the trouble to look over all the papers carefully. There was a full set of faked observations. . . . I saw at once the game the rascals had been playing. The insinuation of their nefarious suggestion for the moment cleared my mind, and a dull anger filled me.

" 'Gentlemen,' I said, 'pack up every scrap of this paper in that dress-suit case. Take all of your belongings and leave this hotel at once.' " Cook said he stood and watched as they "shuffled from the room, ashamed and taken aback."

Cook made provisions to send Lonsdale to Copenhagen three days later with his official report, sixty-one pages of typewritten text and sixteen pages of scientific data. He also explained in his report that Whitney had not been allowed to bring his original observations or instruments from Etah and expressed his hope that the attached material would be adequate.

But the incident with Loose and Dunkle seemed to push Cook over the edge emotionally, and the worry and mounting despair of the two intolerable months he had spent in the United States since arriving to a hero's welcome overwhelmed him. He had not been sleeping well and was afraid that Peary's agents were planning to steal the few original records he had brought back from the North Pole adventure. He was actually being shadowed by men who were presumably in the employ of the Peary cabal, which only increased his anxiety.

The day before Lonsdale was to leave for Copenhagen, he and Cook traveled to Manhattan to bring a copy of the report to Cook's attorney's office. Lonsdale said they were able finally to shake off their shadowers by making several quick changes between street-cars going in different directions. Then Cook made a snap decision to leave the city.

Lonsdale bought him scissors and a razor, and Cook removed his mustache; then he went to get his hair cut short, while Lonsdale bought him a black hat: "Dr. Cook only intended to get away and obtain a needed rest. Without a disguise of some kind this could not be done, for his appearance was too well known and he could not have gone very far without being recognized." When Lonsdale said good-bye to him outside the Pennsylvania Station railroad terminal, Cook said to him, "Now I'll be able to get some sleep."

Three days later, Marie Cook received a note from her husband postmarked Toronto, telling her to meet him in Europe at once. He instructed her to bring all his original records if she could shake the Peary agents, who were also following her; if not, she was to put the records into a safe-deposit box at a bank before boarding a ship bound for Europe.

A few days after that, and one day after Lonsdale had delivered Cook's report in Copenhagen, any doubts about the sponsorship of the Loose-Dunkle affair were cleared up all too well. The December 9 *New York Times* carried an exclusive story alleging that Cook had offered Dunkle and Loose $2,500 to produce a set of fake observations; if the faked material proved capable of fooling the Danish authorities, the pair said, they had been promised a $1,500 bonus.

The story covered seventeen columns in that day's edition of the *Times,* an extraordinary amount of space, especially for an undocumented tale such as this one. Once again, self-confessed coconspirators in an alleged plot by Cook were given credit for newfound veracity worthy of substantial space and attention in a major newspaper. Dunkle later told several people that he had been well paid for the affidavit that appeared in the *Times,* and several reports indicate that Dunkle forged Loose's signature on the document, presumably so he would not have to split the money with him.

Cook was nowhere to be found, so Lonsdale sent a firm denial of Dunkle's story from Copenhagen. But again the damage was already done, adding another stone to the pile that the Peary forces had thrown at the hapless, and seemingly helpless, Cook.

Without his original observations, Cook's new submission to the Danes did not offer much more than had his original report, and the committee was unhappy with some of Cook's efforts to reconstruct his records from memory.

The official verdict of the Copenhagen committee was not unexpected, when it was revealed on December 22: "The material which has been presented to the university for examination does not contain observations or information which could be regarded as proof that Dr. Cook reached the North Pole on his last Polar expedition."

This verdict was hardly an indictment of Cook or a repudiation of his claim, but in tandem with the flood of charges that had been made against him, it was interpreted by much of the press corps—and thus much of the public—as another major defeat for Cook.

This interpretation is well illustrated by the headline of the *Times*'s main story on December 22, which was as big a fabrication as many of the stories the newspaper had carried throughout the entire Great North Pole Controversy: "Cook's Claim to Discovery of the North Pole Rejected; Outraged Denmark Calls Him a Deliberate Swindler; Having No Original Observations, He Used Loose's Fakes."

It wasn't until January 21, after carrying several more stories alleging that Cook had used the forged notes, that the *Times* acknowledged that Cook had not used any of the Loose-Dunkle observations. But, the admission was buried in the middle of a story on an inside page, and again, the damage had already been done.

CHAPTER 18

Dastardly Deeds

Now that Cook was on the run, literally as well as figuratively, the Peary forces decided it was time to dust off their candidate for the North Pole honors and claim the prize while their opponent was out of the picture. The Peary cabal had raised $350,000 to "see Peary through" his trials and tribulations, as they went about securing his claim, Herbert L. Bridgman revealed. As a fanfare for his reemergence, *Hampton's Magazine* began a ten-part serialization in late 1909 titled "The Discovery of the North Pole," under Peary's byline.

Peary's tale contained nothing that conflicted with or expanded upon Cook's already published series, which had run in the *New York Herald*. The two men's descriptions of the Arctic panorama they said they saw were nearly identical, as were their tales about their travels. The only major differences were that Cook had a finer eye both for scenery and for scientific phenomena, and, most important, that Cook's story was told first.

Later evidence showed that one primary reason for this consistency in Cook's and Peary's stories is that Elsa Barker, who actually wrote the series for Peary that appeared in *Hampton's Magazine*, based her articles on information she gleaned from reading Cook's earlier series.

"During the taking of the notes on Mr. Peary's story, as dictated by Elsa Barker, we had very little to go upon," explained Lillian Kiel, the dictationist that *Hampton's Magazine* assigned to assist Mrs. Barker. "There were stacks of the *New York Herald* [which contained Cook's stories] under Mrs. Barker's sink in the kitchen, to which we often were compelled to refer for the next paragraph," she said. "Therefore the two stories are so similar." Kiel came forward several years after the *Hampton's* series ran. She said she had not revealed the truth during the height of the controversy because she was embarrassed to testify because of her cleft palate. She did testify before Congress in 1915, when she had obtained a "speech appliance" that made her words intelligible to all.

The *Hampton's* series was followed by Peary's book, *The North Pole,* which was actually ghostwritten by A. E. Thomas, a novelist, who told one writer that he had written 80 percent of the book— basically all but the chapters about Peary's arrival at the North Pole, which were provided to him. Thomas presumably relied heavily on the *Hampton's* series—since he said Peary was uncommunicative— so, in effect, at least part of *The North Pole* is the result of a ghost-writer rewriting what another ghostwriter had rewritten from Cook's newspaper series.

At the start of 1910, the Great North Pole Controversy was a one-sided affair. Only Peary's forces were making allegations, so only Cook was on the defensive. While the press combed through Cook's story with magnifying glasses in search of any inconsistency or inaccuracy, it quickly accepted Peary's story as true. And Cook's disappearance, the most unwise thing he could have done under the circumstances, served only to convince many others of his guilt.

At this point, Peary could simply have retired to the background and let the campaign his financial backers had set in motion finish the destruction of Cook and his claim. But Peary was much too greedy; he longed to reap the great perquisites of attaining the North Pole he had lusted after for so many years. And by doing so, he made a major mistake: He asked Congress to declare him the official discoverer of the Pole and to retire him as a full rear admiral, which would have provided him with an annual pension of $6,500, a reasonable sum in 1910.

Top officials in the U.S. Navy were outraged by Peary's claim.

Peary had not served a single day as a line officer in the navy and had been referred to as "Civil Engineer Peary" by his military colleagues throughout his career. When Peary's request was referred to the House Subcommittee on Naval Affairs in February 1910, navy officials began a vigorous campaign to deny him his booty. Secretary of the Navy George von Lengerke Meyer wrote the committee that it would be "inappropriate to confer upon him [Peary] a title for which his previous education, training, and service have not fitted him."

The committee heard testimony from two of the men who had served on the National Geographic Society's North Pole committee. Henry Gannett, a society board member and panelist, told the committee "It is hardly believeable that a man would sit down [and give up] within 130 miles of the North Pole [based on Bartlett's questionable observation], and do that after he had undertaken the uncertainties, and the risks of life, leaving outside the question of Peary's personality." That is, of course, almost precisely what these same men had alleged that Cook had done, since even the Peary forces now reported that the Eskimos agreed they had accompanied Cook at least as far as three days' march onto the polar sea. The testimony of O. H. Tittman, who was superintendent of the U.S. Geological Survey and a member of the society's panel, mirrored Gannett's reasoning.

As a result of the hearing, the House panel concluded on March 4, 1910, that the National Geographic Society's review that led the group to endorse Peary as the discoverer of the North Pole was "perfunctory and hasty" and demanded that Peary submit his original records so the members of the House panel could review them. This was the kind of investigation that Peary's forces had demanded of Cook's original records, which were, of course, either still at Etah or had been removed by Peary's agents MacMillan or Bartlett.

Peary flatly refused to submit the records to Congress. A few days later, one of the congressmen who was friendly to Peary's claim offered a questionable excuse for Peary's refusal: It seemed that Peary had already signed a book contract, which specifically precluded his making the records public until after the book was published, many months in the future. Congressman Henry T.

Helgesen of North Dakota opined that the delay was actually intended to give Peary time to "prepare some 'original records' and bring about a climate friendlier to the passage of the bill."

Frustrated in his efforts to gain the promotion and pension he sought, Peary departed for Europe to harvest the many rewards his supporters ensured were awaiting him there. During one of these ceremonies, conducted by the Royal Geographical Society of England on May 4, 1910, another famous, although unrecognized, man was among the spectators in Albert Hall: Frederick Cook. As Cook watched Peary receive a gold medal from the society, he told a writer years later, he "could think of nothing but that the lines of pernicious anemia were more deeply engraved on Peary's face than when he had seen him last," during the rescue attempt three years earlier.

The Peary forces, apparently now convinced that their champion's ultimate victory was still in doubt, continued their villification of the still-absent Cook.

From London, Cook had traveled to Marseilles and then through Portugal and into Spain. His message to Marie had told her simply to meet him in Algeciras, Spain, a small waterfront town opposite Gibraltar, but provided no address. Eventually, the Cooks were reunited when they chanced to meet at a small park in that town. Cook decided he needed a major break from his recent past, and the Cooks headed for the warmth of Paraguay, as far from the frigid Arctic as he could find.

Meanwhile, emboldened by their stunning success in raising an unprecedented uproar over Cook's claim to Mount McKinley—despite the little evidence they could find or manufacture—the Peary forces scoured Cook's history in search of another place to attack. Cook's work on the *Belgica* would have been a likely place, except that he was in the constant company of others, including well-known men such as Amundsen, who would have been too difficult to attack with a campaign of innuendo, perjured testimony, and fantasy.

In their skullduggery involving the *Belgica* trip, however, the

Peary forces did manage to find one convenient topic: the Yaghan Indian dictionary that had been compiled by missionary Thomas Bridges in Tierra del Fuego. Cook had met Bridges when the *Belgica* stopped in Tierra del Fuego on its way to the Antarctica and had offered to convert the dictionary to a standard phonetic language, and to find a publisher to save Bridges's efforts for posterity.

On May 21, 1910, the *New York Times*—never tiring of its role as Peary's loyal and unquestioning canon—offered the latest chapter in the mudslinging, devoting much attention to a story about the dictionary under the headline: "Cook Tried to Steal Parson's Life Work."

The *Times* story portrayed Bridges as an unknown backwoods parson whose life work was usurped by the unscrupulous man from the big city, Cook. Yet standard reference works of the day already listed Bridges as an authority on the Indians of the Tierra del Fuego, on the basis of his previous work, which was well known in the appropriate academic and scientific circles. It is hard to imagine that Cook could ever have dreamed of publishing the dictionary—which undoubtedly took years of study and work—as his own.

In his 1911 book, *My Attainment of the Pole,* Cook called the antics surrounding the Yaghan dictionary "one of the meanest and pettiest charges concocted for Mr. Peary." He quoted from what he said was the already prepared introduction that he had written for the dictionary, a copy of which he said had been provided by the Belgian printer:

My visit among the tribe of Fuegians was not of sufficient length to make a thorough study . . . but I was singularly fortunate in being in the company of Mr. Thomas Bridges and Mr. John Lawrence, men who have made these people their life study. The credit of collecting and making this Yahgan Grammar and Vocabulary belongs solely to Mr. Bridges, who devoted most of his time during 37 years to recording this material. My work is limited to a slight rearrangement of the words, a few additions of notes and words, and a conversion of the Ellis phonetic characters in which the native words were written into ordinary English orthography.

But again, common sense and fairness had long since been cast to the wind, and Cook's reputation suffered still more damage as a result of this incredible charge.

The history of the dictionary is still murky, although an edition was printed in 1933. The original was returned to the Bridges family in England, was lost twice during the wars that ravaged Europe, and ended up in Nazi hands in Germany during the war. After being recovered, it was given to the British Museum, at the Bridges family's request, where it remains.

As blow after blow against Cook and his reputation landed with great success and without retaliation, the Peary cabal seemed more convinced than ever that its work was unfinished, and it stepped up its attacks. The Peary forces were searching for the knockout blow to end the crusade, which was taking much more effort and time than they must have originally anticipated from their leather-chair-furnished headquarters.

The spotlight returned to Mount McKinley in spring 1910, when the Peary Arctic Club—still convinced that it could secure Peary's claim by destroying Cook's claim to having climbed the Alaskan mountain—organized an expensive expedition to climb Mount McKinley under the leadership of Herschel C. Parker and Belmore Browne. The group, it is interesting to note, did not include Edward N. Barrill, Cook's climbing companion whose affidavit had turned the controversy into a serious one and who could presumably show exactly where he and Cook had actually climbed. According to Browne, Barrill was excluded because his "testimony could not be believed by many people."

The group failed to climb to the top of the mountain, but Browne claimed to have discovered proof that Cook's reputed photograph of McKinley's summit was actually taken on a hill on the southern side of the great mountain, twenty miles from the summit of McKinley. They took a photograph that they maintained was identical to Cook's on this distant peak. Of course, neither Browne nor Parker had ever seen the top of McKinley, but they knew well enough that Cook's picture was not taken there. So, after failing to climb Mount McKinley themselves and claiming that they had found Cook's "false peak," they named a peak for Hubbard, the president of the Peary Arctic Club, in thanks for his bankrolling their effort, declared their trek a success and headed home.

Three years later—long after it could make much difference to Cook's claims—photographer E. C. Rost told a congressional investigating committee in Washington that the Peary expedition's "proof"—the photograph that Browne and Parker had made—had actually been doctored. He called it "a combination photograph-drawing-painting" that was purposely altered to make it appear similar to Cook's original photograph, according to the record of the hearing. The Peary forces tried to quash the minutes of the hearing, and hence the evidence of their unmasked chicanery, by preventing the traditional printing of the testimony. And, but for the resourcefulness of one of the committee members, they would have succeeded.

But in 1910, the new and uncontested claims by the Peary forces after the latest expedition served only to reinforce the public's perception that Cook fabricated his climbing of Mount McKinley. This perception led—as the Peary cabal had intended all along—to "proving" that Cook had lied about reaching the North Pole, by "proving" that he had not climbed the mountain. Leaving aside for now that no such "proof" concerning McKinley had been established, the very logic of the argument is without precedent in the history of exploration.

In a noteworthy study of the issue while the controversy was still raging, Edwin Swift Balch, a prolific writer who specialized in books about the polar regions, called this strategy "certainly medieval in its logic." Yet it succeeded or, perhaps more accurately, it contributed, to the success of the overall villification campaign.

Today, Cook's claim to Mount McKinley is at least as difficult to prove as is his claim to the North Pole. But there is more than enough testimony from Cook's supporters to balance the claims of his detractors. And were it not for the Alice in Wonderland–type logic that was applied to Cook, his claim to having climbed Mount McKinley might still stand.

And new kernels of information continue to come to light. In a letter that one of Cook's present leading supporters, Sheldon Cook-Dorough, found in the explorer's files as they were being transferred to the Library of Congress, there is an intriguing tale.

George Kilroy, a writer who spent many years in Alaska, wrote Cook in 1929 about a chance encounter he had in 1913 with the man who is recognized as the first conqueror of Mount McKinley, Hudson Stuck, the so-called Archdeacon of the Yukon. Kilroy said that while he was fishing on the Yukon River, a boat containing Stuck and several companions approached, and he invited them to join him for breakfast:

> During breakfast the archdeacon told the story of the climb (of McKinley) in detail. I specifically asked him if he had seen any trace of the Cook expedition on the higher levels of the mountain and in reply he stated, "It is quite possible that Dr. Cook thought he had reached the summit of McKinley. As you are aware, Mr. Kilroy, the mountain peak is enveloped in dense fog practially 90% of the time. . . . On the 18,000-foot level we came across evidence of some expedition having been there. It was distinctly noticeable that they climbed out on a spur and it is possible they climbed to the apex of this in the fog and decided it was the top of the mountain. Under these conditions it was a natural deduction.

Cook is the only one of the early contestants for the summit of McKinley to have reported making camp at the eighteen-thousand-foot level, of which Stuck was apparently aware. If that camp was Cook's, it would prove that he at least got high up the mountain and did not fabricate his climb from miles away, as the Peary cabal alleged. And given that the last few thousand feet of the climb to the summit are said to be relatively easy, the existence of this camp would lend a great deal of credence to Cook's claim to have reached the top of the mountain.

Peary's ten-part series in *Hampton's Magazine,* despite a heavy publicity campaign, was a money loser for the magazine. So publisher Benjamin Hampton decided to recoup his losses by getting the first-person story of the missing player, who still seemed to attract more interest by readers with his absence than Peary could secure with his presence.

By summer of 1910, Cook had come to grips with the internal emotions the North Pole fiasco had created and decided to re-emerge. Marie went home from Paraguay to tend the children, while Cook returned to London and began to write his story. In the fall, while at least one newspaper was offering one thousand dollars merely for Cook's address, Cook decided to resurface and gave an interview to the *New York World* in London.

Why did he disappear? the reporter asked. "I was like a deer that had been driven into a cold stream. I simply had to get away from the perturbing conditions. The circumstances that surrounded me . . . [filled me with] a disgust . . . the disgust at the conspiracy that was despoiling me of the result of my life's work. . . . I left for anywhere that I could be absolutely alone. . . . I have simply been awaiting the time when my health would permit me to return to the United States. I did not run away from my task."

The reporter told his readers that Cook "stood tall and robust, wearing dark apparel and a black derby hat, carrying grey gloves and a walking stick." Cook had also grown an enormous mustache with drooping ends, to go with his Vandyke beard.

After the story ran, Benjamin Hampton sent editor T. Everett Harre to London to induce Cook to write his own series and present it in the same medium that Peary had used for his: *Hampton's Magazine.* This opportunity to address the same audience to which Peary had made his claims appealed to Cook, and he agreed to meet with the editor.

However, during that meeting, Harre told Cook that Mr. Hampton "would not publish a story reiterating his claim to the North Pole," but rather wanted his side of the entire story, about why he had disappeared. "I told him Mr. Hampton felt there was a great human document there; that perhaps the best thing for him to do would be to relinquish his claim to having reached the Pole. However sincere he might have been in the belief that he had got to the Pole, might there not have been the possibility of error?" Harre said he asked Cook.

Cook refused to budge. "I cabled Hampton that Cook was adamant in holding to his claim, that he was favorably inclined to giving our magazine a story of his disappearance, travels, etc.," Harre said. "But there was to be no 'confession' of fakery." However, Harre did get Cook to make "this concession: that neither he nor Peary could claim to have reached the mathematical North Pole. . . . As both he and Peary had been alone in taking their observations, both could make only a relative claim to getting to the Pole or its approximate vicinity."

Cook agreed to write his series for *Hampton's Magazine* for only four thousand dollars, even though he said he still had one standing offer from a magazine for ten thousand dollars for his side of the tale. "The opportunity of addressing the same public, through the same medium, as Mr. Peary had in his serial story, strongly influenced me" to accept Hampton's offer, Cook later explained.

To heighten the dramatic impact of the series, Harre asked Cook to slip into the United States surreptitiously, through Canada, and to work on the stories without anyone knowing what was planned. Cook made his way to Troy, New York, where he met with Harre and the magazine's new managing editor, Ray Long. According to Cook—and generally confirmed by Harre in a subsequent letter—Long presented an astounding new plan. "I was to go secretly to New York [City], submit myself to several employed alienists who should pronounce me insane, whereupon I was to write several articles in which I should admit having arrived at the conclusion that I reached the Pole while mentally unbalanced! . . . This plan, I was told, would 'put me right' and make a great sensational story!"

"To Long's suggestion Dr. Cook listened in silence, his face inscrutable," Harre later wrote. " 'What you suggest is interesting, Mr. Long,' he said, 'but not true. I got to the Pole.' " When Mr. Hampton himself arrived in Troy and made no such suggestion to Cook, the explorer relaxed and agreed to write the articles. He moved into a hotel in Newburgh, New York, about sixty miles north of New York City, and in three weeks wrote the stories, corrected the printer's proofs, and went back to London to wind up his personal affairs. He was to sail back to New York with much fanfare in time to provide a flood of publicity for the January issue of *Hampton's Magazine,* which would feature the first installment of his story.

Cook was convinced that this opportunity to offer his full story in the same magazine that had carried Peary's tale would remove all the tarnish from his battered reputation and restore not only his claims to having climbed Mount McKinley and to having reached the North Pole but also his life, so he could rejoin his family, head held high, and face the future.

But by the time he was prepared to sail back to America from England with his family, just before Christmas, 1910, Cook learned that he had been hoodwinked one more, and fatal, time: "Imagine my amazed indignation when . . . the cables brought the untrue news, 'Dr. Cook Confesses.' Imagine my heart-aching dismay when, on reaching the shores of my native country, I found the magazine which was running the articles in which I hoped to explain myself, had blazoned the sensation-provoking lie over its cover—'Dr. Cook's Confession.' "

That headline was printed across the cover of the January issue, from border to border, with more text: " 'Did I get to the North Pole?* I confess that I do not know absolutely.* Fully, freely and frankly I shall tell you *everything.'* Dr. Cook's own story in this issue."

While Peary's series in *Hampton's* may not have generated much interest, Cook's "confession" was a big hit, no doubt with some help from the Peary forces.

"The widespread dissemination of the untrue and cruelly unfair 'confession' and 'insanity-plea' stories dazed me," Cook wrote. "I felt impotent, crushed. In my very effort to explain myself I was being irretrievably hurt. I was being made a cats-paw for magazine and newspaper sensation."

Later the outrageous tale of just how the *Hampton's* scam occurred came to light, but again it occurred far too late to help Cook. After Cook had signed the galley proofs and departed, "We, the editorial staff [at the magazine], were sent to work cutting through the galley proofs. . . . We cut through the galley proofs and inserted what has been known to the world as Dr. Cook's confession of mental unbalancement," said Lillian Kiel, the stenographer who had worked on both the Cook and Peary stories for *Hampton's*. During an appearance in 1915 before the House Committee on Education [the same hearing at which photographer Rost accused the Peary forces of having doctored the McKinley photograph of Browne and Parker that was being used to discredit Cook], Kiel revealed that after they cut through the proofs, workers "inserted little scraps of paper, typewritten slips, which, I think, anyone can tell Dr. Cook did not write."

During her testimony, Kiel said their actions represented "A thing, if he [Cook] had not been a strong character, which might have turned his brain. But he was heartbroken, and he refused to look at the magazine." In a tape-recorded statement she made in 1953, Kiel recalled that the chairman of the House Committee on Education had told her at the conclusion of her testimony in 1915, " 'We certainly have been very much entertained by your interesting story.' To which I replied, 'I did not come here, gentlemen, to entertain you. I merely came to show you one of the many wicked methods which were employed to denounce Dr. Frederick A. Cook, who in my opinion, is the discoverer of the North Pole.' . . . Then the chairman closed with this statement: 'This will form the basis for our future actions.' That was in 1915. Today, April 7, 1953, I might add, What action? When?"

In a sworn affidavit that he later gave to Cook's daughter, Helene, editor Harre was even blunter than Kiel:

The so-called 'Confession' of Dr. Cook . . . was a trumped-up fake. . . . Dr. Cook consistently insisted that he had reached the North Pole as closely as he could determine. Working with Cook, I studied and handled his personal diary and films. The notebook was time-worn, stained and greasy from close contact with his body. The copious, tightly written entries were mute evidence of having been written through a long and arduous experience. After Dr. Cook had OKed the galley proofs . . . they were altered without Dr. Cook's permission and without my knowledge, to change the entire meaning.

Harre provided the affidavit on Jan. 21, 1944, when he was no longer employed by *Hampton's*.

O. O. McIntyre called this scheme by Hampton and his magazine the "most dastardly deed in the history of journalism. . . . It was deliberate misrepresentation and chicanery."

Cook floundered for several months after the *Hampton's* series trying to get publishers to print his whole story, but he was met with rejection after rejection. The game was over. The Peary forces had accomplished their goal: Fred Cook's claim to the North Pole was destroyed.

CHAPTER 19

An Official Winner

With Cook out of the picture and no longer contending for the North Pole honors, the Peary cabal decided it was safe to bring their hero out of the closet again. Peary's book, *The North Pole,* was now in print, and Peary had months of solitude to sharpen his story and his still-incomplete explanations for the questions that the members of the congressional committee were sure to ask about his alleged accomplishment.

To help lay the groundwork for Peary's testimony on Capitol Hill, his powerful forces had even gotten the new U.S. president, William Howard Taft, to send a message to Congress in December 1910, citing Peary's "unparalleled accomplishment" of having reached the North Pole, a determination, he said, that was "approved by the most expert scientists. . . . I recommend fitting recognition by Congress of the great achievement of Robert Edwin Peary." Taft's action again showed the value of connections among the rich and powerful elite: The president was a cousin of Gilbert H. Grosvenor, the head of the National Geographic Society, which—at Grosvenor's insistence—was the prime institutional supporter of Peary. In fact, Grosvenor was one of the top organizers of the Peary force's drive to shape history to its own liking by getting Peary confirmed as the North Pole's discoverer. The National Geographic Society was making its support of Peary's expedition a cornerstone of its membership drive at a crucial phase in its quest for status as a serious geographic institution.

Grosvenor also wrote the foreword to Peary's book and is believed to have used all the resources of his growing organization to try to make some sense of Peary's fragmentary, and often contradictory, observations and to construct a plausible explanation for the many obvious flaws in Peary's tale.

Another Peary ally, President Taft's predecessor, Theodore Roosevelt, wrote the introduction to Peary's book, *The North Pole,* in a further attempt to give the book credibility.

Peary's supporters also sent to every member of Congress a pamphlet, titled *How Peary Reached the North Pole: An Expedition over the Ice That Went to Its Mark with the Precision of a Military Campaign and Reached the Goal Sought for Centuries.* And the Peary Arctic Club brought all the lobbying muscle it could muster to influence Congress, especially the members of the House Naval Affairs Subcommittee.

Despite this coordinated campaign, when the subcommittee opened its second round of hearings on Peary's request for a promotion and a pension on January 7, 1911, Peary faced stiff questioning from several congressmen. Peary quickly became petulant and imperious in the face of the questioning, most of which came from Robert B. Macon, an Arkansas Democrat, and Ernest W. Roberts, a Republican from Massachusetts. Both these congressmen said they had no interest in supporting Cook's claim, but were clearly skeptical of Peary's.

Macon and Roberts focused a great deal of attention on the "investigation" of the conflicting claims that the National Geographic Society supposedly conducted before bestowing the laurels on Peary—the man they had helped sponsor. The verdict of the group's study was of great assistance to Peary, especially overseas, where many officials and interested readers believed that the National Geographic Society was an official agency of the American government, since most foreign geographic societies were indeed official bodies.

Under continued questioning, Peary slowly and reluctantly provided some detail on the society's "probe," even though his responses seemed to indicate that he suffered a major memory loss.

Peary told his questioners he could not remember, or, in his own, oft-repeated words, "I could not say," to such questions as how he received the request to appear before the society's committee in Washington, the time of day he arrived in Washington, where he met with the group, and just who was present during the proceedings.

As for the National Geographic Society's "thorough examination" of the instruments Peary used on his trek in the Arctic, under questioning from Roberts it became clear that the probe consisted only of the committee members peering into the box in which Peary had carried them from Maine on the train. The three panel members, Peary, Grosvenor, and unidentified others traveled to the Pennsylvania Railroad Station in Washington and took a peek.

ROBERTS: "Were the instruments all taken out [of the crate at the train station]?

PEARY: That I could not say. Members of the committee will probably remember better than I.

ROBERTS: Well, you do not have any recollection of whether they took them out and examined them?

PEARY: Some were taken out, I should say; whether all were taken out, I could not say.

ROBERTS: Was any test of those instruments made by any member of the committee to ascertain whether or not the instruments were accurate?

PEARY: That I could not say. I should imagine that it would not be possible to make tests there.

Roberts was also skeptical of the one piece of hard evidence that was presented to buttress Peary's claim: Robert A. Bartlett's piece of paper attesting that when he left Peary to return to the *Roosevelt*, as ordered, they were standing at 87 degrees, 46 minutes of latitude, or about 133 miles from the North Pole. Roberts asked Peary when Bartlett had inserted the latitude figures on the note.

PEARY: Immediately after the observation.

ROBERTS: Why did he use two pencils on that record?

PEARY: That I cannot say.

ROBERTS: I should judge that evidently that was a different pencil; that looks like an indelible pencil, and this looks
like an ordinary lead pencil. Do you know whether or
not Bartlett signed that after making his observation,
after putting down the figures?

PEARY: Yes sir, I think he did.

ROBERTS: It looks like a different pencil entirely.

PEARY: Yes sir; that was signed at the time, and of course it
was done after the observation was made.

ROBERTS: It seems rather strange that he had such an assortment
of pencils there—three pencils. Those entries were all
contemporaneous—made that day?

PEARY: Yes sir.

Roberts was also suspicious of how thoroughly clean Peary's
reputed diary was, that it "shows no finger marks or rough usage.
A very cleanly kept book," he called it. In the minority report he
filed in opposition to Peary's demands, Roberts added: "It is a
well-known fact that on a long Arctic journey ablutions even of the
face and hands are too luxurious for the travelers. Pemmican [the
dried-meat, fat, and dried-fruit mixture] is the staple article of food.
Its great value lies in its greasy quality. How was it possible for
Peary to handle this greasy food and, without washing his hands,
write in his diary daily and the end of two months have that same
diary show 'no finger marks or rough usage'?"

Roberts was also perplexed by what else was not in Peary's diary.
The congressman noticed that in his entry for April 6, the day he
now claimed to have reached the North Pole, Peary made no
mention of his accomplishment. And equally peculiar, Peary left
blank the pages for the next two days, April 7 and April 8. Thus,
the only mention of the North Pole during the very days Peary said
he spent in the vicinity of the Big Nail was contained on a loose
piece of paper that was later inserted into the diary and contained
the sentence, "The Pole at last."

Roberts also noted that the shadows on a crucial set of four
photographs, titled "The Four Directions from the Pole," that
Peary included in his book were in the wrong places. Peary had

apparently already been warned by his supporters of the problem with the photographs before he testified and dodged Roberts's direct questions by conveniently forgetting just when the photographs had been taken. He had remembered well enough when he provided the captions for the book, however, and the shadows did not match his claimed location.

It was all too much obfuscation, inaccuracy, and amnesia for Roberts. In his minority report for the subcommittee, he wrote, "A perusal of Captain Peary's testimony shows his recollection of the events of the day to have been delightfully vague and uncertain. The occasion was a most momentous one in his career, for the report of this committee was to settle in the public mind the mooted question of his having attained the Pole, and the fact that the incidents of that day made no sharper impression on his mind than is shown by his testimony, is very conclusive evidence that the examination of his records [by the National Geographic Society's committee] was anything but minute, careful or rigorous."

Peary brought as witnesses several men who were provided by his group of supporters, including two men who worked for the U.S. Coast and Geodetic Survey, men he had paid to recompute his numbers, in the same manner that Cook had originally hired Loose. Those two men testified that Peary's notes showed that he had indeed reached the Pole. In fact, a review of the record shows that the two men, Hugh C. Mitchell and C. R. Duvall, had actually altered Peary's records when it suited their figuring, whenever Peary's records did not support his claims. It is interesting that Peary did not bring along the two men who could presumably have given the strongest testimony about his efforts: Matthew Henson and Robert A. Bartlett.

Just how poor Peary's navigation and record-keeping skills were was underscored while the hearings were still going on. A Danish expedition to northern Greenland at the time was discovering that some of their predecessors had made the mistake of accepting some of Peary's earlier observations. The first group, led by Mylius Erichsen in 1906, was in the area that Peary had explored during his first expedition in 1892. As reconstructed from their records— which they left in a cairn and were recovered around the time of the congressional hearing—the group first learned that Peary's "Independence Bay" was not actually a bay but a fjord. They then set out to explore "Peary Channel," one of Peary's reputed discoveries on the earlier trip. But, according to the later-recovered records, they discovered that Peary Channel "does not exist," that it was dry land. The three men of the Erichsen expedition were never seen again, and several writers and historians said they were clearly victims of Peary's poor navigating and charting.

As ludicrous as it seems in retrospect, the House Naval Affairs Subcommittee approved, albeit by a 4 to 3 margin, Peary's bid, although it did make several amendments, such as retiring him as a civil engineer with the rank of rear admiral, instead of promoting him to rear admiral and retiring him, and fudging a bit on the question of whether he had actually "discovered" the North Pole.

But even Peary's supporters were disturbed by what they had heard during the congressional hearing. Subcommittee chairman Thomas S. Butler told Peary, "We have your word for it, and we have these observations to show you were at the North Pole. This is the plain way of putting it, your word and your proofs. To me, as a member of this committee, I accept your word; but your proofs I know nothing about at all."

Congressman Macon saved his fire for the debate before the full House of Representatives, which considered the Peary bill after the subcommittee approved it. "I realize that my efforts to defeat the passage of the bill to promote and retire Captain Peary are herculean in their proportions when I consider that I have the combined influence of the administration [as well as] a paid lobby of the Peary Arctic Club and the National Geographic Society to contend with."

While several committee members wanted to get to the bottom of the issue, Macon said, "The best information or so-called proofs that they could get from the alleged discoverer, when summed up, were a lot of guesses, assumptions, estimates, and evasions. And from these, four of the subcommittee of seven solemnly reported that the proofs were sufficient to establish the self-serving declaration of the gentleman to the effect that he had discovered the Pole."

Macon said that once Bartlett left him, Peary's actions were "uncertain, unstable and as unreliable as the wind." Of Peary's pristine diary, Macon said, "It is much more reasonable to believe that he prepared it in some office after his return home than it is to believe that he prepared it in an igloo under the circumstances and conditions described by him."

In summation, Macon said, "I have given more time and thought to this alleged discovery than I have to any other public question that I remember to have undertaken to investigate in my whole life; and the more I have investigated and studied the story, the more thoroughly convinced have I become that it is a fake, pure and simple."

Nevertheless, the full House of Representatives approved Peary's application 153 to 34, and President Taft signed it on March 4, 1911.

Astoundingly, the House subcommittee had received a letter from Cook in January that said: "From various sources I am informed that my prior claim stands as a bar to Mr. Peary for national honor. My object in writing you is to clear the way for Mr. Peary. My claim of attainment of the Pole is a personal one." The Peary forces scoffed at the letter as another sign of Cook's meddling in their hero's affairs.

CHAPTER 20

Cook Carries On

Despite the obvious commercial value of Cook's tale, his reputation had sunk so low because of the Peary cabal's unrelenting campaign that no publisher wanted to risk public criticism for being associated with him. After several months of unsuccessfully trying to find a publisher, Cook, in desperation, formed the Polar Publishing Company in Chicago and printed the book himself. He titled his work *My Attainment of the Pole* and offered it to the public in 1911 in a large-format book with many of his original photographs at five dollars a copy. Then Cook disappeared from view again.

There are few records of Cook's activities during this period. Cook apparently traveled extensively, speaking in meeting halls wherever he could draw a crowd.

His book sold well, which fed the lingering doubts that continued to nag Peary's claim to the North Pole, despite all the official endorsements. Encouraged by this spontaneous support for his claim, Cook returned to New York and found that Mitchell Kennerly, a large commercial publisher, wanted to reprint *My Attainment of the Pole* in an inexpensive trade version. This edition was immensely popular, running through several printings within months of publication, as sales quickly exceeded sixty thousand copies.

Cook also found that one the nation's largest speakers' bureaus, the Chautauqua Managers Association in Chicago, was prepared to put him on its prestigious lecture circuit. In those days, before radio and television replaced it, the lecture circuit was the most effective way of reaching a large number of people from coast to coast, spurred by the extensive newspaper coverage the lectures attracted.

Announcing the group's decision to sponsor Cook in May 1913, the association stated, "In placing Dr. Cook on the Chautauqua platform as a lecturer, we have been compelled to study the statements issued for and against the rival polar claims, with special reference to the facts bearing upon the present status of the Polar Controversy. Though the question has been argued during four years, we find that it is almost the unanimous opinion of arctic explorers today that Dr. Cook reached the North Pole on April 21, 1908."

The statement, which was reprinted in later editions of *My Attainment of the Pole,* included a long list of explorers and notables who supported Cook and ended with the declaration: "We are inclined to agree with Capt. E. B. Baldwin [who headed the Baldwin-Ziegler Expedition to the Arctic] and other Arctic explorers who say—'Putting aside the academic and idle argument of pin-point accuracy, the North Pole has been honestly reached by Dr. Cook, three hundred and fifty days before any one else claimed to have been there.'" (Baldwin would later repudiate his support of Cook, in another shameful display of disloyalty. One writer reported that after he turned on Cook, Baldwin "soon paid up $1,000 in personal debts and came forth in a new wardrobe, acting the part of the well-to-do gentleman.")

Cook proved to be an exciting, popular speaker, moving from engagement to engagement in the wake of such men as William Jennings Bryan and Robert M. La Follette. Cook told one writer that after he had spoken to a large audience in Fort Myers, Florida, in winter 1913, Henry Ford came through a long line of well-wishers to greet him. Cook said that Ford told him, "Doctor, I've read everything you've written, and I'm with you." Ford then introduced Cook to his two companions: inventor Thomas A. Edison and naturalist John Burroughs. Cook spent the next two days at Ford's house in Florida discussing life in the Arctic. He reported that they did not discuss the controversy until Cook was preparing to leave, when Ford told him, "Keep up your fight and stand on your own feet."

In virtually every city and town Cook visited on his speaking tour, he found that the Peary cabal was continuing its efforts against him, unsatisfied with having stolen his glory and his reputation and concerned about Cook's continuing popularity. Editors of the local newspapers in towns where he was to speak received anonymous packets containing detailed information on the Great North Pole Controversy and copies of the primary affidavits that the Peary Arctic Club had used to destroy Cook's claim to having climbed Mount McKinley. The *Des Moines* (Iowa) *Evening Tribune* reported on June 23, 1914, when Cook visited, "Whatever else Dr. Cook may be right or wrong about, he is most certainly right about the efforts that are being made to suppress him and his contention over the North Pole discovery." The newspaper reported it had been sent "a mass of printed matter from no acknowledged source" that had obviously taken weeks of labor and a good deal of money to produce. "The question that naturally suggests itself is why such an effort should now be considered necessary to discredit the doctor, and who is financially interested enough to go the expense?"

The Peary forces apparently still feared, and perhaps rightfully so, that their man might somehow lose his claim. Three federal legislators—Representatives Charles B. Smith, of Cook's home district in New York; Henry T. Helgesen, of North Dakota; and Senator Miles Poindexter, of Washington—were indeed ready to pick up Cook's banner when he returned from his period of exile. Peary's claim had drawn few new supporters over the years outside officialdom, and his behavior had not won him many new friends.

In late April 1914, Poindexter introduced a resolution in the Senate in support of Cook and to offer the nation's "thanks . . . [for] his discovery of the North Pole." The senator said that since Congress had already investigated Peary's claims, "it is but right it should also investigate those of Cook, and if an injustice has been done and merited honor has been withheld, we should now bestow it." This resolution was referred to the Committee on Libraries, where it died a silent legislative death.

Cook's supporters, although lacking the money and coordination of the rich Peary cabal, circulated petitions urging Congress to recognize Cook's efforts and collected thousands of signatures. Congressman Smith then introduced a resolution into the House of Representatives late that year, and it was referred to the Committee on Education. That committee held a brief hearing on January 28, 1915, at which stenographer Lillian Kiel revealed how the staff of *Hampton's Magazine* had altered Cook's manuscript to create his "confession" and E. C. Rost testified that the photograph the Peary forces had used to discredit Cook's claim to Mount McKinley had been doctored. Also that day, noted geographer and author Edwin Swift Balch introduced evidence that some climbers who had made the trek up Mount McKinley since Cook's climb had confirmed many of the things he noted in his writings.

A few days after the hearing, the Committee on Education voted not to pursue the matter. Were it not for the resourcefulness of some of Cook's supporters, the testimony would have been erased from history because the original transcript was destroyed soon after the committee's vote. Fortunately, a copy was made, and, much to the chagrin of the Peary cabal, Representative T. H. Caraway of Arkansas had the entire transcript entered in the *Congressional Record,* for all to see.

Caraway's action occasioned an angry denunciation of Cook and his claims from Representative Simeon D. Fess of Ohio, a member of the Committee on Education. Representative Helgesen later revealed that Fess's tirade had been made into a twenty-seven-page pamphlet and that 400,000 copies of it had been distributed anonymously around the nation, in still another attempt to discredit Cook. In his rebuttal of Fess, Helgesen attacked Peary, Peary's claims, and Peary's supporters.

But just as Helgesen had attempted to unmask Peary as a fraud, he was soon attacking Cook in similarly vehement terms. He had been pushing to give Cook his long-sought hearing in Congress, but just when he believed he was going to accomplish it, Cook inexplicably chose to accompany a close friend, Dr. Frank P.

Thompson of Chicago, on a long foreign expedition, which was to include an attempt to climb Mount Everest.

This chapter in Cook's story is perplexing to understand. Some of his modern-day supporters believe he suffered a nervous break-down or was at least unable to stand the rigors of continuing the fight. Others say Cook was simply being realistic, knowing he would never be able to outgun Peary's wealthy and influential lobby.

Cook's supporters at the time stated that he had simply accepted that he was not going to prevail before Congress and decided to accept his friend's offer to join him on an expedition to climb Mount Everest to put the painful issue behind him.

Helgesen chose to interpret Cook's decision as proof that Cook knew his story would not stand the scrutiny of such a congressional review. In a blistering speech on the floor of the House, Helgesen recalled that Cook had "suddenly disappeared for about a year" during the height of the Great North Pole Controversy, and that the Peary cabal had pointed to his disappearance as proof that he sought to "avoid further investigation into his claim." Now, Helgesen said, "when matters looked as though a hearing might be granted him, he decided on an eight months' tour around the world. . . . [This lends] color to the theory that Cook does not desire a bona fide hearing or investigation."

Finally, to what must have been the immense relief of the Peary forces, world events pushed the Great North Pole Controversy off the front pages of the nation's newspapers after six long years. The sinking by a German submarine of the British passenger liner *Lusitania* on May 7, 1915, off the coast of Ireland, focused public opinion on more pressing issues than determining the true discoverer of the North Pole.

This diminution in interest helped Peary, who had taken himself out of the limelight soon after Congress approved his pension, for it signaled a halt to the embarrassing questions that continued to hound him whenever he appeared in public. During his infrequent lectures after that, he generally avoided talking about the North Pole and adamantly refused to discuss the controversy with Cook. Instead, he lectured on his new passion: the growing field of aviation.

Cook, meanwhile, sailed on the ship *Magnolia* from San Francisco a few weeks after the *Lusitania's* sinking, bound for India and Mount Everest. When he and Thompson arrived in Penang, however, they were arrested because the British authorities believed they were part of a German plot to foment a rebellion in India. They were eventually allowed to sail with the *Magnolia* when it departed, but they were again detained when the ship reached Rangoon.

Years after the events, Cook explained to one writer that a series of coincidences and innocent activities had combined to raise the suspicions of the British. It seems that Indian revolutionaries had also sailed on the *Magnolia* and that unaware of the Indians' political leanings, Cook and Thompson had become friendly with them. The pair also had spent an evening with the German consul in Honolulu when the ship stopped there because he was an old friend of Cook. Cook's father, of course, had come to the United States from Germany. Cook and Thompson carried picture postcards made near the military fortifications around Rangoon, postcards that, it turned out, had coincidentally been produced in Germany. And Cook and Thompson requested permission from the British authorities to visit Sudharam, a town on the Ganges River, the same day that the British aborted an attempt to land forty thousand rifles there to equip a revolutionary army.

Some of the mystery of the astounding series of coincidences was cleared up two years later, during a conspiracy trial in Chicago. According to witnesses at the trial, the Germans "had planned to kill Dr. Cook and his crew [he actually had no such crew] who were to make an expedition in the vicinity of the Himalaya Mountains." One of the conspirators "was to assume the name of Dr. Cook . . . [and] go through India under the guise of the explorer and foment a revolt among the natives," he told the court.

Meanwhile, Cook and Thompson managed to convince the British to release them, although they were denied permission to travel to the Himalayas, which ended their plans to climb Mount Everest. They were, however, allowed to journey to Borneo—where there was apparently no threat of a revolution—and where the two men spent two months studying tribes of primitive Indians.

The next obstacle Cook and Thompson faced was getting home,

while World War I raged around the globe. Unable to book passage to the United States in Manila or Yokohama, they traveled over land through Russia to Copenhagen. There they learned of a Norwegian ship bound for the United States, but were told that it was filled to capacity with Americans fleeing the war in Europe. However, when the ship line's management learned that both Cook and Thompson were physicians, it offered them free passage to New York in return for their services as ship's surgeons.

The two men quietly arrived home on January 23, 1916, to a nation preoccupied with the war, which by now seemed sure to spread to its shores.

CHAPTER 21

Kangaroo Court

By the time the United States entered World War I in 1917, Cook found himself unable to continue his campaign for justice and without a means of support, since Congress was preoccupied and the lecture circuits had been taken over by speakers who sought to fuel patriotic fervor and raise money to finance the war effort through the sale of Liberty Bonds.

At age fifty-two, he had by now lost all interest in pursuing his medical practice, and his marriage was suffering serious strain caused, in good part, by his repeated absences. When his friend and traveling companion, Dr. Thompson, offered him a job investigating an oil company in Wyoming in which Thompson had a part-interest, Cook jumped at the chance. The oil industry had become a hotbed of investment speculation, since the Industrial Revolution required increasing amounts of petroleum products to fuel and to lubricate the rapidly rising number of machines that were taking over production tasks.

Cook had developed a working knowledge of geology as a result of his exploration activities and had the kind of personality that could well benefit an investigator, since he could quickly put people at ease. After several months of probing the company's operations and prospects, he advised Thompson that the firm's oil was coming from seepage, not from a large pool, and advised him to pull his money out of it.

Cook obviously enjoyed the gold-rush-like excitement of the burgeoning oil business and quickly found himself back in Wyoming directing the field work of the New York Oil Company in Casper. That company's president, Frank G. Curtis, created a new company, the Cook Oil Company—with Cook as president—to develop one of the oil fields that Cook had studied for the New York Oil Company in the Salt Creek district. The field was close to the Teapot Dome, which the federal government owned and was holding for a reserve source of oil for the navy in case a war shut off other sources of petroleum. The company brought in a large well, and the Cook Oil Company, and its president, prospered.

Late the next year, 1918, Cook was swept up by the oil mania developing in Texas and resigned from the Cook Oil Company. He was a geologist on projects for Marriner Eccles, who later became chairman of the Federal Reserve Board, and for a boxing promoter; both explorations brought in gushers. Cook then financed his own well in the vicinity of the two he had worked on, but came up dry. So he remained in the oil business as a geologist or prospector in the larger fields in Texas and Arkansas.

While Cook was working in the oil fields, Peary had retreated even further from public view during the war years. He was last seen in public in January 1919. Then, on February 20, 1920, after a lengthy illness, he died of pernicious anemia and was buried in Arlington National Cemetery. Despite his death, his rich supporters remained vigilant to his cause and continued to carry his banner for many years. Two years after his death, the National Geographic Society placed a huge monument on Peary's grave that bore his motto: "I shall find a way or make one."

In March 1922, Cook, along with several associates, formed the Petroleum Producers Association in Fort Worth. The company was designed to take advantage of the myriad oil companies that came up dry and shut down or simply never raised enough capital for extensive exploration. It offered the stockholders of these moribund companies shares in the new firm, in exchange for their stock and some additional cash. This way, the association acquired land and equipment, as well as some working capital, to explore the fields, from people who would otherwise have lost all the money they had put into their earlier investments.

Cook and his associates were successful at attracting stockholder-investors, and in less than a year had merged more than 340 little oil companies into the Petroleum Producers Association.

But Cook was to pay once again for his audacity in trying to claim "Peary's Pole." In a speech that came out of the blue on January 10, 1923, at a meeting of the National Advertising Commission of the Associated Advertising Clubs of the World in Washington, D.C., a former member of the Peary Arctic Club charged that Cook was conducting a massive oil swindle of unsuspecting investors.

Herbert S. Houston, a publisher who had been a staunch supporter of Peary and was then the head of a group called the National Vigilance Committee, which purported to be a "Better Business Bureau" in New York, charged that the Petroleum Producers Association was "a gigantic reloading scheme."

Once again, Cook was accused of being guilty of one thing for supposedly having done, or not done, something else, just the way the Peary cabal manufactured evidence that he had not climbed Mount McKinley and then used that "evidence" to "prove" he had not reached the North Pole. This time, the North Pole fiasco was to be used against him in this alleged swindle.

Peary's ever-friendly *New York Times,* in a story on Houston's speech, asserted that "this scheme . . . led to the rediscovery of our old friend Dr. Cook. 'He did not discover the North Pole, but we have certainly discovered him, and it would appear that he is in a fair way toward securing as much publicity for his present exploits as for some of his earlier forays into the realms of fancy and imagination,' the publisher [Houston] said."

According to the *Times,* "Dr. Cook's scheme, he said, was the consolidation of defunct companies, 'probably on some new principle that the combination of nothing equals something.' " Mr. Houston never explained how his organization just happened to find Cook's operation, an interesting coincidence for a group run by an ally of Peary's and for a former member of his chief sponsoring organization.

In fact, Houston was a good friend and protégé of Herbert L. Bridgman, the man who had played such a crucial role in the Peary cabal. Thus, Peary may have been dead, but his gang—and its campaign against Cook—was alive and well.

By now, Cook's relations with his wife had seemingly hit bottom, and on January 31, Marie, accompanied by two Fort Worth policemen, followed him to a hotel, where he was arrested on a Prohibition-era charge of illegal possession of alcohol. This was an era when strong evidence was required to secure a divorce. According to the police report, Cook had the alcohol in the hotel room, which was also occupied by an unidentified young woman. The next day, Marie filed for a divorce in Fort Worth, accusing Cook of cruelty and asking for the custody of their daughter. Marie also asked the court to freeze her husband's funds. Cook denied that he was with a woman at the hotel, although he did not contest that he was in possession of a bottle of whiskey when he was arrested. He was released on a five-hundred-dollar bond.

Mrs. Cook soon agreed not to ask the court to keep the freeze on her husband's funds so he could continue his business. A divorce was quickly granted, with Marie getting custody of their daughter, Helene.

However, it is difficult to obtain unbiased views of the relationship between Cook and Marie. Descendants of Cook, including his daughter and, later, his granddaughter Janet, believed the divorce was a sham to shield Marie and the two children from embarrassment. In fact, Marie clearly stood beside him as his troubles mounted, despite the divorce. And many years later, they would both live in Helene's house, albeit in separate bedrooms.

In any event, fewer than three months after Houston's speech, Cook and nineteen other Fort Worth oilmen were arrested and charged with a federal offense, the fraudulent use of the mails to further several alleged oil schemes. Cook had been in Little Rock, Arkansas, where he said he was arranging for the construction of an oil refinery to process the fruits of the company's wells, when he heard that there was a warrant out for his arrest. He returned to Fort Worth, where after being arrested, he was freed on a twenty-five-thousand-dollar bond.

Cook was caught in the jaws of two dragons: The Peary cabal was obviously still hard at work, apparently sensing an opportunity to bury Cook and his claims for all time, and the Harding administration was looking to remove some of the tarnish from its reputation in the wake of the infamous Teapot Dome Scandal.

In 1921, President Warren G. Harding had transferred the control of two major federal oil reserves—the Teapot Dome in Wyoming and the Elk Hills in California—from the Navy Department to the Department of the Interior; these reserves had been set aside for use by the navy in case of war. Not long before the charges were brought against Cook and the others, it was revealed that Harding's secretary of the interior, Albert B. Fall, had secretly leased those reserves to two of his cronies at terms that were unfavorable to the federal government. It was later uncovered that Fall had received some $330,000 in bribes from his friends, Harry L. Sinclair and Edward L. Doheny.

The government's embarrassment at the Teapot Dome Scandal was immense and led to a witch hunt by the Department of Justice to clean up the entire oil industry and improve its own reputation at the same time. Wrote one historian, "The federal prosecutors were looking for [oil-industry-related] scapegoats to satisfy public opinion." The *Literary Digest* wrote, "After a quarter of a century of ignoring the activities of oil-stock swindlers, the federal government decided to prosecute, and singled out the company headed by the conspicuous Dr. Frederick Cook."

A review of the government's case—aided by its own documents, many of which I obtained under the Freedom of Information Act—raises serious questions about the integrity of the prosecution.

The records show that it was an extremely weak case, fueled primarily by the belief of federal bureaucrats that they "knew" Cook was guilty, even if they could not develop proper evidence to prove it. These weaknesses in their case forced the government to pursue Cook under mail-fraud statutes because it was unable to attack him directly for allegedly bilking the investors. In the end, he was charged with overstating the Petroleum Producers Association's financial results by mailing letters and brochures that contained erroneous statements in an attempt to lure more investors.

The government's chief claim was that Cook was merely using the Petroleum Producers Association to get the frustrated stockholders in already moribund oil companies to come up with still more money, in a vain attempt to salvage their investments, for which they were sure to get nothing. According to a mailing that went out over Cook's signature, stockholders in those companies were issued stock on a dollar-for-dollar basis in the new company, but they were also required to buy additional stock amounting to 25 percent of their original holdings. Thus, a stockholder with $100 worth of stock in a defunct oil company that was being folded into the Petroleum Producers Association was able to get $125 in stock from the new company in return for the old stock and $25 in cash.

The government's entire case hinged on Cook's intent, that is, what he was actually planning to do with the money and the assets he acquired through the stock transfers. Cook maintained that he was allowing investors a second chance and that at the same time they were creating a company that was large enough to fund drilling operations and compete with the large firms that were already beginning to dominate the oil industry. The government's investigators, on the other hand, maintained that Cook was going to take the money and give the unwitting investors nothing in return but unfulfilled promises.

An investigation conducted by H. B. Matheny, a "special bank accountant" for the Department of Justice, established beyond a doubt that for the first few months of operation, Cook ran the Petroleum Producers Association out of his hip pocket, paying its bills out of his checking account, depositing its receipts in the same account, and keeping its records strewn about his personal office. But beyond that, Matheny's report is far less clear cut.

Cook's record keeping improved when the company began attracting more and more investors. When Matheny reconstructed all the company's transactions from Cook's records, he uncovered some peculiar facts that clearly seemed at odds with his, and the government's, contentions.

For example, it was discovered that not only had Cook drawn no salary or commissions from the company, even though he was entitled to approximately $55,000 under the company's bylaws, but he had actually lent the firm another $21,542.76 out of his own pocket. Cook was thus the largest single investor in the Petroleum Producers Association.

Matheny also alleged that Cook had used personnel and material of the Petroleum Producers Association in his efforts to sell stock in two other companies for which he received compensation, but allegedly did not reimburse the company. The government also charged that the Petroleum Producers Association paid dividends to some stockholders with money that came from further stock sales, not oil revenue, in order to cite those dividends as symbols of success to attract more investors.

A review of the internal correspondence involving the case that remains in the files of the U.S. Department of Justice and the Federal Bureau of Investigation reveals the great priority that was assigned to making sure that Cook was convicted. To dishearten the defendants, the government decided to indict in Ohio as well all the major figures involved in the Texas case, to show them that this was not going to be a one-fight war. The rationale for the second case was that Ohio investors had lost money in the purported scheme. Thus, the government could presumably move to indict the oilmen in every state in the country, assuming there were investors from all the states.

After the July 10 indictment of Cook and twenty-five others in Cleveland, David Cahill, a "special assistant" to the U.S. attorney general, wrote, in a letter to Assistant Attorney General John W. H. Crim, quoted here for the first time: "The morale of the defense is now somewhat broken as they realize the power of the government to prosecute them all over the Union and the purpose to use that power." In the letter, Cahill added, "I firmly believe from what I hear that one result of other indictments in other districts will be to drive some of the defendants into the arms of the government here [in Fort Worth] and to materially strengthen the government's cases."

Several of Cook's codefendants clearly saw the handwriting on the wall and entered guilty pleas in return for light penalties, usually a small fine, just as Cahill had predicted in his letter.

The government faced an additional obstacle: The indictments were exceedingly unpopular in Texas, where the case was scheduled to be tried. Cook had become a popular man in Fort Worth, and many of the townspeople had rushed to his aid after the indictment. Lower-ranking bureaucrats urged that the trial be moved to another district. In a coded telegram, Cahill and John S. Pratt, another "special assistant" to the attorney general, urged Crim to move the Cook case, and several others of a similar nature, to a more hospitable environment: "Does not seem desirable to try Revere, Cook, Spoonts, Kingsbury here. Find increasing evidence of unfavorable public feeling. . . . Our plan is to indict and try them in other districts and will do so at earliest possible moment."

But high-ranking government officials in Washington had a different plan, and Crim's coded response was: "Most of these cases must be tried at Fort Worth. It is the exceptional case that may be taken to another district." That there was a bigger scheme is evident by another portion of Crim's response, printed here for the first time: "I cannot be put in a position of asking the Chief Justice [presumably the Chief Justice of the U.S. Supreme Court] to change his program without very great embarrassment."

Besides, the government had another way of dealing with its concerns about how its case would be treated in Texas: It brought in a U.S. district court judge from Ohio. In what may well have been the most important decision in the entire case, Judge James C. Wilson, chief judge in the Northern District of Texas, asked Judge John M. Killits from the Northern District of Ohio to handle the trial of the Petroleum Producers Association.

There were fireworks from the very start of the trial in October 1923, as the defense attorneys and Judge Killits shouted at each other and denounced each other, in what became a ludicrous spectacle. Many of his codefendants, including several of the officers of the company, had by now pleaded guilty, and it quickly became clear that Cook was really on trial for his North Pole claims much more than for this alleged mail fraud. According to the dispatches of Charles P. Stewart, who covered the trial for the now-defunct *Central Press,* Killits "had not forgotten" that Cook had been unable to prove his claims to the North Pole and Mount McKinley. "While these weren't in themselves punishable offenses," Stewart wrote, "the judge appeared to think that they ought to have been, and that a good time to mete out punishment for them was right then with the doctor's conviction on an oil fraud charge to serve as an excuse for it."

When he testified in early November, Cook told the judge and the jury, "I had only altruistic aims in my ventures. I wouldn't deliberately swindle even a swindler." He said his plan had been to salvage as much as possible at a time when oil prices had plummeted, which had driven scores of small companies out of business. The large oil companies, in many cases, ran in and bought out the bankrupt firms for little money. Cook testified that he had not, however, expected the price of oil to fall to one dollar a barrel, which it did. This drop in price led to a sharp cutback in production throughout the oil fields and depressed the value of all oil lands.

Cook acknowledged that he made errors in judgment in pushing hard to make the Petroleum Producers Association a success. But he maintained that such mistakes were the result of his overenthusiasm and his firm belief that the company would eventually succeed. He told the jury that the best evidence of his intentions was that he had invested all his money in it and had not withdrawn any of it or taken any salary or commissions for his efforts.

Just weeks before his indictment, Cook had written, in an article in *World's Work* magazine, that after watching the fire that burned off the natural gas from an oil-well gusher, "I was wondering if all this roaring fire wasn't sent as a kind of warning to the fake promoters—the meanest men in the world. . . . I don't believe that the man who would willingly defraud the public and take from investors . . . the money which they have so carefully saved, without giving them a fair return, deserves much better an end than might be typified by this flaming gas well."

In his solicitation letter to investors, Cook had written, "The struggle between small companies is passing away and they are gathering about the camp fire of the Petroleum Producers Association. United effort makes a strong nation. The same effort forces success in an industrial organization like ours." Cook's chief lawyer, Joseph W. Bailey, a former United States senator, told the jury, "Cook would have made a success of the enterprise if the government had not come along and interfered when it did."

But, amid all the shouting, charges, and countercharges between Cook's lawyers and Killits, the jury, after a trial that ran five weeks and three days, found Cook guilty on November 21. Killits wasted no time in meting out punishment.

In an amazing speech, he denounced Cook in the kind of terms one might expect to hear in a brutal murder case. After Cook declined to make a public statement in the courtroom after the verdict, Killits began:

So, you can say nothing. You have come to the point where your peculiar and persuasive hypnotic personality fails you. The 20th Century should be proud of you. History gave us Ananias [in the New Testament, Ananias is reported to have dropped dead after Peter accused him of lying about how much money he had received from a land sale] and Sapphira [Ananias's wife]. They are forgotten, but we still have Dr. Cook.

Cook, this deal of yours is so damnably rotten that it seems to me your attorneys must have been forced to hold their handkerchiefs to their noses to have represented you. It stinks to high heaven. You should not be allowed to run at large.

Killits was also convinced that Cook had hidden vast sums of money from his dealings and was angry at Cook's wife, who, despite their divorce, had stood by him throughout the trial and brought meals to him at the jail in Fort Worth. He apparently decided that she was being loyal to Cook so she could share in the booty after he went through the trial. "I know that you have your ill-gotten gains put away, but your wife and daughter should not be allowed to touch them. You have stolen this money from widows and orphans."

At one point in his denunciation, Killits stated that he had a far harsher penalty in mind for Cook: "I wish I could do with you as I might, the way I feel about you; I wish I were not circumscribed by some conventions that I think are mistakes." Killits continued, "It is strange . . . that the prosecuting officers have suggested to me that I be not quite so stiff on you. It is my own disposition and my abhorrence for such a crook as you . . ." that led him to want to punish Cook to the extreme. One can only speculate as to what punishment Killits had in mind.

And with that, Killits sentenced Cook to the astounding term of fourteen years, nine months in Leavenworth Penitentiary, fined him twelve thousand dollars, and assessed more than twelve-thousand dollars in court fees against him. He later refused to give Cook any credit for the sixteen months he spent in the Tarrant County Jail in Fort Worth while awaiting the outcome of an appeal he filed.

The day after his conviction, Cook told reporters during an interview through the bars of his cell in the Fort Worth jail, "It seems that an almost impossible burden has been placed upon me. I have no money, in spite of the charges by the judge and the United States attorney that I have many dollars planted away. I only had one dream. Call me visionary if you will, but within me was an abiding desire to find an oil field that would remain a monument to my name and memory, and all the money I received was spent to that end."

The remnants of the Peary cabal, as evidenced by its longtime mouthpiece, the *New York Times,* was besides itself with glee. Two days after his conviction, on November 23, the *Times* editorialized, "If Dr. Cook did not discover the North Pole, he discovered the way to wealth in Texas. But it led to the prison door. It was characteristic of the man that as a promoter of wildcat oil companies he boasted that he had reached the Pole. The fiction was his certificate of integrity."

Unsatisfied with that, the *Times* two days later ran another editorial, this one headlined "A Great Imposter." Again, the *Times* reconvicted him for his alleged transgressions at the North Pole and on Mount McKinley, fiction that it had helped create. "Cook could go nowhere among men without being pointed out as the explorer who pretended that he had climbed Mount McKinley and beaten Admiral Peary to the North Pole, though the fact was that he had not got higher up on McKinley than a spur far from the summit." The *Times* was upset that Cook had written successful books and attracted packed houses to lectures all over the country "before he was exposed as an audacious humbug." It said the "extraordinary thing" about the entire case was "that the perpetrator of two of the greatest impostures of history should have been allowed to represent himself as an honest promoter."

Just how personally involved Killits was in the Cook case is evident from several letters he sent to Justice Department officials complaining that Cook was being allowed to remain in jail in Fort Worth while his appeal to a higher court was pending. Killits wanted Cook sent immediately to Leavenworth, at least, in part, to shut him up. In a long complaining letter to Attorney General Harlan F. Stone in late February 1924, Killits said that Cook, in the local jail, "is given privileges which I am confident the Department [of Justice] does not endorse." Specifically, Cook was interviewed by a reporter and contrasted the treatment he was accorded with that of the defendants in the Teapot Dome trial. (The trial that resulted from that national scandal concluded after Cook had been convicted.) "This he could not have done had he been in proper federal custody following the court's judgment," Killits wrote.

Killits claimed that Cook was the one who was causing the long delay in the appeal process, telling the attorney general that Cook was purposely trying to stall it, to delay being sent to prison. He said that the court reporter wanted cash in advance for the copy of the transcript necessary for Cook's appeal. "Very naturally," Killits wrote, "considering his [Cook's] record from 1909, Cook's prom-ise to pay the expenses of making the transcript is not accepted by the reporter at face value." Why the Great North Pole Controversy would seem to affect Cook's payment for the transcript is unclear.

Eventually, Marie Cook raised the ten thousand dollars necessary for the preparation of the transcript and appeal by personally calling on Cook's associates in the oil business in Houston.

It is important to note that Henry Zweifel, the U.S. attorney who prosecuted Cook, wrote a follow-up letter to Attorney General Stone stating that the court reporter had written him that the delay was caused by his own tardiness and that Cook had paid for the transcript in advance. "This delay was no fault of Cook's," Zweifel wrote. He also told Stone that it was the usual procedure not to send a defendant to prison until his appeal had been heard. The delay in filing was actually working to Cook's detriment by keeping him in jail, since no bond could be set and posted until the appeal was actually under way.

But Killits was unabashed, and just three days after Zweifel's reply to Stone, again wrote to the attorney general to demand that Cook be sent to Leavenworth immediately.

Later, Judge Wilson, who had asked Killits to handle the Cook trial, heard several motions that Cook's attorneys brought prior to their appeal in the circuit court of appeals. On August 4, 1924, he denied a writ of habeas corpus, although he told Cook that if he had jurisdiction in the case, he would have released him immediately. At the time, Cook was being held in jail under a seventy-thousand-dollar bond requirement that Killits set and that Cook's attorney, Bailey, described as the highest ever set in Texas for any crime, including murder.

Wilson told Bailey and his cocounsel, "I find myself in the position of being just about agreed with all of the positions taken by you gentlemen. [But] this court had no power to pass upon this matter."

Soon after that ruling, Wilson wrote an astonishing letter to Attorney General Stone—published here for the first time—that seemed to impeach Killits and draw into question his own impartiality: "For my part, I exceedingly regret that I made the mistake of requesting the assignment of Judge Killits to the trial of this particular case. . . . I say to you frankly that I sometimes think Judge Killits is not quite right. I think that Dr. Cook should have been convicted, I believe the sentence imposed was extreme, but I nevertheless am anxious to see this case affirmed since the matter of the penalty can be taken care of."

Wilson revealed that he had found out that Killits and special assistant Pratt "are conducting a correspondence with the Circuit Court of Appeal of the Fifth District accusing the court of committing error in a decision they reached recently" on a minor part of Cook's appeal. Wilson warned the attorney general that unless Killits and Pratt were "forced to desist . . . this Cook case will be sent back here regardless of whether there was error commited" in the trial. And he ominously warned, "The court will reach the conclusion, and it can do so from the record, for that matter, that it was not possible for any man to get a trial, a fair trial, at the hands of Judge Killits, and particularly that it was not possible for Dr. Cook to do so."

And, Wilson added, that despite his heavy schedule, he would hear the retrial himself if the appeals court ordered one, indicating that there would be no foolishness during the trial rematch.

One is left to wonder how different Cook's fate might have been had Wilson followed through or had the defense been able to obtain copies of Wilson's correspondence.

Wilson went on to tell Stone that Killits's action had had wide-ranging ramifications. "The people [of Texas] generally were shocked at Judge Killits' conduct at the end of that case, regarded his conduct as brutal and inhuman. This to a large extent caused a change of sentiment and a change of attitude toward the government by the public generally."

Wilson also asked Stone why the government's chief prosecutor in the case, Zweifel, was not getting the complete support of Washington in conducting the Cook appeal. Attorney General Stone replied three weeks later that he thought that those men who had been convicted in the oil cases "have not received prison sentences, but have been fined amounts which seem very small when compared with the extent of their operations." He said he believed that Zweifel had failed to request prison sentences, despite Stone's orders to the contrary, and that he had lost confidence in Zweifel as a result. Stone's belief may well help explain Killits's comments during his sentencing of Cook that he was going to ignore the government's recommendations that Cook not be severely punished.

There is no follow-up correspondence remaining in the government's files to detail subsequent events, but Killits apparently did stop writing letters to the court of appeals. The higher court eventually rejected Cook's appeal, and he arrived at Leavenworth on April 6, 1925, just a few months short of his sixtieth birthday.

Killits's reputation was far from sterling. "Proceedings were begun against . . . [him] in the U.S. Supreme Court [in 1918] charging him with contempt for alleged failure to obey a court order forbidding suspension of sentences in criminal cases," the *New York Times* reported many years after the Cook trial. The proceedings were dropped after Killits complied with the order. The newspaper also said that when Killits was prosecuting attorney in a county in Ohio at the end of the nineteenth century, "he was accused of juggling fees and was removed from office, to be later exonerated and reinstated."

———

The Petroleum Producers Association was, of course, moribund from the time of the indictments, and its assets were eventually sold off by the U.S. Marshals Office to help pay some of its debts. Much of the land and leases it had acquired were sold to large oil companies, and in one of the more ironic twists of this bizarre chapter in Cook's life, several of the properties in Texas came in while he was in Leavenworth. Newspaper accounts in the late 1920s reported that several of the properties became major oil producers and eventually earned millions. And research is continuing into a persistent, but as yet unverified, report that one of the properties was part of the Yates Pool, the largest oil reservoir found in the continental United States during the twentieth century.

Some of Cook's allies petitioned for a pardon for Cook, arguing that since the company had actually been working on a well in this field when the government intervened, it would have otherwise struck oil, which would have mooted all the government's claims in the trial because all the stockholders would have made money on their investments. This request for a pardon was denied.

In a letter to *Time* magazine in 1936, Cook wrote, "It is a fact, and this has not been reported by those who have tried to defame me, that some of the lands under question have since produced wealth of millions, far beyond the wildest assertions which I made in literature and letters of the company. . . . I have never in my life taken a penny that did not belong to me, and I am convinced today, as I was in 1923, that my judgment in regard to every phase of my oil development was sound."

A few of Cook's remaining descendants are still waging a campaign to restore his claim to some of the lucrative oil properties.

CHAPTER 22

Hero in Disgrace

Cook entered Leavenworth Penitentiary on April 6, 1925; ironically, that day marked the sixteenth anniversary of Peary's claimed attainment of the North Pole, which was being celebrated in schools around the country as a result of a publicity campaign launched by the ever-adoring National Geographic Society. Cook was nearing his sixtieth birthday when the prison's bars were closed behind him that day, and his enemies had nearly broken his spirit.

Leavenworth's warden, W. I. Biddle, told reporters in San Francisco in July that Cook was in poor health. An Associated Press dispatch quoted Biddle as saying that Cook "is in such a bad mental and physical state that he may never finish his term." The warden also revealed that Cook had "become an expert at needlework."

But after a few more months of incarceration, Cook accepted his fate and, as was his nature throughout his life, decided to make the best of it. According to writer Andrew A. Freeman, who interviewed Cook extensively in the 1930s, "Not long afterward he recovered [from his depression and physical ailments] and embarked on a prison career during which, he told the writer, he experienced some of the happiest days of his life."

Cook became night superintendent of the prison hospital, after turning down the post of day superintendent because, he explained, he did not want to be the person who determined whether his fellow inmates were really sick or were malingering so they could skip their work assignments and take advantage of the superior lodgings and food the hospital offered. He also devised a treatment and rehabilitation plan to assist the many drug addicts among the prison population, since there was no existing therapeutic program, even though some 40 percent of the inmates were said to have been addicts at the time of their imprisonment.

He organized a school to help educate some of the illiterate inmates among the four thousand who were incarcerated in the Kansas prison and ran a monthly magazine called the *New Era.* As it had in private life, Cook's philosophy of life remained cheery. "In his editorials," wrote the *Literary Digest,* "he has struck a consistent note of hope, urging his fellow prisoners to spend their time learning trades and preparing to lead better lives upon release."

Because of his embarrassment at being behind bars, Cook refused to have visitors during his prison stay, denying permission for even his daughter and stepdaughter to see him. The only visitor he did not refuse was Roald Amundsen, who appeared unannounced in the warden's office on January 20, 1926. Amundsen was in the United States to conduct a speaking tour to raise money for his latest project, a planned flight from Spitsbergen, Norway, to the North Pole on the dirigible *Norge.*

Amundsen's visit took a great deal of courage, since the anti-Cook frenzy had still not abated, six years after Peary's death. Amundsen and Cook had not seen each other since Cook's triumphant return to Copenhagen in 1909, after his return from Greenland, during which he had advised Amundsen to pursue the South Pole.

His old friend from the *Belgica* "took it as the most natural thing" to visit him, according to Amundsen's biographer Roland Huntford. But it is unclear who was the doctor and who the patient during this visit. "It was a moot point, however, who stood most in need of comfort [during that hour-long visit]," Huntford continued, "for according to Cook, Amundsen poured out his bitterness, saying amongst other things that 'There is a relation between the tongue and the harpoon. Both can inflict painful wounds. The cut of the lance heals, the cut of the tongue rots.'" Amundsen, of course, was preaching to the choir with these words of world-weary wisdom.

And Amundsen quickly learned just how active the Peary cabal still was. During the next stop on his lecture tour, in Fort Worth—the very city in which Cook had been convicted and whose citizens retained a keen interest in him—Amundsen gave a long and thoughtful answer to a question presented by reporters about the conflicting claims to the North Pole.

"I have read Dr. Cook's story, written months before Peary's, and I have read Peary's. In Peary's story I have not found anything of consequence that Dr. Cook had not already covered. I am not only unconvinced that Dr. Cook was a faker, but, on the contrary, I am of the opinion that his story of the discovery is just as plausible as was Peary's.

"It is possible that neither of them actually reached the Pole, but, regardless, it seems to me that Dr. Cook's claims were just as sound as Peary's."

Amundsen also had a few words for Peary camp follower Donald MacMillan, who had taken it upon himself to be the cabal's chief attacker, now that Peary was dead and the Peary Arctic Club was inactive. MacMillan had made some new claims that the Eskimos had told him that Cook had never gotten near the Pole. To that, Amundsen told the reporters, "My experience with Eskimos has been that they will give you the kind of answer you want. MacMillan said to the Eskimos: 'Dr. Cook only away from camp one sleep?' and laid his head on his hands to denote the passing of one night, and the Eskimo nodded, 'Yes.' That kind of evidence was used to discredit Dr. Cook."

Recalling their efforts together during the *Belgica* expedition, Amundsen told the Associated Press that "Cook was the finest traveler I ever saw. He was practical. He never would say quit. Why, I remember once when he needed a camera in the worst way. Cook had a lens. Around that lens he built a camera and it worked. I've never been able to duplicate some of his feats. He was a fine physician, too."

MacMillan's response, which was carried in the same story, was an outright lie: "Peary's claim to having reached the North Pole is fully as good as Amundsen's to having reached the South Pole." In fact, Amundsen had well learned the lesson of the Great North Pole Controversy. While Peary and Cook had no witnesses to verify their positions, when Amundsen and his expedition arrived at the South Pole on December 15, 1911, the explorers took independent readings; he then sent members of his party out across the ice to plant flags that created a large box pattern, to prevent any later claim that he had missed the actual Pole.

Another great contrast between Amundsen and Peary was that while Peary had sent all others away so any claim would be his alone, Amundsen wrote that as they approached the South Pole: "I had decided that we would all take part in the historic event; the act itself of planting the flag. It was not the privilege of ONE man [Amundsen's emphasis], it was the privilege of ALL those who had risked their lives in the fight and stood together through thick and thin."

The Peary cabal was livid at Amundsen's candor after his visit with Cook. The *New York Times*'s headline on the story was, "Amundsen In Role Of Cook's Defender." Gilbert H. Grosvenor, by now the director of the Peary cabal and the president of the National Geographic Society, was beside himself with anger. While Amundsen tried to contain the furor by pointing out that he was not declaring Peary's claim invalid, Grosvenor haughtily canceled a planned lecture that Amundsen was to give to the National Geographic Society, which cost the Norwegian a lot of money. Soon after he reached the South Pole in 1913, the society had provided Amundsen with twenty thousand dollars to help pay his debts. Despite his accomplishments, Amundsen had little support from his government; he was always short of money and was hounded by creditors for debts related to his expeditions.

But in this latest controversy, Amundsen managed to keep his sense of humor, even as Grosvenor stoked the flames by canceling the speaking engagement. When he returned to New York at the end of the shortened tour, without addressing the society, Amundsen was asked by reporters if stories that he was very angry about the cancellation were true. "I don't want to get into any controversy," he said. "I am told I am very indignant, but I am not.

I am rather amused than otherwise at the childishness of things. Maybe they will grow up some day."

Cook, of course, was elated by Amundsen's words and wrote a long letter to the *Kansas City Journal–Post,* in which he said the incident went a long way toward proving his claims and "positively disprov[ing] most of Peary's. It is by his production that a pioneer must stand or fail, and I am willing to rest my case with future generations by my published records."

When Amundsen got to his hotel room after arriving in New York City at the end of his tour, he found a small package, which contained an embroidered linen tablecloth about four feet long and fifteen inches wide. "Well, and whom do you think this is from?" he asked an accompanying reporter. "The man I once thought was going to discover both the North and South Poles. . . . And he did every stitch of it with his own hands. It is pathetic. Yes, it is from Dr. Cook. I am more touched by this gift than by almost anything that has happened to me in a long time."

That wave of rekindled interest in the Great North Pole Controversy abated, and the nation's newspapers went on to other subjects, while Cook remained trapped in the reality of prison life. His health declined the next year, and in early 1928, he petitioned President Calvin Coolidge for executive clemency. Cook cited his poor health, the fact that the average term of the other men who were convicted for similar crimes was less than one year, and the fact that several of the former properties of the Petroleum Producers Association had been found to contain vast amounts of oil and natural gas by their new owners as reasons he should be released.

Newspaper accounts in 1928 marked the progress of Cook's old properties and often cited him by using the word "vindicated," at least when they discussed his judgments in the oil business: "That oil was flowing bounteously beneath the sand-, cactus- and mesquite-covered prairies of western Texas exactly where Dr. Cook believed it to be, is some vindication for him, but certainly not wholly satisfying to a penniless man who languishes in prison, reported one newspaper." Nevertheless, his petition for clemency was denied thirteen months after it was filed and only one year before he would be eligible for parole. He decided not to pursue his request.

But his embarrassments were still not over. During summer 1929, Cook was approached by James R. Crowell of *American Magazine,* who offered him twenty thousand dollars for the story of his journey to the North Pole and the things that had happened to him as a result of his claim. Cook readily agreed, and three weeks later sent a manuscript to Crowell. The magazine's editors liked the tale, Crowell replied, except for the part about the North Pole. What the magazine actually had in mind, Crowell told writer Andrew A. Freeman in 1937, was for Cook to tell its readers how he had fabricated his claim of reaching the Pole.

"I informed Mr. Crowell that I appreciated his offer and that I needed the money badly," Cook said. "However, I also told him I did not need money to the extent of telling an untruth, which any repudiation of my claim . . . would really be. To a man in prison, $20,000 is a lot of money. It was indeed a fortune to me, since I am without funds. But a million dollars would not be enough to cause me to waver from my claim to the discovery of the North Pole."

As the date of Cook's possible parole approached, the remnants of the Peary cabal, led by one of Peary's adoring biographers, William H. Hobbs, launched a letter-writing campaign against his release, some of the fruits of which still sleep in the National Archives. The letters claimed that Cook had not suffered enough for his real crime: claiming to have discovered Peary's North Pole.

Despite this drive, on March 9, 1930, four years and eleven months after he arrived at Leavenworth, the sixty-four-year-old Cook walked out of prison. The cover of the prison's magazine, the *New Era,* the night before he left, contained an editorial that stated, "Perhaps no more noted prisoner was ever committed to a federal penitentiary. None was ever held in higher esteem by officials and inmates alike. . . . The world of freedom has reclaimed a man meek and loving, asking for nothing more than an even break with his fellow man."

Fittingly, when he walked out the gates of the prison on that Sunday morning, the first people he met as a free man were a group of reporters, and he immediately resumed his campaign for vindication.

After a flurry of rumors about his future plans made headlines in newspapers around the nation, Cook settled down to a quiet existence, writing a new book, speaking before groups whenever asked, and spending time with various family members and friends around the country.

Over the next several years, while living as a virtual pauper, he vainly sued some of his detractors for libel for their comments about him, including the publishing firm of the Macmillan Company and the *Encyclopedia Britannica,* which stated that Cook's claims were "universally rejected." He would occasionally find a friendly ear, and there would be a burst of new stories, but, in general, the world seemed uninterested in what had happened so far away and so long ago. Still, he carried on—speaking to groups when he could and writing letters; a book titled *Return From the Pole,* which was not published for many years; and a still-unpublished book about his life.

Somehow, he managed to maintain his positive outlook and his belief in his eventual vindication, according to those who knew him then. Fortunately for history, Cook spent many weeks in the 1930s with his biographer, writer Andrew A. Freeman, discussing the events of his life and his exploration. "Of the people I met during the years I worked on this case [the book, *The Case for Doctor Cook,* was not published until 1961]," Freeman noted, "the least partisan and the calmest was Cook. . . . Although in those last years [of his life] he was dependent for support upon a few friends and relatives—which explained his shabby clothes—he never complained of his indigence or the meagerness of his worldy goods or of the unsavory repuation he bore."

On May 3, 1940, while he was visiting Ralph Shainwald von Ahlefeldt—who had been part of his first Mount McKinley expedition—in Larchmont, New York, Cook suffered a stroke. He had come to New York to help care for von Ahlefeldt's ailing wife. Cook was taken to a hospital in nearby Port Chester, where he was listed in critical condition and in a coma.

A group of Cook's friends, led by von Ahlefeldt, petitioned President Franklin D. Roosevelt for a pardon, which was granted on May 16. Cook was still in a semicomatose state when he received the news from von Ahlefeldt. When he was shown the document, "he gasped 'great—happy day, pardon' before settling back into the comatose state," according to one newspaper account.

Cook rallied after the pardon and left the hospital on June 4 to return to von Ahlefeldt's Larchmont home. He suffered a relapse, however, in late July, and at 8:06 A.M. on August 5, 1940, Frederick Albert Cook, one of history's greatest explorers, died at New Rochelle Hospital at the age of seventy-five, still a hero in disgrace.

EPILOGUE

CHAPTER 23

Last Words

From the time the first doubts were cast about his accomplishments, Cook always maintained that history would someday exonerate him. He believed, he said, that the future travelers who would inevitably follow in his footsteps would confirm his findings and remove the tarnish from his claims to the North Pole and Mount McKinley.

Many of the early writers and historians who studied the Great North Pole Controversy also agreed that the ultimate test of Cook's and Peary's claims would be time. Because Cook made his claim first and published his detailed observations first—and because Peary contradicted none of Cook's observations—most early writers agreed that it was Cook who stood to gain the most, or lose the most, by the comparison of his claims with the observations of future explorers.

And those predictions have proved to be at least half right. Today, after some three-quarters of a century of erosion, Peary's claim to the North Pole has been destroyed. Now, by reading Peary's own evidence and by dispassionately reviewing the record, nearly all historians and geographers believe that Peary not only failed to reach the Pole by at least dozens, and more likely hundreds, of statute miles, but that he knew he had failed and consciously conspired to foist a grand fraud on the world at the same time that he and his henchmen were systematically destroying Cook's claims and Cook's life.

The death of Peary's crumbling hold on the North Pole came out of the blue during summer 1988, and from a most unexpected source. The last die-hard Pearyites—those pseudoscientists and mail-order salesmen at the National Geographic Society—realized that their continuing defense of Peary's claim in the face of ever-mounting evidence to the contrary was continuing to make them a laughingstock among serious geographers and historians. And the damage was continuing because the Great North Pole Controversy has refused to die over the decades since it began.

After years of steadfast and unflinching support for all Peary's claims, the society decided it needed to reach a more defensible position in the late 1980s. So, the organization commissioned a British writer, Wally Herbert, to examine Peary's long-hidden records and issue a new report on his claim. In earlier works, Herbert had been pro-Peary enough, and anti-Cook enough, to put the society members' minds at ease about what he would come up with.

But, presented with Peary's unvarnished records, Herbert was aghast. He said he realized after studying the records that Peary's navigating was so reckless and haphazard and his record keeping so scant and disorganized, that Peary most likely did not make it to the North Pole. While he put as happy a face on it as he could, Herbert concluded that Peary had made several navigational errors and that he "most likely" got only within thirty to sixty nautical miles of the Pole.

Herbert did not stray too far from the fold, however. In the September 1988 issue of *National Geographic* magazine, he wrote that Peary probably did not make it to the North Pole, but that his failure was due only to incompetence, not malice. While Herbert's article diminished Peary's claim, it still left Peary the hero of the North, since, as Cook said so many years ago, arguing over a few miles, considering the conditions endured by Arctic explorers, is truly quibbling.

Peary's failing as a navigator and as a record keeper should hardly have been a surprise to Herbert, since nearly everyone who has studied the controversy since 1910 knew full well of the enormous holes in Peary's story. Indeed, Herbert cited virtually no new information in making his "new" determination that Peary had not reached the North Pole.

Even this half-hearted correction, however, ruffled feathers at the top of the roost of the National Geographic Society, where the grandson of one of Peary's chief supporters, Gilbert H. Grosvenor, still rules. After reportedly stalling publication for many months after receiving Herbert's manuscript, the society reportedly put the article into its monthly magazine only when it became clear that Herbert was planning a book about his work on Peary's records.

By printing it first, the National Geographic Society could put the most positive face possible on the report, salvage Peary's place in history, and contain the damage to the society's reputation for having championed Peary's cause so vehemently for so many years. Thus, while the National Geographic Society bigwigs might be a bit embarrassed by the episode, Peary would still be king. But after seventy-five years on the throne of polar exploration, Peary was clearly on the way out.

The latest North Pole controversy took an even more peculiar turn. Less than two months after Herbert's article—which was based entirely on information available in 1910, nearly all of which had been cited in earlier books, magazines, and newspapers—Dennis Rawlins, a Baltimore-based historian and astronomer, struck a blow that seemed to mark Peary once and for all as a liar and a cheat.

Rawlins—ironically a Peary fan who, even after his discovery, said, "I consider Peary the greatest American polar explorer from the United States"—revealed that he had found Peary's long-missing navigational sightings from the day Peary later claimed to have reached the North Pole: April 6, 1909. This is the same record that Peary maintained never existed, while the world was clamoring for proof of his claim.

Now, according to Rawlins, explorers and historians knew why Peary had claimed there were no records: Peary's own reading showed that he was 121 statute miles—105 nautical miles—short of his goal on April 6, at the most northerly point he ever reached.

With this one document, much of Peary's seemingly peculiar

behavior following his alleged discovery began to make sense, and most of the missing pieces of the puzzle seemed to fall into place.

The importance of Rawlins's find was underscored by the *Washington Post,* which broke the story of the discovery, saying, "If Peary knew he was far short of the Pole when he turned back, his claim would be one of the biggest scientific frauds ever perpetrated."

Peary had apparently given the document containing his observations to his wife, claiming that the information in it could be used to destroy "that goddamned son-of-a-bitch Cook." Josephine, who could not decipher the calculations, eventually put them into a safe-deposit box at a bank in Portland, Maine. In 1935, some fifteen years after Peary's death, his daughter, Marie, went to the bank vault, hand copied the mysterious document, and sent it to Isaiah Bowman, the new president of prestigious Johns Hopkins University and the director of the American Geographical Society, an association of professional geographers.

By 1935, Cook was out of prison, and once again a wave of popular support was building for his claim. Josephine and Marie apparently thought it was a precipitous moment to use the mysterious and long-hidden record that Peary had entrusted to his family. The mother and daughter, of course, thought that the document somehow proved that Peary had reached the North Pole.

Sometime after Peary gave her the document, Mrs. Peary wrote on its envelope: "Original Observations made by R. E. Peary U.S.N. at 90 degrees N. Lat. April 5 & 6 1909." Why she thought Peary would have kept secret a document that could have resolved the Great North Pole Controversy years earlier is unknown.

When Marie sent the copy of the document off to Bowman, an avowed admirer of Peary, she hoped he would interpret the document and advise her how to use it to the best advantage against Cook. Although he was unable to interpret the numbers on the paper himself, he sent the document to Harry Raymond, an astronomer at the Carnegie Institution in Washington. Raymond had no trouble deciphering the numbers and told Bowman they represented a sextant reading taken about two hundred nautical miles from the North Pole.

Bowman and Raymond tried hard to devise a scenario that would make the figures work to buttress Peary's claim, but were unable to do so. Incredibly, Bowman—a man of science and education— chose to join the Peary conspiracy rather than to unmask it or at least to release the documents or to attempt to determine what they really represented, even though Cook was still alive and could have had the terrible blemish removed from his reputation.

Bowman went so far, according to documents found in his files, as to recommend to Marie that the records she sent him be sealed for fifty more years, which is precisely what was done.

The secret would remain hidden in Bowman's files for those fifty years, until Rawlins, who was researching a far different topic at the time, came upon correspondence between Bowman and Marie in which the note was discussed. He eventually obtained a copy of the document that contained the observations from Peary's records, which the family had finally agreed to open to the public in 1984 at the National Archives in Washington. After deciphering the calculations, Rawlins said that Peary was clearly never closer than 121 statute miles from the North Pole. According to Rawlins, Peary was so inept with his instruments that he believes Peary never really knew exactly where he was, although he clearly realized he was not at the Pole, since the sun was still rising and falling in the sky, as evidenced by the readings on the historic document.

When asked why Peary had retained a document that proved him to be a liar and a fraud, Rawlins replied that he thought he did so because "he was so proud of what he really had done." Rawlins, who does not believe that Cook got anywhere near the Pole, claimed, "He [Peary] hadn't made it to the Pole, but he did get farther north than anyone else ever had."

Rawlins said, "But he also knew it would be his last try for the Pole and that he didn't want to go home as a failure. He decided to stake a claim, knowing full well that it might not stick. If it didn't he would at least have the documentation for what was legitimately his life's greatest achievement."

While the destruction of Peary's claim has not led him to pick up Cook's banner, Rawlins commented, "I get along with the Cook people, in that I've proven them to be at least half-right, that Peary did indeed not make it." And, he said, Cook deserves some credit for being the first man to have wintered in both the Arctic and the Antarctic.

Rawlins's claim sent the National Geographic Society scurrying for cover. In an all-out bid to preserve at least the remnants of Peary's honor, the society turned to a virtually unknown club of amateur navigators, the Navigation Foundation, to examine Rawlins's claim and Peary's stale proofs. It is not surprising that the Navigation Foundation was able to do what no one had been able to do since the claim was made: It "proved" that Peary had indeed gotten right to the North Pole.

By stringing together a downright humorous group of assumptions, presumption, and outright fabrications, the club "proved" that Peary had walked right up to the Big Nail.

In a seeming repeat of the activities of the National Geographic Society in the days after Peary returned from the Arctic, Gilbert M. Grosvenor, the president of the society, told the press in early 1990 that he was relieved, since the Navigation Foundation's finding was "unimpeachable . . . and should lay the controversy to rest."

The foundation did apparently discover that the navigational sighting Rawlins had found was apparently not the claimed North Pole sighting after all. However, no one has been able to figure out why Marie Peary kept it in the safe for so many years, apparently on Peary's instruction that it was the proof positive of his claim.

That discovery, while clearly embarrassing to Rawlins, hardly dissuaded him. After the Navigation Foundation's study was released by the National Geographic Society, Rawlins said that it "has more fiddle factors than the New York Philharmonic. . . . There are large errors running around in the analysis."

Another analyst, an astronomer at the Space Telescope Science Institute in Baltimore, added, "What I resent is the way the Geographic is trying at all costs to be an advocate for Peary. That's not the proper stance for an educational or scientific organization."

With Peary's claim now virtually destroyed, Cook's reputation and his place in history have not benefited. The myriad lies put forth by the Peary cabal have a strong afterlife, much like nuclear waste. In many of the flood of newspaper stories that followed in the wake of Herbert's and Rawlins's revelations, Cook was dispatched in a scant paragraph or two as a minor claimant, at best, or a discredited hoaxer, at worst. This treatment of Cook stemmed more from ignorance and the byproducts of the conspiracy generated by the Peary forces than it did from any reexamination of the record.

The passage of time, coupled with a natural diminution of interest by the scientific community in a seemingly long-settled issue, have worked against Cook by dimming the light of historical curiosity. But, as evidenced by the amazing amount of publicity that the destruction of Peary's claim attracted in 1988, there remains a strong, if unofficial, interest in the topic.

The members of the small Frederick A. Cook Society have struggled to keep the flame burning. The society, which is based at the Sullivan County Historical Society, near Cook's birthplace in New York State, is led these days by a grandnephew of Cook and others, including Sheldon Cook-Dorough, an Atlanta attorney and the group's historian, who is not a Cook relation.

Cook-Dorough has no doubt that Cook reached the North Pole, or was at least close enough to it to deserve the claim as its discoverer. "Historically, the proof rests in the corroboration by later exploration of a discoverer's original description of the area first seen and trod by him," according to Cook-Dorough.

Cook-Dorough noted that much evidence has been presented in the years since Cook and Peary made their competing claims— evidence that presents a unique yardstick with which to measure the previous claims. "Historians have carefully and conscientiously studied and examined these facts, and the evidence now presents an extraordinarily strong, indeed a compelling, case supporting Dr. Cook's discovery of the North Pole," he said.

Cook-Dorough and other believers in Cook cite several experts who have come to support Cook's claims in recent years, including the following:

• Dr. A. F. Treshnikov, director of the Arctic and Antarctic Institute of Leningrad, who "has concluded that the evidence overwhelmingly indicates that Cook journeyed deep into the Central

Arctic basin and to the immediate vicinity, at least, of the North Pole."

• Rear Admiral Charles W. Thomas, a retired officer in the U.S. Coast Guard, who spent much time in the Arctic and who was also a glaciologist and oceanographer.

• Dr. V. S. Koryakin, a member of the Soviet Academy of Sciences and a glaciologist, who, after studying Cook's writings and comparing his descriptions of conditions around the Pole with what is known to exist today, "has concluded that the evidence without serious question confirms Cook's journey to the Pole."

• Noted historian Frederick J. Pohl, who, after a great deal of initial skepticism, concluded that Cook had indeed reached the North Pole. As a result, Pohl agreed to edit Cook's book, *Return From the Pole,* which was published posthumously in 1951. Pohl added a compelling introduction, detailing his vivid recollection of the events as a young newspaper reader,

> my growing doubt [in 1909–10] that he had reached the Pole, because of my assumption that a man against whom there were so many accusations was probably dishonest. Then through the years came a reaction, the feeling that something about the story as it had come to me was not right; but I had no moving desire to study the facts until I read "Return From the Pole" [in manuscript form] and realized that the experiences Cook recorded were in some ways unparalleled in Arctic annals. Only a man of extraordinary power of observation could have described so vividly the animal, marine and vegetable life—the Arctic dawn, the awaking of the ravens and rats and foxes, and the first impact of light. I then re-examined in great detail all the records I could locate and I found Cook's claim had strong supporting evidence.

Pohl's reexamination led to his agreement to edit the book and later to appear on radio shows and in other forums to champion Cook's cause.

Cook-Dorough also places much stock in Cook's observations about the ice conditions and currents around the North Pole, none of which was known at the time and all of which have since been confirmed. He stated: "The cumulative effect of the corroboration of Cook's original descriptions of natural conditions in the Arctic Ocean . . . and at the North Pole itself is staggering. He correctly reported the condition of the pack ice at various latitudes, up to, and including, the Pole; islands of glacial land ice; the prevailing [ocean] drifts in the region. . . . Cook gave to the world the first information concerning natural conditions in areas of the high Arctic which had never been seen or traversed before his historic journey."

Cook's granddaughter, Janet Cook Vetter, who died some months after I interviewed her in 1989, said of the new information about Peary: "It doesn't solve my problem. I'm glad they've finally admitted what they have, what they know, but it doesn't solve my problem [of getting people to reexamine her grandfather's claim]." She had taken on the responsibility for what became a crusade for her mother: proving that Cook did, indeed, reach the North Pole.

At her riverfront house on the Atlantic Coast of Florida, Janet Vetter maintained a room full of filing cabinets loaded with Cook's records, photographs, newspaper accounts, and correspondence that were compiled by her mother. The more her mother, Helene Cook Vetter, "collected material [about Cook] and read it, the more she became convinced he was right," Janet Vetter said. Throughout her mother's life, she "never had any doubt" about her father's veracity, except during the darkest days of the oil-swindle trial in Texas.

Janet Vetter said that, in retrospect, a major turning point in her grandfather's life was the death during childbirth of his first wife, Libby Forbes Cook, in 1890. "After his first wife died, and the child died, he developed a wanderlust. You couldn't keep him in a single place for very long."

Not long before Helene's death in 1977, Janet Vetter said her mother told her "that vindication would not come during her lifetime, but that she hoped that it would come during my lifetime." And, she said, she herself was still hopeful, which was why she has picked up the baton and continued her lonely task to undo almost eighty years of injustice.

Cook himself left his own conclusion and obituary in the form of an unpublished autobiography that he wrote in the 1930s. In the manuscript, which is now in the Library of Congress, along with most of the records Janet Vetter was keeping, it is clear that Cook had come to terms with his fate and was remarkably free of bitterness. He wrote:

> The test of an explorer's work must always be in context of the quality of his work. His published narrative, with its complete data, is his book of rights. Peary's book and mine were printed 20 years ago. Nothing can be added, nothing subtracted. The material thus presented, re-examined and compared with later work of later explorers, verifies or condemns. History thus gives each explorer his award of merit. It can be done no other way. Public opinion, news reports, encyclopedic information, may influence the casual observer—but writers of history get their information from original sources. This takes time, but I am willing to rest my case in this system of adjustment.
>
> I reached the Pole. I climbed Mount McKinley. The controversy from my angle is at an end. I now have other, and still more important, exploration at hand. This will occupy my attention until the frost of the next world arrives.

Notes

Chapter One

page

5:     Quoted in *New York Herald Tribune*, March 10, 1930.

Chapter Two

8:     Robert E. Peary, *Northward Over the Great Ice* (New York: Frederick A. Stokes, 1898), vol. 1, p. xxxvii.

8:     Quoted in Roland Huntford, *The Last Place on Earth* (New York: Atheneum, 1986), pp. 211–212.

8:     J. Gordon Hayes, *Robert E. Peary* (London: Grant Richards & Humphrey Toulmin, 1929), p. 32.

12:    Andrew A. Freeman, *The Case for Doctor Cook* (New York: Coward-McCann, 1961), p. 26.

14:    Peary, *Northward Over the Great Ice*, p. 347.

15:    Ibid., p. 94.

Chapter Three

17:    Quoted in Andrew A. Freeman, *The Case for Doctor Cook,* (New York: Coward-McCann, 1961), p. 35.

17–18: W. T. Stead, "Character Sketch and Interview, Dr. F. A. Cook," *Review of Reviews* (London), October 1909, p. 331.

20:    Herbert L. Bridgman, *Brooklyn Standard Union,* December 2, 1893.

21–22: Quoted in Freeman, *The Case for Doctor Cook,* p. 39.

24:    William Libby, Jr., *Journal of the American Geographical Society* 27:1 (1895), p. 62.

24:    Robert E. Peary, *Northward Over the Great Ice* (New York: Frederick A. Stokes, 1898), vol. 2, p. 155.

25:    Frederick A. Cook, *My Attainment of the Pole* (New York: Mitchell Kennerley, 1913), pp. 38–39.

26:    J. Gordon Hayes, *Robert E. Peary* (London: Grant Richards & Humphrey Toulmin, 1929), p. 269.

Chapter Four

29:    Frederick A. Cook, *Through the First Antarctic Night* (reprint) (Montreal: McGill-Queen's University Press, 1980), p. 48.

29:    Ibid., p. 3.

30:    Ibid., p. viii.

31:    Quoted in Roland Huntford, *The Last Place on Earth* (New York: Atheneum, 1986), p. 20.

32:    Cook, *Through the First Antarctic Night,* p. 55.

33:    Quoted in Andrew A. Freeman, *The Case for Doctor Cook* (New York: Coward-McCann, 1961), p. 52.

34–35: Cook, *Through the First Antarctic Night,* pp. 198–199.

35:    Ibid., p. 208.

35:    Ibid., p. 213.

36:    Ibid., p. 214.

36:    Ibid., p. 215.

37:    Roald Amundsen, *My Life As an Explorer* (New York: Doubleday & Co., 1928).

38:    Cook: *Through the First Antarctic Night,* p. 312.

38–39: Ibid., p. 234.

39:    Amundsen, *My Life As an Explorer,* p. 35.

39:    Huntford, *The Last Place on Earth,* pp. 71–72.

39–40: Quoted in ibid., p. 73.

40:    Amundsen, *My Life As an Explorer,* pp. 28–29.

41:    Cook, *Through the First Antarctic Night,* p. 399.

41:    Amundsen, *My Life As an Explorer,* p. 31.

42:    Frederick A. Cook, *My Attainment of the Pole* (New York: Mitchell Kennerley, 1913), p. 498.

Chapter Five

44–45: Quoted in Fitzhugh Green, *Peary, The Man Who Refused to Fail* (New York: G. P. Putnam's Sons, 1926), p. 167.

46: Quoted in Bradley Robinson, *Dark Companion* (New York: Robert McBride & Co., 1947), p. 132.

49: Robert E. Peary, *Nearest the Pole* (New York: Doubleday, Page & Co., 1907), p. 344.

50: Quoted in Andrew A. Freeman, *The Case for Doctor Cook* (New York: Coward-McCann, 1961), pp. 73–74.

Chapter Six

54: Frederick A. Cook, *The Top of the Continent* (New York: Doubleday, Page & Co., 1908), p. 51.

54: Ibid., p. 96.

56: Frederick A. Cook, "The Conquest of Mount McKinley," *Harper's Magazine,* May 1907, p. 824.

56: Ibid., p. 824.

57: Ibid., p. 828.

57: Ibid., p. 829.

57: Ibid., p. 834.

58: Cook, *The Top of the Continent,* p. 218.

58: Ibid., p. 225–226.

58: Ibid., p. 226.

58: Ibid., p. 231.

58–59: Ibid., p. 232.

Chapter Seven

61: Quoted in Andrew A. Freeman, *The Case for Doctor Cook,* (New York: Coward-McCann, 1961), p. 92.

61: Quoted in ibid., p. 92.

61: Alexander Graham Bell, quoted in *National Geographic Magazine,* January 1907.

62: Robert E. Peary, *Nearest the Pole* (New York: Doubleday, Page & Co., 1907), p. xi.

62: Frederick A. Cook, *My Attainment of the Pole* (New York: Mitchell Kennerley, 1913), p. 29.

62: Ibid.

62:        Quoted in Freeman, *The Case for Doctor Cook,* p. 95.

63:        John R. Bradley, "My Knowledge of Dr. Cook's Polar Expedition," *The Independent,* September 16, 1909.

65:        Fitzhugh Green, *Peary, The Man Who Refused to Fail* (New York: G. P. Putnam's Sons, 1926), p. 196.

65:        Ibid.

67:        J. Gordon Hayes, *Robert E. Peary* (London: Grant Richards & Humphrey Toulmin, 1929), p. 68.

Chapter Eight

71:        W. T. Stead "Character Sketch and Interview, Dr. F. A. Cook," *Review of Reviews* (London), October 1909, p. 331.

73–74:   Ibid., pp. 330–331.

77:        Ibid., p. 331.

Chapter Nine

79:        Frederick A. Cook, *My Attainment of the Pole* (New York: Mitchell Kennerley, 1913), p. 67.

79:        Ibid., pp. 69–70.

80:        Quoted in Frederick J. Pohl, Introduction to Frederick A. Cook, *Return From the Pole* (New York: Pellegrini & Cudahy, 1951), p. 12.

80–81:   Cook, *My Attainment of the Pole,* p. 74.

82:        Ibid., p. 79.

82:        Ibid., p. 77.

83:        Editorial, *New York Times,* October 4, 1907.

84:        Andrew A. Freeman, *The Case for Doctor Cook* (New York: Coward-McCann, 1961), p. 99.

84:        Robert E. Peary, Letter to the Editor, *New York Times,* September 9, 1909.

85:        Quoted in Robert E. Peary, *The North Pole* (New York: Frederick A. Stokes Co., 1910), p. 27.

Chapter Ten

86:        Frederick A. Cook, *My Attainment of the Pole* (New York: Mitchell Kennerley, 1913), p. 80.

86–87:   Ibid., pp. 93–96.

89:        Ibid., p. 200.

90:        Ibid., p. 196.

91:     Ibid., p. 205.

91:     Ibid., p. 217.

91:     Ibid., p. 222.

91:     Ibid., p. 223.

92:     Ibid., p. 206.

92:     Walter Wager, *Camp Century, City Under the Ice* (Philadelphia: Chilton Books, 1962), pp. 58–59.

93:     Cook, *My Attainment of the Pole,* p. 224.

93:     Ibid., p. 223.

94:     Ibid., pp. 250–251.

94:     Ibid., p. 261.

94:     Ibid., p. 270.

95:     Ibid., p. 284.

Chapter Eleven

96:     Frederick A. Cook, *My Attainment of the Pole* (New York: Mitchell Kennerley, 1913), pp. 287–288.

97:     Ibid., p. 266.

98:     Ibid., pp. 301–302.

98:     Ibid., p. 309.

98:     Ibid., p. 313.

98–99: Ibid., p. 312.

100:    Ibid., pp. 327–328.

100:    Ibid., p. 577.

101:    Ibid., pp. 330–331.

102–103: Quoted in Andrew A. Freeman, *The Case for Doctor Cook* (New York: Coward-McCann, 1961), p. 112.

104:    Ibid., p. 113.

104:    Frederick A. Cook, *Return From the Pole* (New York: Pellegrini & Cudahy, 1951), p. 14.

104:    Cook, *My Attainment of the Pole,* p. 444.

Chapter Twelve

106–107: Frederick A. Cook, *My Attainment of the Pole* (New York: Mitchell Kennerley, 1913), p. 343.

108:    Frederick A. Cook, *Return From the Pole* (New York: Pellegrini & Cudahy, 1951), p. 220.

108:    Ibid., pp. 222–223.

109:     Ibid., p. 233.

110:     Ibid.

110:     Ibid., pp. 259–260.

111:     Robert E. Peary, *The North Pole* (New York: Frederick A. Stokes Co., 1910), p. 192.

111:     Quoted in Andrew A. Freeman, *The Case for Doctor Cook* (New York: Coward-McCann, 1961), p. 117.

112:     Quoted in Theon Wright, *The Big Nail: The Story of the Cook-Peary Controversy* (New York: John Day, 1970), p. 234.

112:     Peary, *The North Pole*, pp. 272–273.

113:     Ibid., p. 274.

113:     Quoted in *Boston American*, July 17, 1910.

114:     J. Gordon Hayes, *Robert E. Peary* (London: Grant Richards & Humphrey Toulmin, 1929), p. 173.

114:     Peary, *The North Pole*, p. 288.

114:     Frederick J. Pohl, Introduction to Cook, *Return From the Pole*, p. 39.

115:     Quoted in Freeman, *The Case for Doctor Cook*, p. 121.

Chapter Thirteen

117:     Frederick A. Cook, *My Attainment of the Pole* (New York: Mitchell Kennerley, 1913), p. 413–415.

117–118: Ibid.

118:     Ibid.

119:     Ibid., pp. 436–437.

120:     Ibid., p. 437.

121:     Ibid.

122:     Quoted in Andrew A. Freeman, *The Case for Doctor Cook* (New York: Coward-McCann, 1961), p. 131.

124:     Quoted in Theon Wright, *The Big Nail: The Story of the Cook-Peary Controversy* (New York: John Day, 1970), p. 218.

125:     Paul J. Rainey, "Bagging Arctic Monsters With Rope, Gun and Camera," *Cosmopolitan Magazine*, December 1910, p. 97.

Chapter Fourteen

128:     Frederick A. Cook, *My Attainment of the Pole* (New York: Mitchell Kennerley, 1913), pp. 466–467.

129:     Ibid., pp. 470–471.

129:        Frederick A. Cook, *Return From the Pole* (New York: Pellegrini & Cudahy, 1951), pp. 19–20.

129–130: Quoted in ibid.

130:        Quoted in Andrew A. Freeman, *The Case for Doctor Cook* (New York: Coward-McCann, 1961), p. 148.

131:        W. T. Stead "Character Sketch and Interview, Dr. F. A. Cook," *Review of Reviews* (London), October 1909, pp. 327–328.

132:        Cook, *My Attainment of the Pole,* p. 474.

132:        Quoted in *New York Herald,* September 8, 1909.

132:        Ibid.

132–133 *New York Times,* Sept. 9, 1909.

133:        Cook, *My Attainment of the Pole,* p. 475.

Chapter Fifteen

137–138: Quoted in Andrew A. Freeman, *The Case for Doctor Cook* (New York: Coward-McCann, 1961), p. 158.

138:        Quoted in Russell W. Gibbons, *An Historical Evaluation of the Cook-Peary Controversy* (Ada: Ohio Northern University, 1954), p. 2.

139:        John Edward Weems, *Race for the Pole* (New York: Henry Holt & Co., 1960), p. 12.

139:        Gibbons, *An Historical Evaluation of the Cook-Peary Controversy,* p. 2

Chapter Sixteen

143:        Frederick A. Cook, *My Attainment of the Pole* (New York: Mitchell Kennerly, 1913), p. 477.

144:        Ibid., p. 478.

145:        Ibid., p. 480.

145:        *New York Sun,* September 22, 1909.

147:        Quoted in Andrew A. Freeman, *The Case for Doctor Cook* (New York: Coward-McCann, 1961), pp. 145–146.

148:        Quoted in *New York Times,* September 7, 1909.

149:        Quoted in *New York Times,* September 9, 1909.

149:        *New York Herald,* September 18, 1909.

Chapter Seventeen

152:        Quoted in *New York Sun,* September 6, 1909.

152:        Quoted in *New York Herald,* September 6, 1909.

152–153: Quoted in *New York Herald,* September 16, 1909.

153: Frederick A. Cook, *My Attainment of the Pole* (New York: Mitchell Kennerly, 1913), p. 527.

153: Hugh Eames, *Winner Lose All: Doctor Cook and the Theft of the North Pole* (Boston: Little, Brown & Co., 1973), p. 188.

154: Ibid., p. 189.

154: Cook, *My Attainment of the Pole,* p. 528.

155: Quoted in *New York Times,* October 16, 1909.

155: Quoted in Eames *Winner Lose All,* p. 191.

156: Quoted in *New York Times,* September 28, 1909.

156: Cook, *My Attainment of the Pole,* pp. 200–201.

157–158: Quoted in *New York Times,* Oct. 21, 1909.

158–159: Quoted in Andrew A. Freeman, *The Case for Doctor Cook* (New York: Coward-McCann, 1961), p. 196.

160: Cook, *My Attainment of the Pole,* p. 537.

161: Ibid., pp. 538–539.

162: Quoted in Freeman, *The Case for Doctor Cook,* p. 200.

163: Quoted in ibid., p. 203.

Chapter Eighteen

164: Frederick A. Cook, *Return From the Pole* (New York: Pellegrini & Cudahy, 1951), p. 30.

164–165: Taped statement of Lillian Kiel, April 7, 1953.

166: Thomas F. Hall, *Has the North Pole Been Discovered?* (Boston: Richard G. Badger, 1917), p. 220.

166–167: Quoted in Andrew A. Freeman, *The Case for Doctor Cook* (New York: Coward-McCann, 1961), p. 211.

167: Ibid., p. 211.

168: Frederick A. Cook, *My Attainment of the Pole* (New York: Mitchell Kennerly, 1913), p. 498.

169: Quoted in Freeman, *The Case for Doctor Cook,* p. 217.

170: Edwin Swift Balch, *Mount McKinley and Mount Climbers' Proofs* (Philadelphia: Campion & Co., 1914), p. 75.

171: Copy of letter from Kilroy to Cook in author's files.

172: Quoted in *New York World,* October 2, 1910.

172: Quoted in Freeman, *The Case for Doctor Cook,* pp. 220–221.

173: Quoted in ibid.

173: Cook, *My Attainment of the Pole,* p. 552.

173:     Ibid., p. 553.

173:     Quoted in Freeman, *The Case for Doctor Cook,* p. 221.

174:     Cook, *My Attainment of the Pole,* p. 554.

174:     Ibid., p. 555.

174–175: Taped statement of Lillian Kiel, April 7, 1953.

175:     Ibid.

175:     Affidavit by T. Everett Harre, now in the Library of Congress.

176:     Charles B. Driscoll, *The Life of O. O. McIntyre* (New York: Greystone Press, 1938), pp. 222–223.

Chapter Nineteen

177:     Quoted in Andrew A. Freeman, *The Case for Doctor Cook* (New York: Coward-McCann, 1961), p. 210.

179:     U.S. House of Representatives, Private Calendar No. 733, 61st Cong., 3rd Sess.

180:     Ibid.

180:     Ibid.

181:     U.S. House of Representatives, 61st Congress, 3rd Session, Private Calendar 733, Report 1961, p. 18.

182:     Quoted in Freeman, *The Case for Doctor Cook,* p. 234, and W. Henry Lewin, *The Great North Pole Fraud* (London: C. W. Daniel) pp. 88–90.

Chapter Twenty

185:     Quoted in Andrew A. Freeman, *The Case for Doctor Cook* (New York: Coward-McCann, 1961), p. 238.

185–186: Ibid.

186:     *Congressional Record,* 63rd Cong., 2nd Sess., Vol. 51, No. 116, p. 8065.

188:     Cited in Theon Wright, *The Big Nail: The Story of the Cook-Peary Controversy* (New York: John Day, 1970), pp. 275–276.

189:     Freeman, *The Case for Doctor Cook,* p. 240.

189:     *New York Times,* October 19, 1917.

Chapter Twenty-One

193:     *New York Times,* January 11, 1923.

195:     Quoted in Russell B. Gibbons, *An Historical Evaluation of the Cook-Peary Controversy* (Ada: Ohio Northern University, 1954), pp. 37–38.

197:     Copy of letter from David Cahill to John W. H. Crim, in the author's files.

198:      Ibid.

198:      Ibid.

198–199: Quoted in Andrew A. Freeman, *The Case for Doctor Cook* (New York: Coward-McCann, 1961), p. 245.

199:      Cook, quote in *New York Times*, November 10, 1923.

199:      Quoted in Frederick A. Cook, *Return From the Pole* (New York: Pellegrini & Cudahy, 1951), p. 43.

199:      Copy of Cook's letter in the author's files.

199–200: Quoted in *New York Times*, November 22, 1923.

200:      Quoted in ibid.

200:      Ibid.

200–201: Judge John M. Killits, court record, quoted in Freeman, *The Case for Doctor Cook*, p. 245.

201:      Cook, quoted in *New York Times*, Nov. 23, 1923.

202:      Copy of letter by Killits in the author's files.

202–203: Copy of letter by Zweifel in the author's files.

203:      Quoted in *Fort Worth Star-Telegram*, August 4, 1924.

203:      Copy of Wilson's letter to Harlan F. Stone in the author's files.

203–204: Ibid.

204:      Ibid.

204–205: *New York Times*, September 14, 1938.

205:      Quoted in Cook, *Return From the Pole*, pp. 44–45.

Chapter Twenty-Two

206:      W. I. Biddle, quoted in *New York Times*, July 25, 1925.

206:      Andrew A. Freeman, *The Case for Doctor Cook* (New York: Coward-McCann, 1961), p. 247.

207:      Quoted in Russell W. Gibbons, *An Historical Evaluation of the Cook-Peary Controversy* (Ada: Ohio Northern University), p. 37.

207:      Roland Huntford, *The Last Place on Earth* (New York: Atheneum, 1986), p. 537.

208:      Roald Amundsen, quoted in *New York Times*, January 24, 1926.

208:      Ibid.

209:      Amundsen, quoted in Huntford, *The Last Place on Earth*, p. 455.

209–210: Amundsen, quoted in *New York Times*, March 4, 1926.

210:      Cook, quoted in *New York Times*, January 25, 1926.

210:      Amundsen, quoted in *New York Times*, March 4, 1926.

210:     *New York World,* November 4, 1928.

211:     Cook, quoted in *Kansas City Star,* March 10, 1930.

211:     Quoted in Freeman, *The Case for Doctor Cook,* p. 256.

212:     Ibid., p. 10.

213:     *Buffalo Evening News,* May 18, 1940.

Chapter Twenty-Three

219:     Dennis Rawlins, interviews with the author in the fall of 1988.

220:     *Washington Post,* October 2, 1988.

221:     Rawlins, interviews with the author, fall of 1988.

221:     Rawlins, quoted in the *Washington Post,* October 12, 1988.

222:     Rawlins, quoted in the *Washington Post,* April 12, 1990.

222:     Quoted in ibid.

223:     Sheldon Cook-Dorough, interviews and correspondence with the author.

224:     Ibid.

224:     Ibid.

224:     Frederick J. Pohl, Introduction to Frederick A. Cook, *Return From the Pole* (New York: Pellegrini & Cudahy, 1951), pp. 42–43.

225:     Sheldon Cook-Dorough, *Frederick A. Cook: The Major Explorations, a Brief Summary* (Atlanta) 1988, p. 11.

225:     Janet Vetter, interview with the author, 1989.

225:     Ibid.

226:     Frederick A. Cook, unpublished manuscript.

Selected Bibliography

Amundsen, Roald. My Life as an Explorer. New York: Doubleday & Co., 1928.

Balch, Edwin S. Mount McKinley and Mountain Climbers' Proofs. Philadelphia: Campion & Co., 1914.

Cook, Frederick A. My Attainment of the Pole. New York and London: Mitchell A. Kennerley, 1913.

———Return From the Pole. New York: Pellegrini & Cudahy, 1951.

———Through the First Antarctic Night (reprint). Montreal: McGill-Queen's University Press, 1980.

———To the Top of the Continent. New York: Doubleday, Page & Co., 1908.

Freeman, Andrew A. The Case for Doctor Cook. New York: Coward McCann, 1961.

Gibbons, Russell W. An Historical Evaluation of the Cook-Peary Controversy. Ada, Ohio: Ohio Northern University, 1954.

Hayes, J. Gordon. Robert E. Peary. London: Grant Richards & Humphrey Toulmin, 1929.

Huntford, Roland. The Last Place on Earth. New York: Atheneum, 1986.

Peary, Robert E. Nearest the Pole. New York: Doubleday, Page & Co., 1907.

———The North Pole. New York: Frederick A. Stokes Co., 1910.

———Northward Over the Great Ice. New York: Frederick A. Stokes, 1898.

Weems, John E. Race for the Pole. New York: Mitchell Kennerly, 1913.

Wright, Theon. The Big Nail: The Story of the Cook-Peary Feud. New York: John Day, 1970.

Index

About the Author

Howard S. Abramson is the author of *National Geographic: Behind America's Lens on the World* and is the editor of *Traffic World,* a weekly newsmagazine that covers the transportation industry. During his years in the news business, Abramson cofounded States News Service and has worked for the *New Haven Register, Washington Post,* and *Journal of Commerce.* He lives in the suburbs of Washington, D.C., is married, and has three children.